ADVENTURES
in Black and White

ADVENTURES
in Black and White

by Philippa Duke Schuyler

Foreword by Deems Taylor

EDITED WITH A CRITICAL INTRODUCTION BY TARA BETTS

2LP CLASSICS

NEW YORK
www.2leafpress.org

P.O. Box 4378
Grand Central Station
New York, New York 10163-4378
editor@2leafpress.org
www.2leafpress.org

2LEAF PRESS
is an imprint of the
Intercultural Alliance of Artists & Scholars, Inc. (IAAS),
a NY-based nonprofit 501(c)(3) organization that promotes
multicultural literature and literacy.
www.theiaas.org

Copyright © 2018 Phillipa Duke Schuyler and Tara Betts

ADVENTURES IN BLACK AND WHITE
by Philippa Duke Schuyler, with a Foreword by Deems Taylor was first published by
Robert Speller & Sons, Publishers, Inc. (New York, 1960)

Cover photo: Portrait of Philippa Duke Schuyler (May 9, 1951)
Carl Van Vechten, 1880-1964, photographer
Library of Congress, Prints & Photographs Division,
Carl Van Vechten Collection, LC-USZ62-132150

Bio photo: Photo of Philippa Duke Schuyler (1959)
Fred Palumbo, photographer
Library of Congress. New York World-Telegram & Sun Collection, LC-USZ62-109640
Bio photo: Photo of Deems Taylor (December 1943)
Publicity photo/WNYC Archive Collections

Book layout and design: Gabrielle David, *Copy editor:* Carolina Fung Feng

Library of Congress Control Number: 2017963327
ISBN-13: 978-1-940939-77-3 (Paperback)
ISBN-13: 978-1-940939-89-6 (eBook)

10   9   8   7   6   5   4   3   2   1

Published in the United States of America

First Edition | First Printing

2LEAF PRESS trade distribution is handled by University of Chicago Press / Chicago Distribution Center (www.press.uchicago.edu), 773.702.7000. Titles are also available for corporate, premium, and special sales. Please direct inquiries to the UCP Sales Department, 773.702.7248.

For my parents
Bennie H. Betts Jr. and Maureen Terrell

—Tara Betts, 2018

ADVENTURES IN BLACK AND WHITE
is dedicated to
Delta Sigma Theta Sorority

I also wish to express appreciative acknowledgments
for their kind interest through the years to
Deems Taylor, Irl Allison, and George B. Russell.

—Philippa Duke Schuyler, 1960

CONTENTS

The Case of the Missing Piano

NEW YORK IS A SOMBER CITY, one of perpetual turmoil.
Restless, striving, beautiful, impressive, dangerous, cruel, full of calumny and rivalry.

I did not realize its intense competitiveness when I was a child. Rather, I found wonder in each new discovery—museums, concerts, theaters, books, and parks.

Only when I was thirteen did my parents show me my clippings, press releases, and inform me that I had a career for the past nine years.

Before then, I had played for enjoyment, without realization of the weighty importance of each concert. As soon as I knew, I felt a sense of responsibility about each appearance, which precluded enjoyment, and opened the door to anxieties and nervous apprehension.

I even felt anxious, at thirteen, when I heard the New York Philharmonic Young People's Orchestra, under the direction of Rudolph Ganz, give the first performance of my symphonic tone poem, "Manhattan Nocturne."

"They're playing it too slow!" I thought, in anguish to myself at the rehearsal, and though this was remedied at the performance, I lived years of self-torture listening to each note. One can never enjoy hearing others play a work one has written, for one goes through in one's mind, as the music spins out, all the torments one underwent during the composition: the uncertainties, confusion, anger, months of revision, and hundreds of wee morning hours spent laboriously copying out scores and parts. My teacher, Otto Cesana, always insisted that

I copy scores and parts of my orchestral works myself, so I would realize the significance of it.

Composition, to me, recalls a series of thousands of hours of "copying out," replete with such horrifying moments as when one suddenly realizes one has just copied five pages of the Flute II part on Oboe I line, or forgot to transpose ten measures of the A Clarinet. Then out must come razor blade, glue, and scissors again.

On a fine July morning the following year, I arrived with my mother at the back entrance of Lewisohn Stadium for the one and only rehearsal I would have with Thor Johnson, the conductor, and the New York Philharmonic Orchestra for my orchestral debut that evening.

A worried stage manager met us and announced that no piano had been delivered from Steinway Hall. The Stadium Society, which had been in constant touch with us, had forgotten to order it, or to tell us to do so. He added that it was impossible now to order a piano because Steinway Hall was closed on Saturday, and besides, the unions did not permit Saturday deliveries.

We did find a small, battered piano in the wings, used by City College students for rallies, and it was rolled out for the rehearsal. Mr. Johnson and the men of the orchestra entered into the spirit of the adventure, and we optimistically went through my concerto. At the same time, my mother was making frantic telephone calls. Through mutual friends, she located Mr. Theodore Steinway just fifteen minutes before his departure for Europe. He graciously agreed to order his watchman at the store to have Rubenstein's favorite instrument ready for the truck; but he said that his contract with the union did not allow him to request delivery.

Fortunately, my mother recalled that Mother Josephine Morgan, my first harmony teacher at Manhattanville College and Convent of the Sacred Heart (which was just across the street from the Stadium), had a family in the trucking business. She contacted Mother Morgan who promised to do her best.

The piano arrived just before concert time, too late for me to try it. The people were already cued up to buy tickets.

I stood trembling in the wings while the orchestra performed my scherzo, "Rumpelstiltskin." Then I walked to the open piano, painfully aware that the Stadium was full. The "Saint Saens Concerto in G Minor" opens with a fateful, passionate series of arpeggios. Playing them, I forgot everything else.

Afterwards, Jean Tennyson, Gladys Swarthout, Carl Van Vechten, Deems Taylor and many others embraced me; and hundreds of young people walked me the short distance home. There was a party, but I was too stunned to enjoy it.

Next day, to my surprise, the reviews were glowing.

In 1953 and 1954, I gave Town Hall recitals, and in July 1955, reappeared at Lewisohn Stadium with Thomas Scherman conducting. Seven months later, I flew from Spain to New York to play with the Brooklyn Philharmonia under Siegfried Landau, in a Gershwin-Copland Festival. At Idlewild Airport, my practice keyboard, which I had carried everywhere, was stolen. However, I had a new one made in two sections which could fold up and was much easier to handle. That October, I gave my third Town Hall recital.

In June 1959, after a world tour, I made my Carnegie Hall recital debut. It was a benefit for the Church of the Master to help build a Youth Center on West 122nd Street, drawing a large, colorful, and international audience.

Among our sponsors were the United Nations ambassadors from Liberia, the Philippines, and Korea; the consuls of France, Belgium, Dominican Republic, and Haiti; members of United Nations delegations from Nationalist China, Ghana, Lebanon, Britain and Malaya.

Among the prominent New York sponsors were Colonel Archibald Roosevelt, Spruille Braden, Alfred Kohlberg, Reverend James Robinson, Dr. and Mrs. Max Yergan, Roy Cohn, Bishop R. Lawson, Monsignor Cornelius Drew, J. Raymond Jones, Roy Wilkins, Elmer Carter, Clarence Holte, the Richard E. Webbs, Lester Grangers, Edgar Hendersons, and George Meares; Doctors Vernon Ayer, J. B. Matthews, Leslie Allen, Cecil Marquez, Arthur Grieg, and Arthur Gellis; Mesdames A. A. Austin, Carolyn Mitchell, Ellen Dammond, Regina Andréws, Frances Anderson, Leonard Bernstein, The Musical Art Group, and delegations from three unions. Elegant Fania Marinoff and Carl Van Vechten had front seats. Carlo applauded vigorously after each group; at seventy-nine, he was the most distinguished looking man there. Old friends like Captain William Spears, Henry Steigner, Deems Taylor, Laura Jane Musser, and Joyce Cooper made me forget I had just risen from a hospital bed after an attack of tropical virus contracted in Africa.

Marion Preminger, radiant and beautiful, came backstage accompanied by Charles Ross, who was carrying a huge package. I unwrapped it wonderingly. It was a bust of Dr. Albert Schweitzer! A gift from Marion.

The management reported that we had the largest audience for classical music of the season, with a box office of $7,000.

Outside, New York is hard and pitiless. But if you can reach its heart, you find it to be warm and generous.

Then my friends urged me to write a book. It seemed an intriguing idea — to try to share one's experiences with others. Little did I realize the difficulties! I had always kept a diary. It would be a simple thing, I thought, just to transcribe it. I soon discovered my mistake. A book is as different from a diary as a concerto is from a collection of songs.

I decided that if it was to have any value, it would have to show me as I was at the time of the experience, not after I had thought it out. That is, not always wise, and sometimes very foolish.

It could not be consecutive. Tours are not straight lines but mazes.

Since I had to learn about life on the run, the form would have to be looser than a sonata, yet held together. I beg the reader's indulgence for the way I worked it out. (And for so much use of the personal pronoun.)

This book is a series of snapshots of adventure, of exotic people, ideas, and scenes caught swiftly in passing.

Wherever I traveled, people confided their intimate lives to me, as if they were still puzzled themselves by what had happened. I listened eagerly, often shocked but fascinated. This was my college education. It all helped me form a more accurate picture of life.

To protect identities, a few names have been changed.

This is how I have lived for over a decade, in sixty countries, in black and white moods, among black and white people, and with my only permanent companion, a black and white keyboard. ✠

—Philippa Duke Schuyler

My Recollection of an Extraordinary Artist

THE EXACT DATE ESCAPES ME. I do know it was some time in 1938 that CBS telephoned to ask if I would go on the "We, the People" program to interview a remarkable six-year-old pianist and composer named Philippa Schuyler. Now various painful experiences in the past had caused me to view child prodigies with dark suspicion. They almost invariably turned out to be little monsters who, by threats or promises, had managed to attain an extraordinary digital dexterity. They could play fast, heaven knows, and they could play loud. But of what we roughly call "soul" there was little if any trace. And why should there be? Only by a miracle could a six-year-old possess the emotional and intellectual depth of a mature artist.

But then I thought, "Oh, well, if it will make CBS happy, I'll go along. Thank God she isn't a violinist. At least she'll play in tune, the piano permitting." So I went to the studio, and the moppet and I gravely discussed this and that, and she played me some of her own works, and some by other composers. And at the close of the broadcast, as she and I faced the studio audience, a small hand tucked confidingly in my own, I suddenly realized something. "Why?" I thought to myself, "This is no infant. This is a born musician." The miracle had happened.

This discovery of her extraordinary talents was not exactly what a reporter would call a "beat," as I found out when I began to explore her past. She is the child of a mixed marriage—a Negro newspaper man and a white Texan. Her mother had taught her to read and write simple words by the time she was two-years-old. When news of this was noised abroad it provoked an amusing reaction in educational circles. Some of the educators seemed to feel that for an infant to perform such a feat was vaguely indecent. Columbia's Teachers' College heartily disapproved of such goings on. Tested at New York University, she was found to have an I.Q. of 185 and an E.Q. (educational quotient) of 200. This promptly brought a warning that she would turn into a lopsided bookworm. Whereupon she further annoyed the pedagogues by studying piano and musical composition. By the time she was four she had composed ten pieces, thus breaking Mozart's record of only one at that age. Then began a series of "firsts" never equaled by children of Negro ancestry.

At five, she played her first public recital at Fuld Hall in Newark, New Jersey, and was a regular fixture at NBC. At seven and eight she was playing her own works at the New York World's Fair. She graduated from grammar school at ten, finishing the course in three years and down-graded by her teachers so as not to discourage the other girls. At twelve she won first and second prizes in a contest for young composers sponsored by Wayne University, in Detroit, took the trip alone to receive them, and heard the Detroit Symphony Orchestra play her "Manhattan Nocturne," which she had orchestrated herself. Soon after that she made her debut as a concert soloist, playing the "Saint-Saens Second Piano Concerto" with the New York Philharmonic. On the same program was an orchestral work of her own, "Rumpelstiltskin." At fourteen she repeated the performance with the Boston Pops Orchestra.

By this time she was a full-fledged performer, with agents making noises like concert tours. Her parents, however, refused to commercialize her talent. She did play concert and recital dates; but any money they yielded went either to charity or to pay for her piano lessons. She was fortunate in having for her teacher Gaston Dethier, the famous Belgian organist and pianist, who devoutly believed in her genius, and gave his time unsparingly.

"We kept her non-commercial," writes her mother, "as long as she was in her teens. She has been allowed to be independent, to travel alone. We were fortunate in being able to give her more than money or position. We gave her an intellectual and artistic companionship. That was our gift to her. We had nothing else, but we gave that lovingly and freely."

One striking feature of her career is the fact that even as a child—meaning six-years-old—she was always taken seriously by the critics. When she was fourteen, the *New York World Telegram* remarked, "The talk of the town this morning is Philippa Schuyler. Both as a performer and a composer she demonstrated enough talent to last her for a long lifetime. She is the kind of wunderkind who will grow with the years."

Or, as Frank Perkins of the *New York Herald Tribune* put it, "Miss Schuyler has been well known since very early childhood for her musical and intellectual attainments, and has also impressed her listeners as an adult artist."

One of her intellectual attainments you will soon discover: she writes delightfully. Among her other virtues is her ability to convey the mood, the feel of a place or a person in a sentence or two. Consider these:

ICELAND: "The glassy dawn sky was dismal. It hovered like a stigma over the shroud-like earth."

STOCKHOLM: "One had to pay extra for baths, of course."

COPENHAGEN: "The sparkling atmosphere, the rich good food, the sight of hundreds of bicycle-riders pedaling to work each morning."

HELSINGFORS: "One was ever conscious of the proximity of Russia."

SCANDINAVIA: "I decided that it was essential to be hearty in Scandinavia. One must either drink, commit suicide, go mad or be hearty."

SURINAM: "Tiny red ants crawl like sinister bloody veils over everything. I smashed a cockroach as big as a mouse."

RIVER CONGO: "Wearily it flushes into the Atlantic Ocean."

Like most front rank artists, she has a sense of humor, "The orchestral parts of the Gershwin concerto were very heavy. I decided to put them in my sweater, so as not to have to pay excess baggage. When I got on the plane, everyone was most sympathetic about my 'condition'." I also recommend for your perusal the tale of the hotel with one air-conditioned room, the fight with the ants in Usumbura, and the antelope that got a doctor's degree.

You will find comparatively little about music in this book. That seems like an odd omission at first; but it is a logical one. The author is interested in people and places, where she went, what she saw, and what she learned. And she obviously likes to write about them. So there is little room for music. Why should there be? For after all, she *is* music. ⊞

—Deems Taylor

Playing the Notes: A 21st Century Introduction to Philippa Duke Schuyler's *Adventures in Black and White*

Tara Betts

A SENSE OF PLAYFULNESS INHABITS HER NOTES. Among the scant recordings on YouTube, Philippa Duke Schuyler's technical skill as a pianist is clear, and at times almost cheerful and bubbly. I imagine Philippa at a polished black Steinway in an elegant gown and plunking the keys lightly, yet with certainty. Some of these recitals are followed by enthusiastic applause. Considering that Philippa was noted as one of America's first interracial celebrities, we might think that her story would hold a more prominent place by now, especially in this cultural moment where more and more children and celebrities claim a range of experiences yet still experience the brunt of racism. Philippa's story becomes even more timely, not just as an accomplished person who might reflect the experiences of marginalized people, but as someone whose brief life documented a key moment in America's past. Her name recurs in brief stories about interracial celebrities and in the far too few existing histories of Black women composers. Most of Schuyler's life and accomplishments are documented in the assiduous notes and tributes by her parents, Josephine Codgell and George S. Schuyler.

Her parents both had their own individual stories that made them interesting figures in their own rights. Josephine, a bold, blonde heiress to a wealthy Texas oil family who had lived a bohemian life as a painter and figure model, and she wrote as well. She left one lover in San Francisco to follow her artistic pursuits in New York City, where she read the works of George Schuyler, a journalist at the black left-wing publication *The Messenger*.

On July 27, 1927, Josephine met George at his office to express her admiration for his writing, the two struck up a long conversation that began their courtship. Shortly thereafter, they were living together. They married in early 1928. The Schuylers made their home in Sugar Hill at 321 Edgecombe Avenue, where Philippa was born on August 2, 1931. Josephine did not tell her family that she married a black man, much less had a child with one, for years. A blatant contradiction revealed itself later. Her father kept a black mistress for decades and one of her brothers provided for a black daughter. Josephine kept her secret, presumably because white men were permitted to sexually exploit black women, while white women must be pure and protected—an ideology that pervaded the justification for lynching that were still occurring in record numbers in the United States.

Josephine kept detailed daily journals of Philippa's progress and included press clippings in these notes. These very journals, which were revealed to her as part of carefully engineered upbringing horrified Philippa and inevitably became one of the reasons why Philippa tried to break away from her family and declare some sort of independence. A child like Philippa made people feel hopeful about possibilities during the Depression, but she was also only two-years-old when award-winning pianist and composer Florence Beatrice Price became the first African American woman to have her work, namely "Symphony in E Minor" performed by a major symphony at the Chicago Symphony Orchestra in 1933. There are not many more who have been able to duplicate this success.

Celebrated as a child prodigy who won spelling bees at age two and wrote musical compositions and poems as early as age four, Philippa was often featured in newspapers and even interviewed on television, which highlighted her conversational grace and her performances. She was often compared to Shirley Temple, and black girls all over the country dressed like Philippa in organdy dresses with big ribbons in their hair. Philippa won numerous New York piano competitions several times. At a certain point, Philippa was banned from some of those competitions so other young pianists would have the opportunity to win. When Philippa was age twelve, her composition "Manhattan Nocturne" was performed at the Detroit Symphony Orchestra and at the New York Philharmonic Orchestra. At age fourteen, she played with the New York Philharmonic and the Boston Symphony. When she performed at the 1939 World's Fair, they named that day of the fair after her. Philippa performed at Carnegie Hall in April 1945 and made her much later debut at Town Hall in 1953.

Although George was often traveling away as a correspondent journalist, Philippa and her father were fond of each other. Philippa's childhood was filled with a parade of African American intellectuals and artists. Carl Van Vechten, who captured the cover image of this volume, was Philippa's godfather. Even Mayor Fiorello La Guardia was a regular visitor at the Schuyler home, and he was completely charmed by the precocious, talented Philippa. George, and especially Josephine, closely managed Philippa's childhood and career so intensely that eventually Philippa did begin to assert herself. Philippa's rigorous piano practices had a range of teachers and much tutelage to allow for her performance schedule, so she often spent more time with adults than children her own age. As Philippa grew older, it also became clear that her parents' ideas about "hybrid vigor" that related to plants, and not necessarily to people with parents of different races, did not cohere with race relations of that time or the present day.

The premise of race mixing creating heartier, superior people is not something readily proven, and as Philippa matured white members of her audiences dwindled considerably. This disappearance, and overall lack of acknowledgment in her home country of America, inevitably took its toll. As readers of *Adventures in Black and White* will see, Philippa performed for the leaders of countries all over the world—most notably Ethiopia's Haile Selassie and many others. However, Philippa did note that the President of the United States never requested a performance from her. There were only six presidents during her lifetime, and several with more than two terms (Herbert Hoover, Franklin Roosevelt, Harry Truman, Dwight D. Eisenhower, John F. Kennedy, Lyndon B. Johnson). Not one of them ever invited her to perform.

Philippa found herself breaking away from her parents' regimentation in a vocal manner for several reasons. One was her mother's reliance on her for companionship and income. As George spent more time away from home and she was not employed herself, she was basically working as Philippa's stage mother. That controlling presence and the shift to her audiences becoming almost entirely black and Quaker disenchanted her willingness to pursue a career as a pianist. Philippa's writing was one area of her life that may have been managed with far less rigidity. Eventually, Philippa asserted herself. She forbade her father from writing about her life, and insisted that she be allowed to travel alone. Once Philippa began traveling more, she spent less and less time in the United States and constructed a new identity for herself as Felipa Monterro. Although she was passing in some contexts, this identity could have also been a way for Philippa to construct herself as distinct from her parents and expectations that people had for her as a pianist, especially as she traveled. The writing was another matter.

Her parents provided an intellectually stimulating environment that any child could have used to their benefit as a writer later in life. Some called it eccentric because of their raw food diet, structured schedules, and constant documentation. Philippa's second half of life as a writer marks her break from her parents, documents her travels, and finally expresses her sense of autonomy in several books—namely, *Adventures in Black and White* (1960), *Who Killed the Congo?* (1962), *Jungle Saints: Africa's Heroic Catholic Missionaries* (1963), *Kingdom of Dreams* (co-authored with her mother Josephine in 1966), and the posthumously published *Good Men Die* (1969). These titles have long been out of print until now.

Philippa's first book *Adventures in Black and White,* reprinted here for the first time in decades, embodies her expression as a young adult woman. In her archives, there is a novelized version of what became the book you are holding now. *Adventures in Black and White,* a memoir and a travelogue, documents her travels as a pianist as she explores a life that most women then could not have imagined. Some still fantasize about such a life in the twenty-first century.

Throughout her travels, she meets a variety of worldly intellectuals. Philippa elaborates on ornate dresses and cheongsams that she wears and describes in detail some of the luxurious and less than lush locales that she encounters with poetic sensibility. She narrowly escapes several attempted sexual assaults and performs at Marion Preminger's (former wife of Hollywood's Otto Preminger) leper colony in Hawaii. Although this book also captures her burgeoning interests in the music of "her homeland," Philippa also witnesses and documents the traumatizing ritual of female circumcision, decades before Alice Walker and Pratibha Parmar's 1993 book *Warrior Marks* or Fauziya Kassindja's 1998 autobiography *Do They Hear You When You Cry?* Reading this young woman's testimony about the hard, unpaid labor of women around the globe, even though it only appears in brief descriptions, is so telling about how far the rights of women as workers have yet to evolve. Then there are moments when Philippa seems unaware of the politics of certain countries, especially Trujillo's violent tyranny over the Dominican Republic and the Haitian people or the malaise induced in European countries post-World War II. Part of this certainly relates to her right-wing politics evident in some of her interviews and her writing. Still, her story bridges an interesting timeframe—the bounty of Harlem Renaissance intelligentsia, and Philippa's adulthood coincided with the growing consciousness of the Civil Rights Movement, Black Power, and the anti-war sentiment against Vietnam. She is also a figure engaging a host of issues that are still salient for women of color today.

In Katherine Talalay's book *Composition in Black and White,* some critics discounted her disciplined craft and abilities and chalked them up to being too forceful or intuitive, a heavy-handed criticism that often plagues astounding black female athletes like tennis players Serena and Venus Williams or figure skater Surya Bonaly. Talalay's *Composition in Black and White* is the one comprehensive biography about Philippa Duke Schuyler, which elaborates on her parents in more detail. Talalay's book relies heavily on interviews with surviving acquaintances, the papers of the Schuylers, and Philippa's own writings. Further support for Philippa's narrative is readily accessible at Schomburg Center in New York City and in a small collection of Philippa's papers at Syracuse University. Copies of many of Philippa's actual musical compositions are in the Helen Walker-Hill Collection at the University of Colorado-Boulder. One of her portraits captured by her godfather prominently appears in the Yale University's online exhibition "Extravagant Crowd: Carl Van Vechten's Portraits of Women" alongside musicians like Diana Sands, Leontyne Price, Ethel Waters, Pearl Primus, Bessie Smith, Billie Holiday, Ella Fitzgerald, and Harlem Renaissance literary figures Nella Larsen, Zora Neale Hurston, and Dorothy West, in addition to a breathtaking number of authors, actresses, and vocalists.

There are a few changes in this volume to note. The original text set the titles with roman numerals and often relied on phonetic spellings for terms in other countries. There were also some antiquated European spellings of adjectives and some previously hyphenated compound words. Such words have been updated to reflect current grammatical practices. Unfortunately, the wonderful folio of black and white photos where Philippa is posing with political leaders, family, and friends are omitted from this edition. Some of the photos can be easily found online, but the photos were specifically chosen to support points in the narrative that Philippa relays in *Adventures in Black and White*. On the page preceding the first edition's title page, there is a photo of adult Philippa in a full-length ball gown with a fitted bodice poised in a graceful lean against the piano behind her. The center of the book contained thirty-two glossy pages featuring a total of fifty-eight images. Most of these photos are clearly taken at social functions and before or after recitals and performances. The series begins with Philippa smiling intently at Mayor Fiorello La Guardia, and she looks like an almost replica of Shirley Temple. The photos progress very quickly to a maturing and beautiful young woman in the foreground of scenes in various countries. There are some notable photos worth mentioning. One small photo shows Philippa's parents sitting in the audience with Carl Van Vechten, Van Vechten's wife, James Weldon Johnson's wife, and Roy Wilkins at her 1953 debut at Town Hall. A July 1960 photo features Philippa next to a serious looking Prime Minister of Ghana, Dr. Kwame Nkrumah. There are more photos of Philippa on the African continent in this section than any of the other locations that she visited. There is a photo of Philippa holding hands with the artist Ben Enwonwu in Nigeria. Although there is not much documentation of her romantic life and Philippa never married, Enwonwu was one of her love interests. These photos are an indication of the amount of material unpublished or digitized, and they illustrate how Philippa's adventurous life is still not fully explored in a meaningful way.

Although Philippa has no direct survivors, her memory has been celebrated to some degree. In 2002, Tamar Brott produced a 9-minute segment entitled "What Happened to Philippa Schuyler?" for WNYC, New York City's National Public Radio affiliate. In it, Brott succinctly covered much of Philippa's biography that people often repeat. However, it was notable that Brott interviewed Don Shirley, who was also discouraged from pursuing classical music, even after debuting at the Boston Pops in 1945. This critical trend has always followed any African American excelling in any field, but the adoration of cute, small children shifts dramatically when children mature, and consequently, become criminalized and ignored as more threatening adults. Although she never broke through the glass ceiling and the racial discrimination that was bound to it, Philippa left behind a considerable number of musical compositions, writings (out of print and unpublished), and a path for others. In 1963, after she had assumed her identity as Felipa Monterro, and at times, passed for white, Andre Watts, an African American classical pianist, was able to break into classical music when he accompanied Leonard Bernstein in a televised appearance.

Some 2004 news articles stated that Alicia Keys and Halle Berry were discussing making a movie based on Philippa Duke Schuyler's life. Keys certainly would have been an ideal candidate to portray Schuyler's virtuosity as a pianist. There is also the arts education-focused J.H.S. 383 Philippa Schuyler, also known as Philippa Duke Schuyler Middle School in Bushwick, Brooklyn, which celebrates her memory. In 2011, the late jazz trumpeter Abram Wilson began sharing work he composed and toured with based on Philippa's life. He was collaborating on developing this project with director Pia Furtado to create a more expansive experience entitled "The Philippa Project." After his death, the Abram Wilson Foundation conducted a successful fundraising campaign to continue developing "The Philippa Project" into a music theater production based in the U.K. Performers continued to workshop this production as recently as 2014-2016. Her father George Schuyler is remembered for his contradictory political stances as a journalist, but was recently noted by novelist Danzy Senna as a precursor to Afrofuturism with his speculative novel *Black No More*. Josephine has also been written about for contribution to the Harlem Renaissance in Carla Kaplan's *Miss Anne in Harlem*—an exploration of white women involved in that artistic movement.

By reissuing Philippa Duke Schuyler's first book *Adventures in Black and White*, my hope is that this volume will consider that there are voids in the histories of women of color, including women of African American heritage, who confronted the lived realities at complex points in America's history. In Philippa's case, she may have confronted her identity on some occasions and dodged it at other times, but here it is clear that she is a multi-faceted woman, who was only beginning to offer much more when her life was cut short in a tragic helicopter accident on May 9, 1967 in Vietnam, where she was working on her last book *Good Men Die*. She was 35 years old. At this point, her story has extended well beyond her short life. By sharing her story, the notes of a significant story are still being resolutely played. ⊞

CHAPTER 1

Black Mass in Mexico
Mexico: 1945, 1954

T HE STREET ON WHICH WE LIVED in Mexico City was a busy thoroughfare leading into the heart of the town: it was hot, dusty and dirty, fragrant with flowers, and full of the delicate aroma of centuries of corruption. On the corners, amiable street vendors stood behind improvised counters and made fresh orange juice while ragged children played and sold lottery tickets.

This was war-time Mexico, and the narrow street was congested with fine American cars driven by wealthy Mexicans in spotless tropical suits, and Army cars packed with soldiers in the uniforms of a dozen nations. Weaving in and out of the traffic were serape-draped Indians in huge peasant hats walking with bare feet in silent and morose dignity. Sometimes, handsome officers of the Mexican Army galloped by on blooded horses. The architecture was faintly Moorish. The ghosts of Cortez and Montezuma hovered over the city.

We had come by train from San Antonio, a long, uncomfortable dusty ride through arid blackish mountains and parched desert, only occasionally relieved by monstrous cacti.

We had stayed for a few days in a musty midtown hotel near the magnificent white Palacio of Fine Arts, then moved to a more reasonably priced flat.

The large market place under an open roof sold fresh native food of all kinds: meat stalls from which hung carcasses of lamb, *cabrito,* beef and fowl aswarm with millions of flies, did not tempt us, in spite of the memory of meat-rationing at home. The fruit and melons did.

In search of a piano for practice we visited a conservatory. A flight of steps led to rooms that had once been painted with figures of Soler, de Falla, Albeniz. Now the walls were cracked and crumbly, and the paintings flaked into smeary leprous horrors. The pianos were ghastly wrecks, wretched, and forlorn.

One day, we tried to telephone a Hungarian lady, Marie Nepkoz Baudré, whom a New York friend had recommended to us. She was a refugee, her husband had been French, and she had escaped from Europe with her son and came to Mexico City.

We drove to her house, past frightful decrepit hovels with ulcerated walls and ravaged fronts—wounded battered houses that quivered with the cankerous poison of warp and mutilation—buildings whose blighted rotten sides were gnawed with many colored mangled corrosion.

We reached a stained, moldering stucco dwelling.

But inside was a French-style flat with exquisite Louis Seize furniture.

Madame Baudré was attractive, red-haired, vaguely in her thirties. Her son, Stepan, about nineteen, had black hair, sharp, severe features and an introverted, indrawn expression.

She, had a rosewood Bechstein piano, which she said I might use for practice.

Daily, I began to come. Often, she was absent and her son was there alone. Though I was only twelve, he did not treat me as a child but talked to me on an adult level.

The grim, sour-looking maid who had first let us in, was always there, hovering. She was fat, in a swollen way, like a water bag, but her face was narrow and malicious, and she had sharp little eyes.

One day, when I came over, she was there alone.

After an hour's practice, during which she stared at me with unblinking intensity, I started to go towards the bathroom. She pulled me back, saying:

"Oh, no. Not zat one. Zat ees out of order. Today you go to zee other one. Come here."

She led me into another room, magnificently furnished, all black and silver, with silver lame draperies, and an enormous bed with black silk brocade bedspread and a black satin canopy. At the foot of the bed lay gray pajamas, and a sheer green silk nightgown of chiffon and lace.

She pointed to the bed, and said, "Zat ees where zey sleep. Zey sleep togezzer. Eet ees a sin. She sleep weeth her son. God weel punish zem."

Indeed, this was the only bedroom in the flat, except for a small room off the kitchen for the maid.

I left, and never returned.

A week later, Madame Baudré visited my mother and told her a long story. Her son, she said, had been killed before her eyes in a bombing raid in Central Europe. This boy, who was now supposed to be her son, had been his best friend. He somewhat resembled her son, and she had given him her son's passport. They had escaped together, in a very complicated way, and came to Mexico. They had hoped to get into the U.S., but had been unable to. Now they were waiting, just waiting. They had fallen in love, and since they had nothing left but each other, they had seen no reason to hesitate in consummating it.

But we never did quite believe her.

Now we started to visit some of the old ruins.

The Desierto de Los Leones was high in the mountains, a monastery where, for three centuries, a secret order of monks had existed. The story was that they had stolen girls from the nearby countryside, tortured them, and misused them in every way. The confessional was strange, oval-shaped, built so it made the slightest whisper resound like a booming shout when listened to from a certain point on the outside. This supposedly enabled the head of the monastery to keep informed on all he wished to know. In an underground chamber, torture-instruments still hung from the moldy green walls.

At the Cathedral of the Blessed Virgin of Guadalupe, there were multitudes of representations in silver and gold of parts of the human body cured by the intercession of the Blessed Virgin, set in mosaics on the walls.

In the floating gardens of Xochimilco the gondolas on the canals were flower-laden; some of the boatmen sang dreamily to guitars while others tended braziers, selling spicy hot food.

After climbing to the top of the Pyramid of the Sun where, five centuries ago, sacrificial youths had their still-beating hearts pulled from their breasts by Aztec priests, I stood in the sweeping wind on the spot where the live hearts had been immolated. This pyramid was not built as the Egyptian ones had been, but rather by pouring cement over the top of an already existing mountain, and setting stones in the cement.

At the great Cathedral in Mexico City, where people were permitted to worship, we saw the magnificent twisted gold Altar of the Monarchs, and a big crater in the floor where a bomb had exploded.

After seeing the Lake of Blood in Guanajuato, on which scarlet flowers float in the spring, we visited the nearby Yuririapundaro with its bas-relief statues of St. Nicholas Torentino, the province's patron saint.

At a museum, one day, we met a strange man, by chance. He had an egg-shaped head, and a distant, evasive manner.

He invited us to a ceremony given by a group of Mexicans descended from African slaves, who had preserved traditions of a strange religion of their own, of Guinea African mixed with diabolic European blood. It took place in a chapel that had been closed when Mexico's trouble with the church began, and had been part of a mansion outside the city that had passed into other hands. Having lost our way, we were late arriving.

To get to the chapel, we had to climb down a flight of steps by the wearily dripping fountain of a flag-tiled patio. At the bottom of the rusty stairway we passed through a black velvet curtain, into a stone room with pews filled with weird-looking people. Statues of pagan idols and Christian saints were in niches on the moldy corrupt walls. The altar was spread with red velvet, and over it hung an enormous upside down ebony cross, with a green serpent twined round it. A pyramid of skulls sat on the red velvet, and strange geometrical shapes and obscene symbols were painted on the wall behind it. A priest came out, in a red satin robe embroidered with goats and devils. The altar boys wore long black silk robes covered with red triangles. They, like the priest, were barefoot, and had phallic symbols tattooed on the soles of their feet, and long toenails painted gold.

The Mass began, in a strange language, like Latin spoken backwards and mingled with African and Spanish words. It was a direct parody of the Catholic mass, with a demoniac addition of a rather sadistic and satanic humor. I was terrified as it grew wilder and more devilish. A sweetish, pungent, smoky incense seemed to fill the room. We took advantage of this cloudy haze to escape up the stairway to the patio and street.

The closing of the Catholic churches by the revolutionary government making it unlawful even to appear on the street in Roman vestments, had encouraged strange cults to spring up.

Eventually, all visitors to Mexico attend a bullfight.

I had hoped to compose something characteristic of the country, so one Sunday afternoon we arrived at the Plaza de toro. At this time, it was surrounded by a high, unpainted wooden fence. Within, there was an open-air oval of seats perched safely above the arena into which you looked to watch the elegant, subtle spectacle of torture and death. That afternoon, with pomp and ceremony, six sleek, defiant bulls and eight luckless, blindfolded horses were killed. My mother wept openly for the poor animals.

An intellectual Spaniard seated next to us explained that the baiting of bulls had been introduced to Spain by their Moorish conquerors, and that the "game" expressed the pagan acceptance and enjoyment of death. It had been banned by many popes but to no avail. The Spaniards had to learn to surpass their conquerors in the bullring before they became ruthless enough to drive them from

Spain. Though this reason has now been forgotten, the Spanish ethos unconsciously associates the bullring with virility and self-esteem.

I returned to the flat to start my composition. Instead, I wrote the melodies for my first orchestral work, "Manhattan Nocturne," a tone poem expressing my longing for home.

In 1954, I returned to Mexico, playing in the quaint border town of Juarez; and then in Mexico City. Curiosity led me to look for the chapel of the Black Mass again. The district had changed. A modern movie theatre advertising a film with Mapy Cortés was there instead. ⊞

CHAPTER 2

Thieves and Plots in Cuba
1950, 1952, 1953

STAYED AT THE HOTEL PLAZA on my first visit to Havana in 1950. In the center of the city, it was near everything one might wish to see or avoid. The staff was friendly, they went out of their way to be, not official, but human.

I gave performances at the University of Havana and the Club Atenas.

I also visited the Club Atenas when l revisited Cuba in the spring of 1952.

The Club had some mysterious origins and had probably been a luxurious private dwelling in the days of the Spanish rule.

It was of white stone, with winding marble staircases. It was subdued, silken luxury within, and the walls hung with heavy, flowing drapery. The curtains were like diaphanous full-blown roses, the spacious upper rooms were a sanctuary of muffled silence, and the rich furniture was covered with petit point and pink and grey brocades.

One man I met there, Ernesto Ramírez y Quiroga, had a curious life story.

Of Spanish ancestry, he had regular features, with eyes that were amiable, but a shade too unobtrusive, and his black hair carefully combed. While engaging, he seemed almost too careful.

Then, taking me for a naive person, and perhaps feeling the need to reveal his inner self that bedevils all of us at times, he spoke extensively.

"I was born in Barranquilla, Colombia. As you have been there, you know it is not very interesting, and lacks the potentialities for a person of my qualifications that are offered by such a metropolis as Havana. My parents, Spaniards, from Asturias, had decided to immigrate to the New World despite its continuous upset of revolutionary disturbances. Barranquilla was a small place of only 30,000 people when they arrived in 1896, and the poor lived in desolate mud-walled cabins, thatched with rushes, on bamboo framework, just as they had in the seventeenth century, but my parents were happy. They never even saw Bogota, the capital, communications were so difficult then, and Colombia was like a nation of city-states, as medieval Spain had been. Civil war broke out in 1899, and, after my birth in 1900, my parents fled."

"They went to Nicaragua, but it was suffering under the tyranny of José Santos Zelaya. They journeyed on to Guatemala, but it was writhing under the dictatorship of Manuel Estrada Cabrera. They sailed to the Dominican Republic, but it was in hopeless anarchy. They voyaged on to Cuba, which was still under U.S. domination, arriving four months before the official withdrawal of General Wood, and the American Army in May 1902."

"They stayed in Havana. My father grew fairly prosperous. I grew older. My two sisters were born. I was sent to Spain to attend school. The postwar collapse in Cuban sugar prices ruined my father. I had to leave school, but I remained in Europe. My parents were accidentally killed by the *porristas,* or gunmen of President Gerardo Machado. One of my sisters entered a convent, one married and moved to Camaguey. I lost touch with them. Now, l felt alone in the world, l began to live by my wits."

DRINKING CUP AFTER CUP of heavily sugared coffee, Ernesto told me of his life as a dancer. Yet you would have almost thought he was talking to himself, or to a fantasy-image, and was unaware that l was there, listening.

He told me of his success at dancing in hotels and nightclubs in Europe, and at gallantry with women, until an unfortunate accident occurred.

"I was dancing at a luxury hotel in Milan, and was carrying on simultaneous love affairs with the wife and daughter of a wealthy Italian businessman. A business enterprise, on my part, in the beginning, for I had intended later to blackmail the wife, but the affair grew unwisely complex when the daughter who disliked, and was jealous of her mother, grew enamored of me. After maneuvering to find me alone she began to flirt, perhaps meaning to go no further. I never resisted temptation, everything suddenly went black, and when I awoke the bed was covered with blood. She blamed me, but I did not see why I should be accused, for had I not assaulted her, undoubtedly someone else would have. In any case, it made her life more interesting, and she should have been grateful for being diverted from her boredom."

"Then a shocking thing happened. I had been gambling heavily, and losing. Luck was against me. In a bad humor, I went rashly to visit the businessman's wife one evening, to ask her for some money. She did not give me as much as I wanted, as she was of a rather stingy and avaricious nature. While we were arguing, her husband had the effrontery to return from Genoa much sooner than I had been led to expect. Misunderstanding my presence, and thinking I was there for some lascivious purpose, he caught me unaware, knocking me down violently. I rose, and struggled with him. Soon we were fighting on the balcony."

"I did not know the extent of the balcony, and his blows, coming in the dark, stunned me and I toppled and fell over the low railing, to the stone-flagged garden path two stories below."

"My right leg was broken. In agony, I crawled to the street, and into my car. Though the pain was grueling, I had already formulated a plan."

"In response to my signal, a street urchin came over to me, accepted some lire, and promised to telephone my Cuban friend, José Portales. In twenty minutes that seemed like as many hours, José arrived. He took the wheel, and drove us out of the city, while I told him what he must do."

"Only the Blessed Virgin could have given me the strength to bear the physical anguish. On the outskirts of Milan, José rammed the car into a tree in such a way as to make it seem my injuries resulted from this automobile accident. He gave himself a few minor cuts, left the car, walked to the nearby villa of a physician I knew. My next awareness was of being rushed to the doctor's private clinic in a screaming ambulance."

"While I could have had the businessman arrested and tried for assault and battery, I preferred this more roundabout method, which would enable me to defraud my insurance company of a large sum, as well as to blackmail the businessman. And I had reason to wish no connection with the police."

"José was adroit, cooperative, as was the doctor. If the latter had any suspicion that my injuries were not totally a result of the accident, he quelled them, for he would not have liked my knowledge of the abortions he had performed on society ladies made public."

"Though the insurance company's doctors and lawyers were not entirely satisfied they gave me, at last, a fat settlement, which I was forced to split with José. We also bled the businessman and his wife heavily. The husband paid to avoid prosecution and to get back some incriminating photographs of his wife. The wife paid for the return of her gushing and passionate letters, and the diary I had taken the precaution of abstracting from her room one day, and which revealed in earthy and indelicate detail, her relations, not only with me, but with other lovers."

"As soon as I could, I left Milan."

"I convalesced for a month in Naples, in the villa of my former dancing partner, María del Toro that she shared with the wealthy Roberto Paccini. Both had reason to be grateful to me. Roberto had been in the audience nightly to watch María when she danced with me, and had grown enamored of her. He had approached me for advice. Realizing that virginity commands a higher price, I had told him that María was a good girl, whose parents back in Cuba, had entrusted her to my care. Adding that María had planned to take the veil, and only left the convent to earn money for her family, I made him feel she would be shocked by dishonorable intentions. This increased his passion. I coached María carefully in her role of innocence. Indeed, we found a skilled plastic surgeon who recreated what time and man had long destroyed. Then, I coached Roberto in how to seduce the angel. This fool had brought María's parents over from Santiago del Estero, Cuba, to Italy by boat, and bought them an annuity and a villa in their name, and had given María a sizable amount of money before she succumbed."

"María, in her gratitude, gave me this platinum and diamond watch before I left. I sailed for Havana, where Batista had just assumed control."

"I had intended to buy a *latifundia,* with my European earnings, and retire, but a devil possessed me. I began to gamble, lost heavily. My wits had been somewhat dulled by my long absence from Havana. I was robbed by my own countrymen."

"A windfall came. I met an American whom I rescued from drowning. I had arranged his falling in the sea in the first place, and I knew he could not swim. When I saved him, he was grateful, kept me as his guest at a luxury hotel, and paid my bills for months. He never knew the treachery of the act by which I gained his favor."

"He died. I was disappointed he had only willed me a few thousand dollars."

"Then, I joined forces with a high-class fortune teller and astrologer."

"She had a clientele among American tourists, mostly female. Women always want to know their future in love. That appears to be the only subject that interests them, and they rarely have as much male attention as they crave."

"Margarita Quintero, the astrologer, would recommend me to some of her bored, rich clients, always indicating that my horoscope matched theirs, and that it was all written in the stars and the cards. I did good business this way, for a while."

"I also began to manage some nightclub singers and dancers. One singer caused me much trouble by claiming I had raped her. I got the case thrown out of court, because I got four friends of mine to testify against her, one claiming that he had been in bed with her at the time of my supposed attack."

"The war was over now. Grau San Martin was President. I was low in funds. Paying my friends for their false testimony in court had impoverished me. Gambling again, I had poor luck at cards. One night, I rashly lost a greater sum than I could pay, but a man later offered to cancel out my debt, and pay me. In addition, he asked if I would join in a revolutionary plot he was concocting."

"I agreed. What did I have to lose? I thought. I was wrong. We were caught and I lost my liberty. Are you listening?"

"Of course. But why do you tell me all of this?"

"Because your youth and innocence recalls my own to me and makes me sad. Besides, I enjoy shocking you."

"But why? I have not hurt you. I am a stranger to you."

"For that very reason, I can speak more freely."

"But why do you want to shock me?"

"Oh, for several reasons." He looked at me and smiled bitterly. "You believe that the world is good and that offends me. The world is not good. It is bad or it is indifferent. But when I was young, like you, I believed it was good. That was my undoing. I kept thinking that if I could only get a sizable nest egg, I could turn over a new leaf and be good. It is so much more comfortable to be good." He shrugged, "But I was forty-four. I had squandered my youth and talents. My leg had not healed properly. I could never dance again. I had a jail record. What was I to do?" He lit a cigarette and looked at me ironically.

"Perhaps you should have married. That might have saved you."

"Exactly what I planned to do next. But since I couldn't keep a wife, I would have to get one who could keep me. Rich women are hard to marry. They are spoiled. Unless you get them very young. Then their money is tied up with guardians."

"First, I had to get enough money to buy a new wardrobe, and a false passport. How do you get money with nothing? You take it from others. But you risk your life doing so. I robbed a woman of her jewelry. I picked one whose jewels were insured so she didn't lose anything. With new identification papers, and a new name, I sailed for Miami. There, at a luxury hotel, I found Mary. She was tall, thin, plain and rich."

"Weren't you ever sincere?"

"Sometimes, but usually with later regret. Mary was accompanied by her mother, a bitch of the first order, a tyrannical, fat hypochondriac. I had the good sense to play up to her mother, by listening to her endless stories about her health and her family, carefully losing to her at dominoes."

"The mother grew so attached to me that she herself got the idea of 'catching' me for her daughter. I had represented myself as a wealthy Cuban, and spent money freely. Soon she was practically forcing her daughter to see me. They came from Michigan, and though not worldly-wise, were solidly wealthy. The only drawback was the girl, who when I made love to her, showed unexpected resistance. A cold, frigid neurotic."

"I was determined to seduce her, so she would feel grateful, and that I would be doing her a favor by marrying her. It was a difficult job. She was preoccupied with ideas about righteousness and sin. I was sure this indicated that once seduced, she would go overboard with desire. But how to start? When all else failed, I appealed to her sense of pity; told her I was ill, my life was dead, I was about to kill myself, and showed her the pistol. I wept. Her maternal instinct aroused, she gave in."

"I intended to make her pregnant, so she would be desperate, and plead with me to marry her. Thus, we would enter matrimony with the advantage psychologically on my side, and I could assume control of her money without difficulty. I did not intend to let these two women dominate me. She did become pregnant, but was too ignorant to realize it until two months had passed. Then, instead of falling more passionately in love with me, she got torn by conscience-stricken guilt, and a feeling that she was ruined in the sight of God. She began to weep and castigate herself."

"She committed suicide."

"It was terrible. She slashed her wrists and bled to death. I was entering the hotel lobby when one of the bellboys told me that she had just been discovered, dying, and the doctors were unable to save her. I left the hotel at once. I did not even go back upstairs to get my clothes. I went immediately to the airport, chartered a small plane, and flew to Mexico."

"I was afraid there would be a police investigation. I had become involved in some illegal activities on the side, in Miami, to get the money to keep up my front as a wealthy Cuban. I could not risk contact with police."

"In Mexico, I bought false passport and credentials. After Carlos Prío Socarrás became President, I returned to Cuba in 1949. Drifting, I tried many schemes. Briefly, I lived with a colored woman who, having amassed money, wished a white escort, which, owing to the color prejudice here, gave her social prestige."

"I gained money smuggling, lost it gambling, then returned to managing nightclub artists."

"Life has not been bad recently, though I have abandoned many former dreams. I am fifty now, and content to direct other people's lives."

ERNESTO RAMÍREZ PAUSED, drank another cup of heavily sugared coffee, and smiled at me, with a smile that was generous, regretful, world-weary, cynical, and yet strangely kind—as though he realized that his life had been weak and corrupt, vicious and deceitful. Through his sins, he assumed, he had grown to know himself, and, thus, all humanity, for the seeds of all evil and all good can be found within the heart of every man. This enabled him to look with tolerance on the sins and failings of all men, and see with more purity and charity, perhaps, into the soul of another, than would one whose life had passed in the ivory tower of cloistered and sheltered tranquility.

I did not betray any sense of shock at what he had told me. I felt strangely humble, shy and abashed, in the presence of a man who had known more, lived more, and suffered more than I ever would. The soul itself can be heaven and hell, and carry within itself the weighty tribulation of the punishment for its own sins. And the sinner can sometimes experience a strange illumination, and be dear to God, as the weakest child is dear to its mother, and the frailest fawn is cherished by the mother doe.

Ernesto Ramírez now told me about the nightclub artists he had managed, their triumphs, and failures, and how he had hoped at times to try classic music management, but found the obstacles difficult.

Latin American social life centers on social clubs like the Club Atenas, which bear no relation to nightclubs. Though not a member of the Atenas, he occasionally visited there, and had heard my 1950 performance. Realizing I could not play at the University that spring, as it had been closed since Batista's return to power in March, he had come to the Atenas in hopes of finding me again, and persuading me to make a try, under his direction, at popular nightclubs in Cuba and South America.

I told him nothing, not even disaster, could make me leave the classic field, to remain in which I had studied, sacrificed, so long.

He urged me to contact him if I ever had difficulties in Havana; though I never again had a conversation with him, he came thereafter to all my public concerts, and I often looked down from the stage to see him sitting, with a party of heartily applauding friends, in the front row.

Soon I found that Cuban affairs have a way of being difficult, unruly, with many a snare for the uncoached and unwary.

I received word from my father that Señor Montenegro, a Havana journalist, had written to say he had to pawn his suit to get money for gas to drive with a friend to the Havana airport to say hello to me, so would my father please send him $35? My father had done so.

I returned to New York. In August, Dr. María Malapuerta, a Cuban intellectual, wrote that she had arranged for me to play at a symphonic festival on August 29. I went to Cuba. The festival had vanished. Only my concert took place. It had turned into a recital at an outdoor stadium. I began the recital with the "A Minor Prelude" and "Fugue" by Bach-Liszt. Men with television cameras rushed onstage, stood all around me, shooting film. A camera tube exploded, a shower of sparks fell on my orange nylon dress. It burst into flames. A cameraman stamped it out while I went on, without interruption, playing Bach to the audience of 7,000.

Four days later, I had an appointment with President Fulgencio Batista. At the last moment, a crowd of thousands of workers marched through the city to the doors of the Presidential Palace, and made a demonstration. The appointment was canceled. Everyone feared revolution. But the worker's leaders made speeches and speeches, and the President talked for hours and hours without stopping, and finally the workers forgot the demonstration, and had a fiesta instead.

Enormously long interviews appeared about me daily in the press. There were an incalculable number of journals in Havana, and they commented on every move I made. One reporter outdid himself to get a scoop. He wrote that I ate the outside husks of pineapples. I telephoned his editor angrily. "I do not eat the outside husks of pineapples!" The reporter came, with photographer, to interview me. Again, I said, "I do not eat the outside husks of pineapples!" The next edition of the newspaper carried an article on the front page, replete with fantastic details about how I ate the outside husks of pineapples.

Cubans did not tend to be punctual.

All day long, I would wait for people to show up.

If I made an appointment for two in the afternoon, the person was likely to phone me at 4:30 p.m. to say he was "on his way" and appear an hour later.

As this went on all day, I had to do my practicing in the evenings.

I would stay all night long, practicing, at the Conservatorio.

As I got almost no sleep at all, I soon grew nervous.

Before I took a taxi, long intricate discussions would take place about the price of the journey. If one were not very shrewd, one would be charged, as a foreigner, twice what Cubans would pay.

Cleanliness would be resplendent and shining in the front rooms of a store or apartment. The contrast would be appalling, in the bathroom.

One American who lived in Havana told me, "The Cubans are so tricky they could steal the gold fillings out of your teeth without your noticing it."

If I strolled alone down the beautiful Avenida Malecon, crowds of little boys would appear from nowhere, surround me, and demand money.

Once, engrossed in reading a book by Pierre Louÿs, I walked aimlessly, until I had unwittingly left the area I knew, and was in a strange, dark, unfamiliar neighborhood. Crowds of men stood on the corners, making obscene gestures, whistling, and shouting Cuban slang at me.

Suddenly, I heard my name called.

Dr. María Malapuerta was running up the street after me, crying, "*Hay que venir inmediatamente! Inmediamente!* I have looked through all Havana for you! You must come to CMQ at once! You have appointment there at four o'clock!" It was now five o'clock. We dashed to CMQ, the great television station. When we arrived breathlessly, the man I was to see had not yet arrived. When he sauntered in, he said, "Hmm. It's Tuesday now. Can you play the Liszt's "E Flat Concerto" with our orchestra over a nationwide television hookup on Friday? Three million people will be watching," I replied, "Sure! *Por supuesto. ¡Ciertamente!*"

I had never studied the Liszt Concerto.

After buying a copy of the music, I practiced for three days and nights.

I still cannot imagine where I got the energy. I hardly ate, did not sleep at all. After seventy-two hours of work and no sleep, I played the concerto with the CMQ orchestra over nationwide television. It was a triumph. Directly afterwards, I dashed by taxi to the Club Atenas, where I gave a recital for a packed house.

Two days later, I met a Catalán impresario, Señor Pedro Alfonso Carlos Paquirito.

A short, thin, nervous man, whose black-rimmed glasses dramatically framed his pale blue eyes, he was sharply proud, well-dressed, and talkative.

His speech rushed out in voluble streams, garrulous rivers, and enthusiastic torrents.

He talked about his awesome Spanish ancestry, his honesty, the thousands of women who had been in love with him, "*¡Marquesas! ¡Condesas! ¡Duquesas! ¡Princesas!* How zey loffs me! Een long lines zey wait for me!" The artists he had presented throughout Latin America, how terrible and ungrateful they all were, how everyone had conspired to be "dreadful" to him everywhere, and how it was not true when people said he talked too much, that really he was "a *santo!*" and "ze mos' silentest man een *zee woorld!*"

By an extraordinary complex and intricate series of happenings, he arrived in Havana. It took hours to tell the details.

"An' zen I go to Panama weeth zees man an' hees wife, only I theenks zey are not marry, an' I am vehry sweet weeth zem, I sacrifices for zem, an' he calls me a thief, ees not kind zat! An' zen I finds zees Spanish dancer, an' she ees mos' greatest dancer een *zee woorld*, only ees not good woman, she like zee reech mens — what kind of wooman ees zat who wants presents? Good wooman does not wants presents — an' I brings her here, I gets her thousan' pesos zee performance an' she says I tries make loff to her — she puts een all the newspaper — an' nevair een my life does I does zat—I am gentleman! I am seerious man—I am like a *santo*—I am hones' *empressario!*"

Then, he went on to say, "But, *es un milagro!* Always, *Dios* make *milagros* for me. Nevair am I depressed. Always, *siempre,* I theenk, 'Tomorrow I make million dollars!' God send me to you. You weel be mos' greatest pianist een *zee woorld!* I weel present you all ovair South America—we weel make all Colombia, all Argentina, all Brazil, all ehverything! Oof! Ees fantastico!"

I did not see him again in Cuba. Later I collided with him briefly in Venezuela, but two years later he presented me in many cities in South America, in a tour that led all the way to Spain.

In a few days, I was given a luxurious reception by American Ambassador Willard Beaulac at the swank American Embassy Residence. Two hundred guests were present, of every conceivable color, an innovation for Havana.

In October, I had a concert scheduled in Santa Clara. A hurricane devastated that area the day before. Hundreds were injured, and there was vast property damage. Dr. María Malapuerta was sure my concert could not take place.

But the next day at 6:00 p.m., she received a cable saying the concert was proceeding as scheduled. (The wire had arrived at noon, but the landlady had not summoned the energy to give it to her for six hours).

We must rush to Santa Clara immediately. Over two hundred miles away. No planes were available due to the storm. No trains. The bus would take eight hours. We must take a taxi. In five minutes, I was dressed to go. But Dr. Malapuerta could not leave so quickly. She had to spend an hour choosing an elaborate costume. Then she must curl her hair. It was past seven when we rushed down Avenida Malecon, searching for a taxi. It couldn't, of course, be just any taxi. She insisted on using the taxi of a friend of hers. We had to find him. We hunted and hunted.

At 8:00 p.m. we were in his car, speeding to Santa Clara. The concert was at 8:30 p.m. Over three hundred kilometers to drive in thirty minutes. She kept shouting to him, "Faster! *Mas rapido!*" He drove faster and faster.

Wildly, we sped southeast, through the hinterlands. I threw on my evening gown in the racing taxi. Time sped.

We arrived in Santa Clara at 11:00 p.m.

By 11:05 p.m., we were at the theatre. A woman in white stood outside, pacing up and down. She told us the entire audience had sat and waited for us until 10:55 p.m., and then left.

We drove back to Havana, in silence, arriving at dawn. I had to pay the taxi driver fifty dollars. Then I had to practice all day without any sleep. That night, I made my debut at the Lyceum Theatre, playing a program of Bach and Ravel.

The next week, we journeyed to Saguas, where we had a beautiful suite at a hotel that looked like it came from the days of the Conquistadors. We trotted to my concert in a horse and buggy.

We voyaged on to Santa Clara, where all the audience that had awaited me the first time, came en masse to my performance. No one even mentioned my tardiness.

Back in Havana, I played over the Cadena Azul radio network. The performance began late. This is the only place I have ever been where a radio program did not start on time.

The next day, we were waiting for a bus, when we collided with Señor Honoré de Renaissance, a French teacher.

After making our acquaintance, he became most friendly, and followed me everywhere.

Dr. Malapuerta told me in confidence, "I theenk he loffs you!"

About fifty, he was sleekly dapper in elegantly cut clothes. He had bright blue eyes, sharp nose like a gargoyle, and an expressionless face.

Wherever I went, he went. I returned to New York.

IN 1953, I WAS BACK IN HAVANA. It was nice to see these charming, warm, hospitable people again.

I had forgotten the difficulties of my previous trip.

I was almost late to my concert at the Auditorium Theatre. The elevator at my hotel broke down while I was in it. It stayed stuck between floors for forty-five minutes. The operator was not upset. He sang Cuban songs while we waited to be rescued.

Señor Honoré de Renaissance came backstage afterwards.

He asked me to sign my autograph on a number of large blank pieces of white paper.

Seven months later, while I was far away on a concert tour he wrote my father to say, "Philippa owes me $200." Of course he had never given me a cent. My father wrote him, "NO."

Seven months after that, he wrote my mother, "Philippa owes me $200. I have her signature on a paper stating that." The third time, he wrote my father again, "Philippa owes me $200. I have witnesses — Señor Montenegro and his wife who saw me hand it to her." I had not even seen Señor Montenegro that year, and he had no wife. Yet, every few months, Señor Honoré de Renaissance would write, adding more and more demands, and more and more names to the number of witnesses, and types of statements I had supposedly put my signature under.

Four years later, I asked a lawyer what to do.

He said, "Ha-ha! Ignore it. I had an American friend in Cuba who was sued by a Cuban for $800 he had purportedly given the American. A lie, of course. When the case came to court, the Cuban had seven false witnesses to swear they had 'seen' him give the American the money. I brought in fourteen false witnesses to swear they had 'seen' the American give the money back! We won the case. That is how to do business in Cuba!" ⊞

CHAPTER 3
Strip-tease in Saint Thomas
Virgin Islands, Puerto Rico: 1950, 1952, 1957

WHEN I LANDED IN ST. THOMAS, VIRGIN ISLANDS, in March 1950, the strong winds whipped one vengefully, as they once lashed buccaneers' sailing vessels long ago. Recollections of St. Thomas' bloody past made her mild, torpid, dormant present seem a little tame.

After my recital, I stayed at the Alton Adams Guest House, an enormous old mansion that had seen pirates and slavers.

Mr. Adams, the patriarch of the island, lived with his wife, and nineteen of his children and grandchildren in the proud, battered white house.

Though nearly sixty, he would run up and down the steep, cruel, dizzying, overhanging steps that rose on the perpendicular hill that led to his historical home like an antelope, while I limped lamely behind. He is tall, dark, with keen blue eyes that miss nothing. Once a Navy band conductor, he is now a Patron of the Arts.

One day, a lobster was prepared in my honor. A Navy Commander had donned diving equipment and swum deep under the ocean to a vast cave where he had speared it especially for me.

Ushering me into the antique kitchen to watch the lobster cooking painfully, doubled up in an open pot, the Commander murmured with a modest air of regret, "What a pity! This one is only four feet long—there was a *nine-foot* lobster I was going to capture for you too, but it got away!"

Some Virgin Islanders came to visit me after supper.

As I had been covered with a painful mass of mosquito bites the night before, I was glad to be distracted by their tales of St. Thomas in the violent buccaneer era.

This history was bloody, fantastic, and colorful.

Then one slender, dark-skinned man, with a face oddly elfin, curious, and strangely cryptic, told me a tale about a friend in one of the British Virgin Islands—perhaps it was Jost van Dyke or Tortola, or Salt Island.

The friend had been captain of a small boat, which had plied lazily between St. John, Snake Island, and some other small islands. He lived in a battered, old, white house, much like Mr. Adams', with his mother and three children.

Like so many Virgin Islanders, his home was sparsely furnished, with only the bare essentials of tables and chairs present. Yet, in the living room, there were three spaces on the walls, here it could be seen very clearly where paintings had once hung.

After the family had lived there a few years, there was a terrific storm one night. Lightning struck the roof, a falling tree crashed into the attic window.

Later, while making repairs, they discovered a recess in the attic wall they had not noticed before. In it were three paintings. They exactly fitted the spaces on the walls downstairs.

They were hung in the living room.

Sometime later, one of the children climbed on a chair and smeared one of the pictures with white paint. My friend took it down and tried to get the white streaks off with paint remover. He found there was another painting underneath the top one, which was an ordinary nature scene. Little by little, a strong and powerful portrait emerged beneath of a man with deep-set, hypnotic eyes, a plumed hat, wearing seventeenth century clothes, and riding a black horse. In one hand, he clutched a piece of yellow parchment.

Amazed, he worked on the other two paintings.

Concealed beneath the mediocre scenes on the surface were more horsemen. With the aid of a magnifying-glass, he was able to see queer figures and symbols on the parchment of the first painting. There were more figures set into the brocade coat of the second horseman. On the third painting, there were a few symbols marked on the sandy ground beneath the black horse.

He copied the marks without commenting on them to his family. After much calculation, he was able to decipher the figures and symbols.

Now he had a vague map, and an explicit series of directions.

Before long, he was digging up the ground in the garden, until it looked like the scene of an air raid. The last place he thought of digging was right under the attic window. He, and a friend, found an oak chest with iron rings.

It was three-fourths empty, but it still contained a mass of doubloons, sequins, goldecus, florins, ducats, and other old coins, and some gold crucifixes, loose sapphires, and massive finger rings.

He kept his findings as secret as possible, never turned them over to the government, sold them little by little, and used the money to educate his family, who were, incidentally, much more unhappy and discontented after the discovery than they had ever been before.

Before leaving St. Thomas, I was received by Governor Morris De Castro the first native Virgin Islander to receive that appointment. A white man, whose family roots were Panamanian, he was most cordial. Everyone I met in St. Thomas was enthusiastic about him, and thought his accession would solve all the problems for the Islands.

MR. ADAMS GAVE ME A LETTER of introduction to the Figueroa family in San Juan, before I flew to Puerto Rico. The new Caribe Hilton Hotel in San Juan was heavenly.

Fresh pineapple awaited us in our modern room. The decor was splendid in a futuristic way. It should have been. The 350-room hotel had cost $7,300,000 to build.

I played a recital for wounded veterans. Señora Figueroa and two of her daughters attended, and we visited them the next day.

The Figueroas were the leading musical family in Puerto Rico. All of them, father, mother, and eight children, were skilled, accomplished musicians. One of the most brilliant had died tragically in Europe. Two of the other girls, though, had studied piano with Alfred Cortot. They showed me finger exercises Cortot had taught them, of enormous value, which helped me with the foundation of my future technique. One sister showed me how to use a practice keyboard with amazing results. Five of the family then played the "Brahms Quintet" for us, with exquisite, profound feeling, and dazzling precision.

Later, the Secretary of Governor Muñoz Marin escorted us through the old Spanish fortress that was the seat of government, showing us magnificent bedrooms, winding staircases, secret passages, and former dungeons and torture-chambers. The spirit of the gruesome victims of the past seemed to hang with seasoned horror, in a cloud over the place.

The Secretary, a slender dark-haired man, spoke to us once we reached the warm, windy street outside, about the interview my father had with Governor Muñoz Marin the previous year. The Secretary was delighted when I told him I loved Spanish literature, and had read Don Quixote and the works of Baroja and Galdos in their Spanish originals.

As we said goodbye and walked down the sunny street, we looked back at his slender figure etched against the Spanish fortress like a Velazquez painting.

That evening, as I sat by a green pool at the Caribe Hilton I saw a blond youth with flawless classic features, soft creamy skin, turquoise-blue eyes, AND dazzling gold hair like flecked sunbeams. He wore a U.S. Army Private First Class uniform. Under his eyes were deep shadows. He was the sleepiest-looking individual I have ever seen.

He would gaze at me fixedly, then look distantly vacant. His head would drop to one side, he would almost topple from the oyster shell chair, then would suddenly sit straight and stare.

His name was George O'Connor.

He invited me to dinner. As we walked into the dining room he said, "Crissake, I'm sleepy. We were on maneuvers in Florida's swampland, and I was eight days and nights without sleep, fighting all the time—I came here to rest. No! I feel fine now, I do not need to lie down!" he shouted, barely keeping from toppling again.

We ordered. I had to ask for salt fish from Boston, for the waters are so fished out around Puerto Rico that it is hard to get fresh sea-food.

In five minutes, the waiter returned, with a note for George who rose with staggering dignity, and cried, "Jesus! Some buddies of mine are outside, I'll have to say hello—be back soon." He went out, knocking into the tables on the way.

In a few minutes, a waiter reopened the door. Outside, I could see George walking away, a U.S.M.P. on either side of him. He had been AWOL.

As he did not return, I dined on two orders of salt fish.

The Governor's Secretary sent a luxurious car to the Caribe Hilton the next day. It drove me throughout San Juan, from monstrous slums to bright new houses in gay pastel colors, derelict shacks to homes of grave Spanish dignity. Then I gave a recital for nuns and students at a beautiful convent.

TWO YEARS LATER, en route to St. Thomas, I passed through San Juan, where I was met at the airport by the musical director of a large radio station.

Engrossed in talking to him, I missed my plane, and arrived two hours late to the windy St. Thomas airfield.

Alton Adams drove me anxiously to Irwin Gross' Theatre.

I noticed that the street names were printed on neat rectangles on corner house walls in Danish as well as English, a reminder of the days when the island had been the Danish West Indies' capital.

My concert at Center Theatre that night was a success, yet St. Thomas seemed subtly, indefinably, to have altered.

For one thing, there was much sour grumbling about Governor De Castro. He had the effrontery not to have immediately solved all troubles in the Virgin Islands, and the audacity not to have instantly given an important government job, with huge salary and prestige, to every single Virgin Islander he had ever known or even shaken hands with.

"They" were muttering about how he had "let people down." The Governor received me warmly, with sincere and charming cordiality.

I met an English painter at Mr. Adam's Guest House, who told me at length how he disagreed with every single thing I had done at my concert, and then spent hours showing me his paintings of flowers.

Before I left, I asked Mr. Adams if I could take a bath.

This rash remark occasioned surprise.

There were showers upstairs, but I do not like to shower. The only bathtub was deep in the bowels of the battered house. I was led down a staircase, then another and another, endlessly. It was like a *Journey to the Center of the Earth.* When I was almost ready for collapse, we arrived abruptly at a dark room with a black, seemingly earthen, floor. A tiny white tub sat there. Otherwise, the room was empty.

As there was no running water, I sat huddled in the middle of the tub, while each one of the nineteen children and grandchildren came in bearing a pot or pan of water, and poured it on me.

WHEN I RETURNED TO SAN JUAN, I made a recording for the radio station.

Before I left, I met a stranger, a British West Indian, who offered to sell me some British West Indian dollars in exchange for U.S. dollars, at a more favorable rate than banks give. His reason, he said, was that he "would not be returning" to Jamaica or Trinidad, and would have no opportunity to use the BWI dollars. I gave him forty dollars in American money, and he gave me a number of bright, new bills. When I tried to use them in Trinidad, I was told they were counterfeit.

IN EARLY 1957, I RETURNED TO ST. THOMAS. It was hotter this time, the air a miasma of humid stifling stillness and burning heat. That was one of the years they had the least rainfall. Before the year ended, 33,000,000 gallons of water had to be exported from Puerto Rico.

It was fantastically hot the evening of my recital at the bright, new, modern High School Auditorium. The air was sodden. The hall was nearly packed. I wore the blue and black Chantilly-lace gown, with six petticoats underneath, in which I had played for Emperor Haile Selassie. The only dress I had brought from New York, it looked grand.

After the first piece on the program, Beethoven's "Pathetique Sonata," I went backstage, and took off my necklace. Then, I returned, played Soler, and went back and removed my earrings. After the "Appasionata Sonata," I took off stockings and garters. After intermission came Chopin "Polonaises." The sweltering heat broiled me. I went off stage and took off my panties. After the Chopin "Scherzi," I went back again, and sliced off three of the petticoats with a razor. The other three went after the "Alborada del Gracioso of Ravel."

My concert ended. Covered with mosquito bites, my feet hurt, so I discarded my shoes in the wings, before coming forth to bow.

The train of the dress hid the fact that I wore nothing underneath, till someone shouted, "Encore!" and I went to the piano.

The train caught on the piano leg and ripped. Halfway through my encore I noticed that it had split way up.

It took sangfroid to finish the encore.

After the concert I received many congratulations, and those who had opposed my coming were, naturally, the first to embrace me.

There were many autographs to sign, questions to answer. One woman asked, "Do you remember me? I met you after the recital you played at the New York World's Fair when you were six!" Others asked me when I was going to get married. One boy muttered, "Gee, how long does it take to play like you? Is it hard?" I replied, "Not when you get the hang of it, but it takes twenty years to get the hang of it!"

Mr. Dell, of the Virgin Isles Hotel, was a cherubic bachelor who loved to say that no woman had ever caught him because no woman could be half so determined as he. He took me sightseeing in his small dark car that sped fleetly up and down the almost vertical hills, as the sun shone down like a sizzling egg yolk from the blue-white sky.

He told me his experiences in managing a hotel in Ireland, and about how the Virgin Isles were named in honor of St. Ursula and her companions.

Now, we drove past the beautiful Virgin Isles Hotel, whose rooms cost $40 a day, and up.

Later, en route to the airport, I looked back nostalgically at the fairytale town, whose pastel-shaded houses seemed like fancily colored cookies and candy on the summits of her chocolate hills.

On gazing at her enchanting serenity, one could not believe buccaneers had once battled in the nearby sea. ⊞

CHAPTER 4

`Voodoo Music for a President
Haiti, Dominican Republic: 1950, 1958

N DECEMBER 1950, I flew via Pan American Airlines to Port-au-Prince, Haiti, to attend President Paul Magloire's inauguration.

It was my first voyage alone.

Alphonse Drouet, a sculptor, and supposedly Haiti's most eligible bachelor met me at the airport, dressed in a flawlessly cut white suit.

His manner bespoke awareness of the languorous perfection of his ebony skin, finely drawn face, and high, arched forehead. He wore blue sunglasses.

His blue car had blue-tinted glass and black and white seat covers.

We drove past Dessaline's statue towards the winding road to Port-au-Prince.

Elusive replies or evasive monosyllable were his response to my every remark. Finally, I asked, "How long do you work every day?"

He said, "Work? I do not work!"

This made it clear that he was of the elite.

We passed barefoot peasants with faces set in fixed malevolence.

He was not interested in them. I introduced what I thought was a safe subject—books. He murmured, "No, I don't read—not in the past five years."

"Do you like to swim?"

"No time."

"What *do* you do?"

"I go to parties."

We passed luxurious modern villas and hideous bedraggled palm-thatched huts, a silent testimony to vast class differences. Trudging by a row of eucalyptus trees were girls bearing huge loads on their heads.

We neared the primitive but colorful Iron Market. Soon Alphonse, who seemed nearer forty-five than thirty-five, dropped me at the Hotel Splendide, where I had a room. Its walls were covered with badly done murals, the ceiling was at least fifteen feet high, and it looked out upon a garden filled with bougainvillea, where the hotel servants came each morning to do laundry and gossip maliciously about the hotel guests.

The food in the mahogany floored dining hall was splendid, and I was glad to find something there that was. I was sitting alone, at eight that evening, eating succulent lobster as tender as avocado when Tom Johnson came over to my table. I had never met him, and did not want to, but such minor details never stood in his way. He wore white shorts, a not very immaculate white shirt open to reveal a hairy chest that was an opulent contrast to his perfectly bald bead, and had indefinite yet insinuating features, and distant blue eyes.

"You know, I'd be all over you in ten minutes if I were alone with you," he said, purring unsteadily.

"You won't be."

"Where you from?"

"America."

"Now I'm an American expatriate. And that's just great. Have you met the woman who runs this place yet? Why, the things she's done would fill six books! I know all the scandals around here. I knew one girl who was the mistress of the last four presidents—let me tell you." He made a long, leering monologue, and then asked, "What're you here for?" His voice wavered.

"I'm going to play a concert in two days, at the Caserne Dessalines, under the patronage of President and Madame Magloire."

"Well, I'll come to it, wearing an athletic supporter, with a picture of Estime hanging around my neck!"

Throughout my stay, he was the only person who dared mention the unmentionable—that I had given two concerts, nine months previously, at the Theatre de Verdure on the Exposition grounds, in honor of President Estime.

That evening, a car took me to the residence of President and Madame Magloire. The weather was splendid, with no trace of the broiling heat one would find in August. The cool breeze enveloped the dusky houses in a mysterious veil of romance. When I arrived, I was taken to a white tile-flagged porch on which many children were playing. Soon, Madame Magloire, a small, pleasant-faced coffee-colored woman with harmonious features, wearing a dark green silk dress, came out and welcomed me warmly. She explained that all of her husband's and her own relatives had come down from the mountains for the inauguration and that, if the house had not been so filled from this, she would have loved for me to stay with them. The small army of children I had seen were only a few of these relatives.

The long yellow buildings of the Army Barracks, otherwise known as the Caserne Dessalines, have a theatre in the rear. The theatre was crammed with government officials and foreign diplomats. The Magloires attended. The President's great frame looked very impressive in the audience. Even seated, he towered over everyone around him.

The recital ended with my composition, "Rhapsody of Youth," written in the President's honor. Then, Dr. Camille Lherisson, Minister of Health, a tall amber-skinned, superbly-dressed man decorated me with a blue and white medal, with the title of Chevalier of Honor and Merit, as conferred on me by the President.

AT DAWN NEXT MORNING, I was in a small rocking plane cabin.

As we flew over the lush Artibonite Valley, I reflected on lights, sounds, smells of Haiti as I had passionately absorbed them the past few days: the brutal, bloody cock-fight, arrogant and uselessly cruel, with the surrounding crowd gazing in the greedy sadism of modern Carthaginians. The voluptuous, scarlet flowers splashing tumultuously over crumbling villas, and the dusty, hilly roads that might end in a magnificent mansion or an atrociously sad and debased heap of pitiful, filthy, degraded huts. The parties with sumptuous food, the fixed look of hatred on the faces of the peasants, the homes of genteel members of the elite now in straightened circumstances — the house decrepit, starkly bare of furnishings save for the barest necessities, while host and hostess sat, exquisitely dressed, charming the polish of their Gallic manners, but unable to fix or clean up the surroundings that so badly needed it, for any manual exertion would lower their aristocratic class status. I remembered the gorgeous new $50,000 dwelling of a government official whose salary was $50 a month, and the rumors about a girl who had been the mistress of each of the four previous presidents, each of whom gave her a banana plantation. The Boulangerie St. Marc, a prosperous bakery owned and managed by Claude Etienne and his family, unique among the Haitians I met in their industry, were of solid sober morality, and hard-working integrity and thrift. The Ibo Lele Hotel, far from Port-au-Prince, with its luxurious, expensive rooms, and unimaginative standardized meals. The Boutillier, with its panorama of sparkling stars, and a child I had seen with webbed feet — a sign it had "eaten" its twin brother in the womb.

I recalled the frightening painting of Baron Samedi, the spirit of death, and the jumbled collection of weird, shabby, exotic and prosaic objects on the *pé,* or altar, of a small voodoo sanctuary, with its grisly bloodstains from the previous nights ritual, and the huge grimacing black cross on the wall, lugubriously clad in a top hat and frock-coat, the flocks of cocks and hens gamboling flirtatiously outside the *humfo*, unaware that they would soon be rent apart in a horrible and repulsive ceremony.

Memories of the meringue dances that lasted until the wee hours of the morning, the mansions of Pétion-Ville, and the evilly quaint paths where one thought on was alone, only to see a profuse myriad of eyes staring satanically at one through the surrounding bushes. The pleasant white Theatre de Verdure, where I had given two concerts at the March Exposition festivities, and the young student who had asked me to elope with him to Cap-Haïtien, all these swarmed through my excited and teeming mind as I flew over the green and violet Province du Nord.

We landed in sad, desolate, Cap-Haïtien, whose grim houses had a secretive decadent look, as if fearing a return of the fires, battle and bloodshed that had so often destroyed the town.

The streets, mostly unpaved, were thick with black squashy mud from which worn stones stuck up listlessly.

The Roi Christophe Hotel was deserted save for two mid-western Americans, and an Englishman who tried to force his way into my room at midnight.

Shivering in the dawn cold, the mid-westerners and I set out for the Citadelle at five o'clock.

We drove down the main south road, branched off some miles from Hippolyte Bridge. We passed groups of black, six foot, totally naked peasant boys, their nudity strange and frightening, who seemed indifferent to their immodesty, as they glared at us with malevolent curiosity.

At the crumbled remains of the Sans Souci Palace, where Christophe shot himself with the silver bullet, we alighted, and mounted some wretched, puny brown horses. We plunged into the cruel jungle and ascended the tortuous matted path.

We were ripped by dense brush, twisted primeval trees vaulted over us in sinister arches, we were seized by vertigo when we looked over the jagged cliff's edge, whose sheer precipitous drop fell hundreds of feet below. The now-burning sun glared pitilessly on us, making us sweat. At last, we reached the ominous stone walls of the Citadelle, devoured like a leprosy with appalling decay and ruin.

Here were the flaming, violent scarlet creepers known as "Christopher's Blood," there forlorn rusted cannon balls, here moss-grown, eroded, strangely phallic-seeming stones, there a wrecked stone cistern, cracked and desolate.

One thought, "This is what a medieval fortress must have been like, after it was gutted and razed by the enemy, and the moss of time had shrouded it in the spider's-web of decay, and it was only visited by passing pilgrims!" My mind recalled Chopin's "F Sharp Impromptu" that has always seemed to me to portray a young man, dreaming near the ruin of a medieval castle, of the thunderous hooves of invading horse men of centuries before. The air, sharp and intense, impelled one to a feeling of vertigo, and the distant unearthly blue sky seemed to hypnotize one with longing to leap from the bare, unsheltered walls to the cruel, bloodthirsty rocks a thousand feet beneath.

We descended the twisted, turning, bramble-ridden path, tormented by the hot afternoon sun. The mahogany, orange, mango and eucalyptus trees were exotic yet sinister.

I flew back to Port-au-Prince.

The next morning, I visited the mountain home of Professor Werner Jaegerhuber. It perched like a mushroom on the cliff-side.

He was a Haitian of German origin.

He gave me some voodoo peasant themes he had collected. I promised to arrange them for concert piano.

Only in 1958 did I return to Haiti.

I was to perform again at the Caserne Dessalines. Presidents had come and gone, but the broad hulking shape of the Barracks remained.

On my previous visit, nobody had mentioned President Estime. On this trip, nobody mentioned President Magloire. My concerts were to honor President Duvalier.

I had made elaborate arrangements of the themes Professor Jaegerhuber had collected, and was eager to play them for him. Unfortunately, I found that he was dead. I felt sad that he had passed. The old Port-au-Prince seemed changed. There were many new beautiful buildings, homes, monuments.

But the elite looked far less gay. Worry over the recent political upsets, fearful dissatisfaction, and uncertainty, was marked on their faces.

Two hours before my concert, the electricity failed in Pétion-Ville. I was unable to iron my green taffeta concert gown. We drove through Port-au-Prince seeking a house where the electricity functioned. When I finally got to the Caserne Theatre, there was no bench in front of the concert grand that had been sent over from the Music Conservatory. No bench was anywhere. The President had arrived. The band was playing the National Anthem.

An American friend found a chair that was far too low. But some bricks lay in a corner. As none of the Haitians could have demeaned themselves by carrying bricks, he rushed onstage, built a platform with the bricks, covered it with a carpet, and set the chair on top.

The concert began. The audience applauded strongly, but one felt they were not paying the least attention to the music.

For days people had been telling me that "certainly" there would be "an incident" during the concert—for it was the first large public gathering since the curfew had been imposed, after an attempted revolution ten days before.

Some people told me the auditorium would be bombed, others that "only" the president would be assassinated. Some predicted shooting or stabbing, others the destruction by fire of the entire barracks or the machine gunning of the entire assembly.

I played the program with some trepidation. Moussorgsky, Beethoven, and Ravel were completed.

Then I played voodoo Haitian music, chants to Erzili, Goddess of Love, Damballah, the Snake God, Marassa, the God of Twins, Legba, the God of Roads, and Ti-Jean-Petro, the tree-dwelling spirit.

I was shivering with fear.

The President kept on his black Homburg hat throughout the concert, never smiled, shook hands with no one during the gloomy reception which followed, but otherwise nothing happened.

After my next concert, at the El Rancho Hotel, the audience fluttered away like swallows.

If they did not get home before curfew, they might be shot. The next day, various people told me they lived in deadly fear of arrest. Others urged me to carry secret messages back to New York co-conspirators.

I declined.

As I drove down from Pétion-Ville to hotter, steamier Port-au-Prince, passing palm-trees dedicated to Ayizan, avocado trees, to Zaka, and mango and bougainvillea trees sacred to Ogu and Damballah, I felt as if the chauffeur and I were not alone, as though a multitude of hostile, curious eyes were staring at us.

In the distance, I heard muffled voices chanting:

> Aizan véléketé
> Imamu tòka
> Lésé bo Loa-a
> Aizâ e, nu tut alé

We passed the dusk-tinted pastel mansions and strange mud-and-straw huts of Port-au-Prince.

As we neared the airport, I wondered if this troubled land would ever know real peace.

When I returned to Hispaniola four months later, I flew, not to Haiti, but to the Dominican Republic, which fills up the east two-thirds of the island. The two nations are in amazing contrast; both tropical, hot, mountainous, with bloody histories, they are far apart in development.

I flew to Ciudad Trujillo, Dominican Republic, via Yang Airlines, which had the most marvelous food I have ever had on an airline. Every luscious delicacy was there. Quite a change from the bad cuisine of most American airlines.

Ciudad Trujillo was beautiful, clean. I stayed at the Hotel Embajador—modern, sumptuously furnished, and air-conditioned. The air-conditioning really worked. It was like the deluxe hotels in the South American capitals. When I drove through the country, everything was safe, everyone wore clothes, and the roads were good and well-kept. The peasantry did not have the look of diabolic, fixed malice I had seen so often in Haiti, but seemed cheerful, and gay.

One wonders what would have happened had the u.s. annexed the Dominican Republic in 1868, as President Baez requested. Some chaotic violence might have been avoided, such as the reign of the cruel Ulises Heureaux, whose assassination was followed by near-anarchy. The u.s. did take over administration of all the customs-houses in 1905, and the entire country in 1916. After the Americans left in 1924, more chaos followed until the assumption of power, by Rafael Leonidas Trujillo, in 1930.

The Generalissimo and his brother. President Hector Trujillo, received me, on December 3, at the Presidential Palace. They were both charming.

The next day, I visited Cristóbal, the Generalissimo's birthplace, and a delightful city. Señor Miguel Gacel, a journalist, drove us there, to meet Dr. Josefina Pimentel Boves, the woman governor of the San Cristóbal Province.

Señor Gacel was a copper-skinned, ebullient middle-aged man, with an enormous warmth of manner. He embraced one continually, with an adorable lack of coldness that did not in the least disrupt his perfect driving.

We had first met him at Havana's Club Atenas six years before. Time had not chastened the innocence of his Pickwickian jollity.

He said, gaily, "Wonderful to see you again! Wonderful! ¡Magnifico! I'll bet you didn't know I was here! I left Cuba three years ago. Couldn't stand any more of that race prejudice there. How do you like it here?"

"I didn't think the West Indies could be like this. The symphony orchestra's wonderful notices is that it is completely racially integrated."

He embraced us all again, enthusiastically and said, "You don't have that in America, do you?"

The orchestra members had been of every shade, and tint, from black to white. I said, "It's almost unheard of for an American symphony orchestra to hire even one colored player, though there are many qualified musicians."

"Have you seen the University of Santo Domingo? The first university to be founded in the Americas. It is wonderful!"

"No, I haven't. Won't you tell me something of the history of the country?"

"*¡Magnifico!* Spain ceded it to France in 1795. Toussaint L'Ouverture swept over it in 1801. The French returned, staying until 1809. Then the Dominicans tried to establish a free republic, but Spain came back in 1814. There was an 1821 revolt. Then Haiti invaded and ruled twenty-two years. Spain returned from 1861 to 1865, otherwise, the country was free until the American intervention. Now we are prosperous."

What a beautiful drive to Cristóbal, past splendid panoramas of mango and coconut trees, shimmering sugar-cane fields.

Dr. Baves greeted us warmly at her cool, spacious villa aired by delicate breezes from the open, tile-floored patio, and filled with solid mahogany furniture.

An attractive woman, she had honey-colored skin, placid brown eyes, shingled black hair, and a relaxed feminine manner. She wore a navy blue linen dress with white piping.

She told us her ex-husband had been an army officer and that he had been a lawyer seven years before becoming governor.

We were served fresh coconut milk, mangoes from her garden, and cinnamon-flavored *majarete* she had fixed herself.

Then, with her, we visited a marvelous palace, sumptuous as those expected to see in the Near East, but never did. Its floors were of a dazzling variety of fine woods from the Republic. The bathrooms were superb: on walls and ceilings were mosaics of deep-sea scenes of pink coral polyps, yellow jelly-fish, brown sea-urchins, golden star-fish, black squid, green sharks, jade mollusks, red lobsters, and turquoise eels, set in brilliant, exotic colors.

From the roof, one viewed the verdant fields and rolling hills for miles. Swirling with pink, purple, gold and lavender clouds, the muted Chinese-red sun sank into the blue horizon. The swift, sharp, profound night of the tropics came. The air was sultry, as we left, with a soft warm sensuous changing atmosphere, like a scented veil.

The next day, I lost my gold fountain pen, given to me six years before, by the Mayor of Havana. I gave up hope of finding it, and returned to the Palacio de Bellas Artes to practice. An art museum and conservatory, as well as school. its upper galleries held scores of striking paintings by modern Dominican artists. They glowed with fiery vitality and craftsmanship.

The air-conditioned, spotless theatre was exquisite, with elegant statuary, bas-reliefs, and luxurious inclined seats.

That evening, the orchestral concert, directed by Manuel Simo, a young composer, began with an excellent performance of Beethoven's "7th Symphony." Then we played the Grieg "A Minor Concerto." The theatre was packed. After my last encore, a man brought me a gold fountain pen he had found on the ground outside the Palacios de Belles Artes' entrance. It was my pen.

My parents were given an award for the sociological achievement they had made by their mixed manage, at a banquet in our honor, the next day.

After we had visited the old cathedral that holds Christopher Columbus' ashes in an interesting tomb, I returned to the theatre to practice.

I worked until a few minutes before my recital, then dashed to dress.

The hall was also packed for my recital. Towards the close, I remembered with a shock that I had left my purse, containing $600, in the Ladies' Lounge.

After my last encore, I rushed back to the Lounge.

Though I had been gone two hours, and the Lounge was open to everyone, my clothes and money were there intact as I had left them.

It was sad, having the next morning to end my Dominican Republic trip, which had been less like work than a gay holiday. Back to Florida in time to get caught in a terrific bottleneck of snarled traffic, arriving worn out in New Orleans, but I was cheered and rejuvenated by the cable I received just before my New Orleans concert:

> "GOOD LUCK FOR YOUR RECITAL WE KNOW IT
> WILL BE A GREAT SUCCESS. FROM MIKE GACEL AND
> YOUR FRIENDS IN THE DOMINICAN REPUBLIC"

NEARLY FOURTEEN MONTHS PASSED.

Great tension had developed between Cuba and the Dominican Republic.

In September, Miguel Gacel and a friend had passed through New York en route to Liberia. Though they had sent us a cable asking us to meet them at Idlewild Airport, every barrier seemed to have been erected to keep us from encountering them when we got there. Finally, by a ruse, we got to his plane. He was warm as ever, but less ebullient, more noncommittal.

When he returned to New York, two weeks later, he visited us. He was affectionate, charming, but even more noncommittal.

In January 1960, we were shocked by news of a vast, though suppressed rebellion in the Republic. On Saturday, January 30, as I walked on 50th Street and the Avenue of the Americas in New York, I heard a sudden screaming and yelling. A crowd of two hundred men and women, soft, brown Latin faces fixed in a barbarous look of hatred mixed with feverish excitement, were carrying a huge, cheap, crude effigy of Trujillo in a bloated, sadistic face of painted cardboard, and dressed in brown jacket, red and white striped cotton pant, with dozens of tinsel medals hanging from the jacket front as from a lurid Christmas tree.

The demonstrators were shouting curses, complaints and vulgarisms, pathetic denunciation and furious sobs, as they thrust garishly-painted placards in the air, reading, "Trujillo Paying Japanese Pilots to Bomb Open Cities," "Trujillo Arresting Catholic Priests," "Offense to Dominican People," "Demand Release of Political Prisoners," and "Red Cross Must Intervene."

Stretching their hands forth in violent gestures, they began to chant the Dominican anthem with desperate fervor.

I asked Dr. Jaime Miguel Charanga y Garcia, who had just arrived in New York from Trujillo City, what he thought of this.

"Trujillo is nearly finished," he said.

"But how can that be? Everything seemed so peaceful, tranquil, when I was there. It seemed an enchanting fairyland. Everyone looked so happy."

"Trujillo does not appreciate people, he only wants to use them. The welfare he has created was not done through idealism, but because, in the long run, that helped his own interests."

"But it has, nevertheless, been effective, and his country has never been more prosperous."

"That is true. And where is there a sincere politician, anywhere? Yet, his era is drawing to a close. No, don't go down there now. Yes, priests have been jailed, and some bombings have occurred. It's dangerous, terribly dangerous."

I could not believe it. One of my happiest trips had been my jaunt to the Dominican Republic, where everything had functioned smoothly, in good taste, and with elegance, art and style, with spotless cleanliness and honesty evident in all I saw, where everything had seemed to be handled in a way that was first class.

Despite present doubts and confusions, I will always recall my week in the Republic, as one of the happiest I ever had. ⊞

CHAPTER 5

Scandal and Calypso

Jamaica, Panama British Guiana, Trinidad
1952, 1956, 1958

N THE FALL OF 1951, I went to hear Marian Anderson sing at Carnegie Hall. Michael Aubry, a West Indian concert manager, had the seat next to mine. He was over six feet, with copper skin and gold-flecked green eyes. He was dressed in black and was the last word in male perfection.

He promised to make a colossal tour of Latin America and the West Indies for me. "I will make you greater than *Guida! Guida* is a god!" He made elaborate promises in the subsequent days, before winging back to Jamaica. There was no further word for six months. Then next April, I got a letter from another West Indian manager, Mr. Mackintosh. He wanted to present me in concert in Kingston in a week.

We cabled him accepting the offer. In reply, we got a telegram, not from Mackintosh but from Aubry. Everyone always knows everything everyone else does, thinks, or receives in Jamaica, so it hadn't taken Aubry long to find that I had new plans afoot. Aubry's telegram startled us:

ABSOLUTELY MUST SAVE YOU FROM MACKINTOSH
STOP HAVE TREMENDOUS COLOSSAL WONDERFUL
TOUR LINED UP FOR PHILIPPA IN JAMAICA TRINI-
DAD CUBA ARUBA PANAMA ST. KITS ST. LUCIA VEN-

EZUELA COLOMBIA ARGENTINA AND THROUGH-OUT MY AREA HAVE SCHEDULED KINGSTON DEBUT NEXT THURSDAY URGENT REPLY.

AUBRY

This astounded us. As no artist would reject such a tour, we canceled Mackintosh, accepted Aubry. On Sunday, I flew to Kingston, where Aubry, green-gold eyes blazing, met me at the airport. Angrily fuming, "This was forced on me! I cannot bear to be forced. I'm only doing this to save you from Mackintosh—I'm a gentleman!" He led me to an uncomfortable, antique car. We drove to a white suburban villa, where I was to stay.

That evening I visited the Aubry residence, which seemed bare of beauty.

Mrs. Aubry, a fluttery brunette, greeted me. Like a tiny, exotic bird, she was never at rest. Her worried speech poured out, with the effect of making me feel I should be sorry for everything they had ever suffered, and that I must do "all I could" to "help."

"Now, dear," she said, "don't be upset by anything Mike said, you know he's devoted to you, he says you have a marvelous future—and *I* think of you as my own daughter. Dear Mike's just nervous over a few worries he's had recently. Why, the Hollywood All-Star Ice Revue came here last month, and Mike had an expert fly down from New York to fix the ice, and he flew back to America just two hours before curtain-time and we thought everything was alright—we had a packed house. But when the performance started, the ice all melted, and the skaters ended by swimming up to their hips in ice water. Mike had to phone to New York and get the expert to fly back the next day and fix it again. This time the ice was fine, but the audience never came back anymore, for they just didn't believe in the show. But we'd contracted to run the show for three weeks, so we had to pay all the salaries anyway, so we ended up losing 7,000 pounds."

Mrs. Aubry was smoking incessantly. She paced up and down the floor, and went on, "And then in January, the Beulah Basie Jazz Quartet was supposed to come—they're four girls, you know, who all play the trumpet, and Mike had the most wonderful tour lined up, in Haiti, Aruba, Curacao, and all over South America, but the girls had forgotten for some reason to get their smallpox vaccinations, and they didn't get vaccinated until two days before they were to fly here. Then they all got sick and came down with smallpox. Poor Mike had to spend all day phoning all the cities to postpone the tour two weeks, and then he had to fly to New York, and some of the cities dropped out-and we ended up losing 2,500 pounds."

She sat down, nervously drank a cup of tea, and continued. "In February, it was really awful — Bralitzky was supposed to come, and he canceled, and those Adagio dancers came, and the man, he's both, you know, got in trouble with his chauffeur here, and I had the flu, and all the children had chickenpox, that's why we didn't write you, dear, we were so afraid of transmitting germs to you via the letter-paper. And these Folk Dancers came, and they were really very difficult — they arrived exactly the same day Lady Cat Crazy and her jazz band were supposed to start their tour — and it seems the Folk Dancers had some strange idea that this was the day *they* were supposed to start *their* tour, and then *they,* the Folk Dancers went around telling everyone that poor Mike was inefficient, I can't imagine why — and then they got in that trouble with the hotel — I mean, you know, Miss Blackfoot who heads the Folk Dancers, is 'both,' and her husband is 'both,' and all the boys and the girls in the troupe are 'both,' and it's all very complicated, and perhaps I'd better not tell you, but poor Mike lost at least 500 pounds from it all. So you'll understand that things really haven't been very easy. But poor Mike is going to start working on your tour next week, and he should be able to get three or four engagements for you at least, perhaps in Curacao or Trinidad — the reviews from your concert Thursday should help a lot, and you know, poor dear Mike is so devoted to your music."

Yet the recital on Thursday did not solve things. There was a furious thunder-storm just before the concert, which was held in an open-air theatre, and this scared off half the audience. Also it drenched the seats so that the ones who came got soaked and it ruined the lights so that they flickered on and off throughout the first half of the concert, totally upset the sound system and made it impossible to tape the performance on a recording machine so they could sell it to the radio. Mr. Aubry had forgotten to get a piano until the night before the concert, and had forgotten to have it moved off the open stage while it rained, so the piano had been soaked too, several keys stuck, and its tone was dull and mushy. At intermission we all rushed around madly looking for flashlights to put in the piano to dry the air so it would be not quite so dull and mushy. Thus it did not sound quite so badly after intermission, and I got rather nice reviews the next day.

This encouraged Mr. Aubry to arrange fourteen more concerts. The next one was set for four days later.

On Sunday, Mr. Aubry informed me that the program was printed, and that he had put the "Scherzo in B Flat Minor" by Chopin on at the end.

"But I don't know that piece!" I cried.

"Well, learn it. You have two days."

"But it's nineteen pages."

"You have to learn it. It'll *bring* the audience. You ought to do *something* for me in return for my saving you from Mackintosh."

"What? Well, I'll try. But anyhow, about Mr. Mackintosh don't you think I ought to write him and his wife to thank him for the flowers they sent me?"

"Do you think you should?" he asked, and left abruptly.

I practiced eleven hours a day until Tuesday night. This concert was held in a closed theatre, and it was steamily hot, with no rain so that the audience nearly suffocated. I performed the B flat minor Scherzo, and there was no applause afterwards.

The next day I had two concerts in Mandeville, at 4:30 and 8:00 p.m. It was over two hours drive from Kingston, but the Aubrys did not arrive until 4:00 p.m. in their car to pick me up. En route, we were caught in a terrible thunderstorm, and we got to my concert at 6:30 p.m. The audience had waited two hours.

Concerts in Montego Bay and at various schools followed. When I left on May 10, Mr. Aubry drove me to the airport and, on the way, haughtily handed me a check for a minute sum.

"This is what you get," he said, disdainfully.

"But I played fifteen concerts! Some days I gave three a day. And this is less than I get for one in America!"

He angrily replied, "You are mercenary! A true artist never thinks of money. This is all you'll get. How ungrateful you are, after I saved you from Mackintosh!"

I had to fly disconsolately back to New York, where, three months later, I received a sudden sharp cable saying:

FLY AT ONCE TO PANAMA YOUR CONCERTS THERE
AUGUST 10TH AND 13TH.

It was from Aubry.

I FLEW TO PANAMA CITY. It was steamingly hot.

The Teatro Nacional was a large hall with very bad acoustics. The piano was battered and its tone did not carry, for humidity had long since swollen the keys and rusted the strings, while insects had nibbled away at the hammer-felts.

I felt nervous the morning of my first concert.

I needed more practice.

Someone had promised to drive me from the house where I was staying (the home of a local politician), to the theatre, which was far away.

No one arrived, so I grew anxious and impatient, left the house, and took a bus to the Teatro Nacional.

The hall seemed empty of all but a few work men when I arrived.

No sooner did I begin to practice on the weary Baldwin piano, than people began miraculously to spring up, like mushrooms after rain.

Some music students trailed through, to ask me why I played with my fingers curved rather than stretched out flat on the keys. A local pianist came and asked me to put all my contacts everywhere at her disposal. A young man asked me to sponsor him into the United States. A journalist asked me whether I was for or against some local political figure of whom I had never heard before, but about whom he was bristlingly intense. A young girl asked me if I had ever been in love, and if so, with whom, and if not, why not?

Then a bilious and self-assured young man strode forth from the deep dim dusty shadows of the wings, and marched arrogantly over to me. He gazed at me contemptuously. His long, pale, disdainful yet Pan-like face had the look of an overgrown and slightly mildewed faun.

In tones of slyly caressing impertinence, he inquired, "Have you known sex?"

Annoyed, I snapped. "Who are you? What a question! A gentleman doesn't...."

"I am not a gentleman, I am a writer! I'm going to write a profile on you for a newspaper in the Canal Zone. I want to know the real you! You must tell me everything, free-associate just as though I were your psychoanalyst."

"I don't have an analyst!" "You're lying!"

"I'm not lying!"

"You are lying. Now, I want to know all your complexes, neuroses and fixations...."

"I haven't got any!"

"And whether you're frigid or a nymphomaniac—what? You haven't any neuroses?"

"No. Yet I do have a few cherished, carefully cultivated eccentricities, like wanting to be alone now."

"Will you marry me?"

"Go away."

"I won't go away."

Eventually, he went away, and another young man, with the improbable name of Ulric St. Cyril Cuthbert Bothwell Bowys, came up. He was tremendously over-dressed, wore spats, and carried a cane. He wanted to know how much money I would be paid for my concert.

"Could I interest you in a little project, in behalf of a dear friend who has a fleet of fishing vessels in Balboa? Would you put up four thousand dollars to help him invest in some modern power launches?" Craftily rumpling his bushy black hair, he elaborated on his scheme.

Suddenly, he stopped short, raced to the wings and disappeared. Another man, flawlessly dressed in a superb white suit, came to the stage. This personage, a Government official, had recently been reelected. His silky aplomb had not been ruffled when the opposition had claimed, after his election, that he had received twice the number of votes as there were voters in his area. He said, "Who was that man who just ran away? I think he belongs to my opposition. Don't talk to these strange characters. Some of these people would like to get money out of an unsuspecting person like you to help further their plots and schemes for revolution. By the way, do you know why we couldn't present your concert the last time it was suggested to us? Well, the last concert we'd had before that, there was a shooting in the street outside the hall during the concert, and then someone rushed in the theatre waving smoking pistols. I say, how did you get here? We went to fetch you and you weren't there—we were frantic."

"I came on the bus."

"The bus! You didn't! The bus. Why you will lose your *ambiente,* your *categoria,* if you do that! The artist cannot travel on a bus-you will lose reputation. You travel on a bus in New York? But *this* is PANAMA!" he shouted.

There was an embarrassing difficulty about the concert that night. The dull, ruined piano had the tired tone of a weary clavichord, and the vast barn-like hall), which was full, had wore acoustics than when empty. To make the program audible was an athletic feat.

The Canal Zone Governor received me in his offices the next day.

Later, the American Ambassador gave a reception in my honor at his elegant residence, with many distinguished guests.

Yet I felt ill at ease. When I had asked my Panamanian friends what I should wear, they had cried, *"¡Si! Si! ¡Es maravillosa!"* at the sight of each piece of clothing I showed them; so now I was dressed in low gold sandals, dark stockings, an ankle-length gown, and a huge cartwheel hat, while the other guests were stockingless, hatless, in high heels and short skirts.

The Ambassador asked me to play on the beautiful rosewood Bechstein piano, inlaid with ivory and painted with cherubic nymphs.

Unprepared for disaster, I did so.

I commenced Schubert's "Impromtu in E Flat," a torrent of glittering scale-runs. As every second key of the piano stuck, the runs were as full of holes as a target after rifle practice. The applause was scant. Then I played a modern work so lacking in melody, form, harmony or rhythm that it would not matter if the notes were there or not.

George Westerman, the brilliant writer for the *Panama Tribune,* who later became Panama's U.N. Ambassador, showed me through the National Brewery the next afternoon. It was immense, with great copper vats, and enormous air-conditioned rooms packed with yeast. The number of processes apparently necessary to make beer were incredible.

The next day, I played before the President-Elect José Antonio Remón, who had won over Roberto Chiari in a hotly contested election filled with violent accusations of fraud and chicanery twelve weeks before.

The forty-four-year-old Colonel Remón, a good-looking man who seemed to be looking forward to his forthcoming inauguration on October 30, was most cordial, as were the many Army Officers and Ministers who were with him.

I played for nearly half an hour. It was a festive occasion, without the slightest premonition that, in less than two and a half years later, Colonel Remón would be the first of Panama's twenty-eight Presidents to be assassinated.

The more I learned of Panama while I was there, the more incredible it seemed to me that a country of less than 900,000 people could be so riddled by factions, counter-factions, counter-counter-factions, plots, sub-plots, multiple-plots, super-plots and ferocious intrigues. The tension between the Spanish Panamanians and those of British West Indies origin was great. George Westerman, whose parents came from Barbados, was the only West Indian Panamanian accepted in Spanish Panamanian society.

After another concert at the Teatro Nacional, I left from Tocurnen Airport.

I TRAVERSED THE CARIBBEAN doing more concerts for Aubry. They were all superlative, that is, superlatively successful, or superlatively catastrophic.

Back in Kingston, I found the city as tranquil as a hornet's nest. Maybe no one was ever for anything in Jamaica, but the city seemed divided in two camps, one anti-Aubry one anti-Mackintosh.

Any word that had been ever said or thought to have been said, any glance that had been given, was repeated, misconstrued, and swollen into balloons of misunderstanding. For example, it seemed that before leaving the airport the previous spring, some woman had overheard me say, "I thought I should have been paid more." Assiduously, she had circulated the legend.

"You wouldn't believe it! I heard that Mrs. Drummond tells everyone this story, and I wouldn't think of passing it on, for you know I never gossip, I cannot bear gossip, and don't you think of telling anyone! But this poor dear desolate child came here and played twenty concerts, some of them four or five or six a day, was simply worked to death, and got no money at all!"

The tale rolled on, gathering momentum like a snowball. The Aubrys grew angry. Blazing with rage, Aubry said, "After all I did for you! I will not stand for this. I am a GENTLEMAN! I will sue everyone. I will sue all for a 100,000 pounds!"

And Mrs. Aubry chirped, "Oh, how could you, dear, you know we think about you as though you were our very own daughter—you know the only reason poor Mike didn't pay you more is that he had to give the money to Gerlinsky, because Gerlinsky wouldn't come at all to play unless he was paid in advance. Mackintosh had been spreading those dreadful tales, quite untrue, dear, that poor dear Mike had been bankrupt four times and owed money to everyone. And Gerlinsky had promised to come, and then canceled after poor Mike had spent 400 pounds on publicity, it was all Gerlinsky's dreadful manager's fault, he's so mercenary. So poor Mike had to spend 50 pounds in one day, phoning long distance to all the places, and then he had to charter a plane to fly to Los Angeles to talk to Gerlinsky alone without his dreadful manager being around, and counteract that awful story Miss Blackfoot had been spreading, quite untrue, dear, so you see, it hasn't been easy, and...."

Now, Mr. Aubry broke in furiously, with, "What hurts me most is that you don't appreciate the presentation I gave you, why there were flowers on the stage...I understand the soul of the artist-you are building your career now, what do you want to think about money for? Can't you appreciate the fact that I saved you from Mackintosh."

IN 1954, I SPENT A FEW DAYS in Kingston in the mansion of some friends who were in England. Cyril Sheridan, a retired British Naval officer, was there too. He was six feet tall, pale and slender, with a sensitive amiable face, partially black teeth, and a totally bald head. He was very intellectual, and was writing a historical verse play about St. Stylus. He enthusiastically suggested that we marry, so he could accompany me on all my tours, while I worked, and he wrote more historical verse plays.

We had splendid conversations alone in that vast deserted house, which had been stripped of almost all furniture by my friends' relatives. Our voices echoed like oboes through the cool empty halls.

One night we visited the only nightclub in Kingston faintly worthy of the name. One lone, plump strip teaser shimmied desperately on the stage, without obtaining any attention from the bored clientele. Throughout, Cyril quoted me verses he had written in my honor.

Later, he introduced me to all his friends, including several interracial couples. In fact, I met many mixed couples in Jamaica, which is an easy-going pleasant island apart from its constant gossip and intrigues.

Jamaica does not have the sinister atmosphere of British Guiana. Kingston is a cross roads, but Georgetown, capital of British Guiana, is far off the beaten track. Guiana comes from an Indian word meaning "wild coast," and it was once thought that El Dorado was there. But Georgetown is no golden city, and the houses are drab, wooden, and weather-beaten by the twice-a-year rains. The atmosphere is poisonous with misunderstanding. The Negroes, Hindus, Mohammedans, Chinese, British, and mixed-bloods are divided by incessant hostile suspicion.

The city, squatted desolately near the jungle, is totally lacking in visual beauty. Yet the jungle itself is exotically beautiful. Monkeys, deers, anteaters, iguana, lizards, baboons, pumas, jaguars, armadillos, alligators, parrots, swarm thorough the lush greenery. The grand primeval mangrove, cedar, crabwood, mahogany and bullet trees are draped and embellished with tangled vines and luxuriant orchids.

Once there were five Guianas—Spanish, Portuguese, English, Dutch and French. Venezuela now has the Spanish Guiana, and Brazil, the Portuguese Guiana. What is now British Guiana was ceded, along with Surinam, to the Dutch in 1667, in exchange for New York. The English took British Guiana back in 1803. The slaves were freed in the 1830's and coolies from India and China were brought in to work the plantations. The Asians, through cunning, foresight and industry have gained ever greater economic control, until they now have the greatest economic power in the Colony.

The original national, racial, and religious divisions remain. They slumber beneath the surface like a serpent ready to strike venomously if provoked.

Two thousand people of all groups were present at my first recital at Queen's College—in their best evening clothes, for it was a social event.

Then came a second recital.

Just beforehand, a Hindu boy telephoned me to ask, "Could I come backstage afterwards to greet you? It's alright? Oh, I thought someone might object because I'm a Hindu."

During the next week, everyone tried to lure me into one rival camp or another. To accomplish this, they told me fantastic tales, peppered with dire detail. One night, I visited some Hindus and listened with amazement to their stories.

Only when a clock chimed two in the morning did I realize the time. It was too late to get a taxi, the phone did not work, the only car at the house was out of order, it would be too dangerous to walk through the deserted streets.

I slept in a hammock at this house until dawn, only to find then that I had done the unforgivable and was wrapped in a veil of scandal.

I decided to go on to Trinidad as quickly as possible. There was a plane to Port-of-Spain in an hour. I took a taxi.

We sped to the airport over the worst road in the world. It was bemired with thick, greasy mud, and had holes in it big enough to throw a chair into. The car rocked wildly from side-to-side of this frightful thoroughfare. The plane had waited for me at the airport when, browned with mud-spray, I finally arrived.

I was glad to board it and soar high in the air over the Guianas, on my way, at last, to Port-of-Spain.

TRINIDAD, THOUGH TINY, seems more fortunate than British Guiana. It has only half a million people in 83,000 square miles, but jungle occupies most of the space. The sugar market has not often been substantially rewarding to them, and the gold, diamonds and bauxite mined are not in enormous quantity.

But Trinidad has, as one of her greater variety of resources, aside from oil, an apparently inexhaustible asphalt lake, and 104 acres in extent.

I did not hear Trinidad's famous steel bands on my 1952 visit, but in 1956, after four concerts in as many days with a different program for each, Cyril Dupre gave a dinner in my honor at his home. Mr. Dupre, who has black eyes and a topaz-colored skin, and is one of Port-of-Spain's leading businessmen, had six handsome Negro and Hindu boys serenade me with sweet music on the odd instruments they make from discarded steel oil drums from the U.S. Naval Base.

I returned in 1958 for a recital at the Public Library, this time in August, when it is searingly hot.

A calypso singer phoned me as soon as I arrived. His name was Caesar the Lion. He wanted to write a calypso especially in my honor.

I did not take him up on it. The next day I was told that Caesar the Lion phoned everyone who came there whom he thought might have some money, and, if they accepted his offer, simply changed two or three words in the standard song he had been using for the last ten years, and milked them for all the money he could get.

I was once almost asphyxiated in Port-of-Spain while I was there. The gas that operated the hot water heater leaked and flooded in from the bathroom into my hotel bedroom, where I lay asleep. I awoke just in time to avert the finis to my career.

Nevertheless, I am very fond of Trinidad, and think it the nicest place in the British West Indies. ⊞

CHAPTER 6

With the Djukas in the Jungle
Dutch West Indies: 1952, 1954, 1958

W ILLEMSTAD, CURAÇAO, WAS TEEMING WITH turbaned East Indians, yellow-skinned Chinese, panther-like Negroes, arrogant Creoles, and heavy cheese-like Dutch. It was a sultry humid evening in 1952.

The faces of the crowd seemed masked, and uncommunicative, only their eyes gave a hint of the twisted cupidity and turmoil underneath. Each was there for gain and gold—to work for Royal Dutch Shell Oil's refineries, to operate strange little shops set in niche-like spaces, to ship out to South American ports, to prostitute oneself, or for other reasons.

The balmy air caressed one insinuatingly. Walking through the tarnished streets, on which no beauty had been lavished, one gazed at the exotic Far Eastern goods piled up in profusion in the shops. Marvelous laces, elegantly carved ivory, and fine silver jewelry, were heaped in sumptuous disarray. They were fantastically cheap. I was unaware of the humming of the crowd, the murmuring vitality of the air one always feels in the tropics. I was lost in dreams.

A sharp voice called to me in bad Spanish from a car.

It slowed down. Four men were inside.

Two of them jumped out and seized me. They yanked me into the car. No bystander had lifted a finger to help me.

The car picked up speed, racing past dim red-roofed houses, straggly trees, and murky gardens. I tried to scream, but one quickly put his hand over my mouth.

The car stopped in front of a drab stucco house.

They pushed me out of the car onto a narrow driveway.

I jumped free of them, and began, furiously, to tell them who I was, pulled out a photo of myself with the Governor of the Canal Zone, and a sheaf of my press notices and clippings from my straw handbag, and flung them at them.

Jake, the first man, who was blue-eyed and dumb-looking, scratched his big blond head in confusion, while Julian toyed nervously with his uniform-sleeve as he read the clippings. Freddy, a tall skinny man with slick black hair, muttered, "Hey, you play long-hair stuff, huh?" Jimmy, the fourth, whined in his unpleasant high pitched voice, "Geeze, we don't mean no harm, honey, maybe we owe you an apology or somepin'—thought sure you came off one of those meat-planes."

I glared at him. He had sickly hazel eyes, and a smell of spirits. They all began to mutter weak explanations, apologizing. They seemed upset by the idea that I was a concert pianist. Their aggressive pugnacity collapsed like a punctured balloon.

Julian, who was partly bald, with horn-rimmed glasses, left the others standing on the driveway, and took me back to where they had seized me.

Back in the car again, he said, "I'm sorry. None of this was my idea. My buddies had heard about the planeload of girls they send here from Venezuela every month. Called the "meat-plane." The girls take care of the men here for a few weeks. Then they're shipped back to South America. My buddies thought you were one of them. We've never been here before. Went to Martinique last time. Saw the Mardi Grass there. Very colorful."

"Were the girls satisfactory?" I asked sarcastically.

"Real cute. But cunning. A trick a minute. One gorgeous little piece took me to a jewelers and asked me to buy her this splendid necklace, all gold and pearls. It only cost about thirty dollars. Seemed like such a bargain, I bought it. Later I found she had seven other boyfriends, whom she'd tapped for the *same* necklace! She used to sing this cute song—'Festin de Fort-de-France'." He sang its fresh gay lilting melody.

Like the others, Julian was a serviceman from the American naval air base in Trinidad, and on leave in Willemstad. He let me out at the corner where they had seized me, and drove off. A voice said from behind me, "So he brought you back."

"Yes. Why? What do you know about it?"

The owner of the voice was standing in the doorway of a narrow shop I had not seen before.

Shadowed by the copper-colored light in the store window which shone on the trinkets, beads, fans and Buddhas of Asian workmanship, he was a dim figure in an open white shirt and grey trousers. I could not see his face clearly.

"I saw them carry you off."

"Why did you not help me?"

"I knew it not to be necessary."

"Why?"

"I knew you'd be brought back."

"How?"

"I foresee things. You are not harmed. I was aware that would be the case."

"You know a great deal, do you not?"

"I do. You are interesting. There is a vibration about you that attracts strange and exciting events. Yet there is, too, a spiritual protection that saves you.

"Who are you?"

"A friend."

"Where are you from?"

"Indonesia."

"I see."

"Come into my shop."

A force seemed to impel me to follow him without hesitation into the drab ill-lighted shop with Eastern bric-à-brac, costumes and jewelry.

He led me through a bead curtain into a back room. Each bead on the curtain seemed to have a quivering, suggestive life of its own as I brushed past.

Offering to make me some Chinese green tea, he ushered me to a cloistral high-backed chair at a round green baize-covered table. The room was lighted by two flickering kerosene lamps.

As he fixed the tea, he told me of his life in Java, before 1946, when he had gone to Holland, then Curaçao. He had been born in Batavia, now Jakarta, of a Dutch father and an Indonesian mother, and his ivory-yellow skin, broad nose, and deep-sunk eyes revealed his ancestry.

We drank the steaming tea, and he told me of his life-long interest in the occult, and offered to show me how to read the Tarot cards.

"The Tarot cards are the Book of Life, which one reads, seeing new meanings. There are seventy-eight cards."

"Where do they come from, Herr Van Kleed?"

"Paris. Grimaud in the Rue de Lancry."

"Rue de Lancry."

"Yes, Juffrouw Schuyler. They originated in medieval France, with a partial heritage from ancient Egypt and the Near East. Fifty-six cards are in the minor *arcanes*, twenty-two in the *arcanes majeurs*."

"Why is this Tarot without number?" I murmured, as he opened a long rectangular orange box and took out the thick, heavy cards, each about twelve centimeters by six, with blue backs splashed with intricate white dots, and I gazed at them.

"It is *Le Mat,* zero—the disordered, confused man on march towards evolution, unaware of his place in the sun. Tarot I is *Le Bateleur,* the sleight-of-hand trickster, juggling with occult forces. Tarot II is *La Papesse,* the all-seeing woman, Isis, The Priestess, moon-goddess, guardian of occult mysteries. Tarot III, the Empress of fixed destiny, is succeeded by the Emperor of temporal power. Tarot V, Le Pape, is a spiritual force. Then follow the Lover, the Chariot, the Hermit, the *Roue de Fortune* or Wheel of Evolution, Force—or the Woman with the Lion, the Hung man, Death, Temperance, the Devil, *Maison-Dieu*—or Catastrophe, and Tarot XVII, the Star—or Revelation. After the Moon and the Sun, comes Tarot XX, the Day of Judgement. Tarot XXI, the nude virgin framed by the four fixed signs of the zodiac—the ox, lion, eagle and angel, is called the World," he softly said.

"And the fifty-six minor *arcanes?*"

"They are in four suits of swords, cups, deniers and batons, representing the fire, water, air, and earth signs. Our modern card-suits of spades, hearts, diamonds and clubs are descended from and are degraded versions thereof. The fourteen cards in each suit begin with Ace through ten, then Valet, Cavalier, Queen and King. The suits indicate respectively—struggle, spiritual riches, material riches, and worldly affairs. Shuffle the cards now, and cut."

I did so, with a queer feeling of thrill and perplexity. "It's Ace of Swords, and six of swords," I said.

"In a few days, you will face a difficult extremity. A letter will call you home from a voyage...."

In fifteen minutes, I had placed all seventy-eight cards in a great circle of twelve packs, to reveal my future Tarot-Horoscope. The yellow lamplight flickered on the strange card-figures. My first house held seven cards: the World, Eight of Batons, the Chariot, Ace of Cups Reversed, Wheel of Fortune, Queen of Batons, Five of Batons.

Lighting an odd brown cigarette, Herr Van Kleed told me, "Unusual. Your life will be perpetual change, almost dizzily exciting. Constant newness, continual travels. Voyages upon voyages, around the world. Your ninth house of foreign trips is extraordinary."

"It holds Force, Judgment, Queen of Cups, Cavalier of Cups, Cavalier of Swords, Cavalier of Deniers, Cavalier of Batons—what does it mean?"

"Travels. Travels. Astonishing to have the four horsemen together."

"The tenth house?"

"Emperor, 3 batons, King of Swords, King of Batons, Star, King of Cups."

"What is it? Tell me."

"Do not be anxious. It is good. Honors. Your star rises. You receive a decoration from an Emperor. You are honored by royalty."

"What about love?"

"Are you sure you want to know? Your fifth house has cards of violence. Nine of Batons, Papesse Reversed, Hermite Reversed, all treachery, delay. The Hung Man Reversed is success without pleasure, Lover Reversed is duplicity, rupture. Turn up the lamp some. The Brown Girl is next to the Lazzarone, or foreigner," he smiled remotely, with a glazed faraway look. The gold and blue flame curled recklessly, like a jungle flower, in the dusty lamp. My eyes riveted on the strange-figured cards.

"Will I marry? Should I? When?"

"After a long delay, you will triumph. The Sun favors you. I shall give you these cards as a present, then you will not need to ask advice, they will guide you. Do not thank me. You will need them. Would you like to look in the crystal ball now?"

He reached in the shadows, and brought out a bronze stand, wrought in gargoyle shapes. In it lay seven glass balls of varying sizes. He placed the stand in the center of the table.

I had a feeling of revulsion, of nervousness. "Should we do this?"

Herr Van Kleed said, in a voluptuous tone, "Why, we might not see anything!" He disappeared into the dim shadows. In a few minutes I smelt an odor of roasting that filled the room with a sickly-sweet acrid vapor.

"What is that?" I asked, with a giddy feeling, as the largest glass ball seemed to sway like a pendulum before my eyes.

"Oh, I'll tell you in a minute," his voice said, seeming miles away. My mouth was dry. The room whirled. The floor leapt and sank like a great ship in a hurricane, while my eyes saw only a hazy blur.

The crystal balls, haloed in mist, began to stare at me with monstrous, livid intensity, like giant, perverse, unblinking cat's eyes. I felt an impulse to laugh. An enormous, diabolical black figure seemed to soar from them, wrapped in serpent-like veils. A procession of elephants, lions, leopards, burst forth from the malignant veils, as though from the tangled trees of a jungle. They looked towards the flaming smoky sky, in which a silver airplane, one wing cracked open, was hurtling to the ground. There were screams of passengers being burnt alive. The earth was crawling with serpents, which swarmed towards their bodies. My hands seemed to fly from my body, my limbs dissolving in every direction.

The sensations grew more frenzied.

As I tried to fight them, I seemed to move, painfully, full of nausea, through a thick, grey cloud. When I opened my eyes, I was sitting on a grey stone bench, under a bent eucalyptus tree, my hand-bag beside me. My head ached, my nose and mouth burned, my stomach retched.

I breathed in the cool fresh air. What had happened? My memory seemed dead. Little by little, recollection took hold of me. The shop. Herr Van Kleed. Tarot cards.

I looked up. Where was the shop? I could not see it anywhere.

Behind me a voice said; "I put some rum in your tea. I hope you don't mind. It will soon wear off."

I stayed away from the Dutch West Indies for a year and a half.

THEN I WENT TO ARUBA, that stark, desolate island, whose few trees are stooped, bent, permanently bowed by the whipping winds.

One heard a strange language there — Papamiento — a potpourri of Dutch, English, Spanish and African words. An almost every other tongue one might imagine, for men from everywhere had flocked to work at the Esso refineries. Men vastly outnumbered women.

When walking through the metal jungle of the refineries, the trumpeting, blasting, chugging sounds were deafening — noisy, cacophonous, screaming with the ear-splitting creak of machinery, with the multilingual shouts of workmen. It was sheer bedlam, like an early Flemish painter's view of hell.

In Oranjestad and San Niccola, I gave concerts. Oranjestad was like a quaint, neat little Dutch village that recalled the days when Aruba was a simple fishing island. In an hour, one could drive across it for the entire Netherlands Antilles, which is comprised of Curaçao, Bonaire, Saba, Eustatius, and part of St. Martin, are only half the size of Rhode Island. They were raised, along with Surinam, to equality with Holland in the Kingdom of the Netherlands in 1954, and are, besides West Irian, all that remains of the once-huge Dutch colonial possessions.

Jungle-covered Surinam, hot and miserable, is a clumsy sprawling giant of 55,400 square miles compared to Aruba. In Paramaribo, the capital, the heat is stagnant, enervating, and poisonous. Twenty miles from the Atlantic, Paramaribo lies on the muddy brown Surinam River. Disease-bearing insects are everywhere, and tiny red ants crawl over everything, like sinister bloody veils.

A quarter of a million people live there.

Perhaps more, for who has counted each Djuka, each Amerindian in the bush?

Four times I went to Surinam, which supplies two-thirds of America's aluminum ore, and bauxite. In August 1952, I played six different programs in five days, while my legs were attacked by swarms of insects.

On one trip, I decided I wanted to see some Djukas. A friend, whom I shall call Mrs. Hoerssler van Reyk, tried to discourage me. We were sitting in her living room, hung with Indian cloths in bright colors, and fancifully-carved Djuka wooden implements. She was a Creole of mixed ancestry, with brown hair and rather tired brown eyes. She looked weary, as though she had undergone too much heat and rain—and she said sharply, "What do you want to see a Djuka for? You should first smell a Djuka!"

"I've heard so much about how these escaped African slaves were able to defeat the Dutch, and establish their own colony in the jungle bush."

Mrs. Hoerssler van Reyk rose, sprayed Flit under the spinet piano at which I sat, and muttered sourly, "They have odd customs. When one of their women has a baby, she returns right off to work in the fields, while the husband rests eight days and receives presents. They don't think a man can die a natural death, and when one passes away, some of the Elders put the corpse on their heads and stalk through the village. If the dead body seems to incline towards a certain hut, the person in it killed him."

"Is your maid a Djuka?" I asked, while noting, dismayed, that a piece of cheese I had been eating had gotten covered with red ants.

"She's a Town Djuka, brought here a few years ago."

"Looks a little queer, isn't she?"

"She's pregnant, and won't believe it. Must be at least six months gone—that's why she ties that big pillow on her behind, to balance the way she sticks out in front, so no one, she thinks, will notice it. She won't eat anything but rice, *nothing* but rice."

She jumped up, sprayed under the spinet again, smashed a cockroach big as a mouse, and went on, "They're terribly promiscuous, you know. They have an aphrodisiac called 'debbil dour,' made from a bush vine bark, that enables them to keep it up for hours—and the Aucaneers use one made from mucca mucca seed, that is even more forceful."

"Don't they have a lot of bastards?" I asked, pulling a fly out of my hair.

She swiped uselessly at a humming mosquito, and said, "They don't care—they don't believe in fatherhood. The mother's brother is the head of the family. The Saramaccers sometimes take a certain yellow berry that produces abortions."

I scratched an insect bite on my foot until it bled, and asked, "Could someone drive me up to one of their villages tomorrow?"

"Drive? By car? There aren't any roads, you can't go by car!"

Yet, several weeks later, I was in a battered wooden coach being hauled up to Kabel by a wheezing locomotive.

I got off at Republiek.

Hindu fruit-dealers, Arawak Indians, and a few Djukas in ill-fitting town clothes were on the platform, selling trinkets. One Bush Negro had a quaint woven mat on the ground laden with exquisite pot stirrers and wooden combs. When I asked if he had any religious items, he replied that he didn't know what God looked like. I wondered if the head of the Kabel trading-post had gotten my wire.

We rumbled on to Kabel. He hadn't.

When I stepped off the train, camera in one hand, automatic tape recorder in the other, no one was there. Finally, I found a Dutchman, Mr. Haarleuw. He was red-faced. His skin looked boiled. He wore wrinkled white pants and a white shirt. He was sour.

"What do you want to go up there for? You'd have to travel by dugout up the river—if they don't like you, they might put you out anywhere, leave you to starve."

I persuaded him, finally, to take me to a near-by village.

As we left, I raised my camera to take a picture of some Arawak Indians. They fled like swallows before a storm, as did the Djukas. My camera was a magic box full of evil spirits who might imprison their souls.

We went to the village, full of thatched-roof huts made from interwoven reeds. Some pendulous-breasted women, naked to the waist, stood in a clearing, pounding cassava root.

They offered us something to eat. Sweet potatoes, okra, rice swimming in *maripa* palm oil, pancakes of cassava flour and fish.

Later, there was a celebration.

The men wore brief loincloths, their hair tightly braided in astonishing patterns. Some of them were beating drums energetically, while their women danced. It became fiercer when some stark naked men, daubed with white clay, burst on the scene, slashing the air with knives and machetes. It went on all night. It was appalling to see how easily man returns to the atavistic.

I left at dawn.

I was as spent as if I had done the dancing, but I had been unable to get a single clear photograph, for no one would risk the spells of my magic box.

Not until my next trip to Paramaribo, in 1958, did I get a photo of a Djuka! And he had long been living in the town. ✠

CHAPTER 7

In the Midst of Revolution, A Night in Maracaibo
Argentina, Chile, Brazil: 1954, 1955, 1958

D RESSED SUPERBLY IN A PINSTRIPED SUIT, Señor Paquirito was at the Buenos Aires Airport to meet me when I arrived in August 1954. I had not seen him since a brief encounter at a Venezuelan airport.

Then he had looked worried, nervous and thin, now he was exuberant, genial, and well filled-out.

He wore the same black-rimmed glasses, which lent dramatic force to his pale blue eyes. His nose was sharply, proudly Catalán as ever.

He had arranged for me to play Gershwin's "Concerto in F" and the "Saint-Saens G Minor Concerto," with the Buenos Aires Philharmonic at the Teatro Opera on September 6. He had gone to tremendous pains to do it, but then, as he said, he was the greatest manager in the world.

With overwhelming eagerness, he embraced me, shouting,"Ees fan-tas-ti-co to see *vous!* Sitzen-sie, *signorina.* I haf arranged ehverything! I am greates' *empressario* een zee world! *Empressario* of zee heart!"

As always, he spoke in six languages simultaneously.

He led me to my suite at the Hotel Claridge.

I loved Buenos Aires, which united the best of the old and new worlds.

The Teatro Opera was splendidly modern. The concert, under the baton of Carlos Cillario, a former violinist who was now one of Argentina's most distinguished conductors, drew rave reviews.

The morning after, Señor Paquirito decided I should play a recital at the Teatro Opera on September 10. "Weel be wonder-fool! What? ¿*Que?* You says three days ees not time enough to promote a concert? Eet ees! What does you mean? To question me? I am greates' *empressario* een zee world! I knows ehverything!"

He planned to put two thousand colorful *afichas,* or posters, throughout the city, to make hordes of people flock to the concert. But it rained — pouring, slashing, and streaming for three days. Not until the morning of the concert could the posters be pasted on the Buenos Aires walls.

Almost nobody came to the concert. Nobody knew about it. A few were present, but the general effect, in the vast dazzling immensity of the Opera, was of nobody. I was nervous before going onstage. Would I remember the "Milonga" by Ginasterra I had gone sleepless to learn? The night before, Señor Flaco, Señor Paquirito's assistant, had arrived at my hotel, lumbering under the ponderous weight of a yard-high pile of music by Argentine composers. It seemed there was a law no one had remembered to tell me about, a law that every performance in Argentina must contain an Argentine work. "Am so sorry. Will you please learn one of these pieces, perhaps a sonata, for the performance tomorrow afternoon?"

I did remember the "Milonga," playing it without music.

The reviews were fine the next day.

"But what happens now?" I asked Señor Paquirito. "Where is the next concert?"

"You American, don't be so *mécanique.* I cannot cut me in two! What cans I do? Eef you has come een June, weel have been wonder-fool. Zee tour I had for you! I hadda zee Colon, zee Opera, zee Wagneriana, an' Tucuman, Mendoza, Cordoba, La Plata, Rosario, an' all Chile, *todo* Brazil, tout Colombia, Venezuela, Uruguay — I hadda ehverything — an' your mother ruin all, she cancel, she *estropea todo* — ees a bad wooman zat!"

"But why didn't you let us know you had all those concerts?"

He dismissed that scurrilous objection with a wave of the hand.

I grew worried.

My only compensation was the joy of discovering the romantic sights of Buenos Aires, one of the world's most outstanding metropolis, and eating the fine food — luscious cheeses, splendid canned goods, and first quality fruits and vegetables.

On September 20 and 27, I gave recitals over Radio Splendid. Before the latter, I had to stay up all night learning an Argentine "Chacarera." I never did get it to sound like tipsy gauchos kicking.

Several times, I visited the soirées given by Gilbert Chase, the outstanding American musicologist.

In October, I gave two performances over the nationwide hook-up of Radio El Mundo, playing the Grieg "A Minor Concerto," and the Gershwin Concerto in F, with orchestra, under the direction of Juan Emilio Martini, the great Argentine conductor. Mr. Martini was exceptionally nice to me.

I gave a recital also at the Salon de Actos of the American Embassy.

American Ambassador Alfred Nufer received me for lunch one day, at his residence, one of the most gorgeous I have seen anywhere, with sweeping marble staircases, exquisite statuary, endless elegant rooms, serene vistas.

The Ambassador, a handsome man, six foot four, with strong features, was a great music lover, and adored animals. Leading me into his garden, he showed me his favorite pet, an elfin grey and white lamb, with a mischievous, droll face, and a pert behind that wiggled as he gamboled happily over leaves and flowers to nibble the daffodils.

I prepared dubiously to leave for Chile. For weeks Señor Paquirito had told me that "ehverything" was arranged in Santiago, "Weel be wonder-fool!"

My mother's advice when she wrote me was, "Don't go." When I showed this to Señor Paquirito, he said, "Ees a bad wooman zat! Ees all arranged. My reputation ees destroyed eef you don't go!"

Yet, a few days later, he told me the Chile concerts had fallen through, "Ees a bad man zat!"

The next week, the news was, "Ees all arrengeda Chile! Ees fan-tas-ti-co! Wunderbar! ¡Muito admirável! Formidable! You weel play three concerts een Santiago, zee 21, zee 23, an' zee 26 of thees month, an' zen weel be zee radio, an' Viña del Mar, Antofagasta, Valdivia, La Serena, Temuco, Concepcion, an' all Chile from Arica to Tierra del Fuego. Ees wonder-fool"

My mother sent cable after cable saying:

> "COME HOME AT ONCE STOP ARGENTINE AIRLINES ONLY FLIES ONCE PER WEEK STOP YOU MUST TAKE NOVEMBER 2ND FLIGHT TO NEW YORK STOP YOU PLAY IN BOSTON NOVEMBER 5TH."

And Señor Paquirito would say, "What I care about Boston? Cancel heem! After all I dooing for-a you!" When, the night before departure, I suggested canceling the trip, he exclaimed, "But ees you who force me to arrange. You cannot ruin now." We flew to Cordoba, where the flight was held up two days, and only arrived in Santiago on October 20.

We found the concerts had not even been announced. No posters were anywhere. No ads had appeared. "Ees bads mens zose!" said Señor Paquirito.

Each concert was only announced the day of the performance. Though there were rave reviews, the audience was smaller each time. Yet I was really taken up socially, and many parties were given for me.

Dr. Alfonso Leng, the great Chilean composer, entertained me, played recordings of his symphonic works, and presented me with an autographed manuscript copy of one of his piano sonatas.

Ambassador Willard Beaulac, who had given me the wonderful reception in Havana, gave me another splendid party at his residence.

Señora Delano de Sierras, a distinguished lady, distantly related to the Delano family in America, and who was of *"La fronda aristocratica,"* gave me a reception.

Her daughter's family had once owned Ambassador Beaulac's luxurious residence. She had just suffered a sad bereavement. Her twelve-year-old child had died of leukemia, after long suffering. She had given repeated transfusions of her own blood to the child, which had so weakened her that she had lost the sight of one eye.

Santiago, truly lovely, has more and more striking modern buildings going up each day. The transparent jade waters of the lucid Mapocho River are overlooked by the aloof rocky slopes of Cerro San Cristóbal.

Never have I seen so many crippled, blind, legless and armless people in the streets of a major city, though, as in Santiago.

Once, when I got lost returning to my hotel from the Teatro Municipal, I found myself in a strange alley among decrepit buildings.

The alley, dirt-encrusted and malodorous, was heaped with garbage, old rags, smashed barrels, broken glass, and ordure piled in the gutters. The crumbling, stained houses leaned over unsteadily, their shadows spreading like wolves' teeth. Soon I emerged into an irregular courtyard that centered around a cracked stone fountain at which lounged seven men.

One had a black beard, two were Indians, one a legless cripple, one had a face covered with eruptions, and one had a gross belly like a swollen wine-skin.

They moved into action on my appearance, and soon relieved me of my scarf, gloves and briefcase.

Some announcements of my last concert at the Teatro Municipal were stuck between the pages of the music. Apparently the Indian could not read. Running one finger through his long straight black hair, he turned it in every direction. Then he looked at the music from every possible angle. The other Indian lighted a kerosene lamp, and the two of them stared at the music, with puzzled intensity, as though it were some kind of map. *"¿Que es esto?"* the Araucanian muttered.

"It's the music I use." I explained that I was a pianist, stammering as I searched for the right words. My tongue twisted on the Spanish phrases. When they finally understood, despite my Castilian accent, that I was a musician, the fifth man, whose face was covered with crusted red sores, laughed raucously, and the Araucanian said, in a malicious voice, that I had better play something then. He pointed to a wooden case that stood on the mendicant's cart. He lifted it down to the ground. It was a small white four octave hand organ, with two pedals.

He pushed an empty wine-case toward it, for me to sit on. I pushed the pedals, and touched a key. It sounded with a flute-like tone. They all gathered around me, passing a wine bottle among themselves. I began the Triana by Albeniz. It went beyond the extent of the organ's keyboard. I began a Bach Fugue. It sounded beautiful on the organ, disciplined, sad, meditative.

I grew lost in its thematic architecture, and the tones soared forth. I thought of the English poet William Wordsworth's lines:

> Action is transitory——a step, a blow,
> The motion of a muscle——this way or that .
> 'Tis done, and in the after-vacancy
> We wonder at ourselves like men betrayed:
> Suffering is permanent, obscure and dark,
> And shares the nature of infinity.

Then I played a passionate Triste from "La Pampa" in Argentina, and a haunting, romantic song from "Patagonia." They were very pleased by this. They smiled, with some appearance of humanity, and said, *"¡Mas! ¡Toca mas! ¡Que ella toque bien!"* I played more Chilean pieces, while they winked, clapped their hands, and stamped their feet.

The Indians, as they drank from several wine bottles, grew less grim and almost friendly. I continued playing, by the flickering light the kerosene lamp shed on the yellow keys, as they sang the melodies in loud voices, evidently enjoying themselves. More Indians emerged from the shadows and began to dance.

This might have lasted forever, had not some sudden screams, followed by what seemed like bullet-shots, caused my audience to disperse in all directions. They disappeared into the shadow so fast one might have thought they had never been there.

One of the Indians gave me back my scarf, gloves, and briefcase, and pushed me toward the edge of the court where there was a stone archway I had not seen before, in which was set a small oak door, studded with nails. He hit a bronze knocker that was on it. The door opened. He led me in, and it closed behind us. A woman with a candle in her hand was standing there. He spoke to her, in a torrent of words, and then the two led me down a long hall until we reached another door. He opened it. It let out onto a fairly busy street. He put his hand outside, pointed to the right I went outside, and he shut the door behind me.

I walked a little way, and found a taxi which took me to my hotel.

Señor Paquirito was pacing up and down in the lobby of the hotel when I arrived. "Where has you been? I been lookeeng ehverywhere for you!" he shouted.

"Well, you see, I got lost. I was walking back."

"Walking! You mus' not walk! You weel spoily our *ambiente?* Zee arteest cannot walk. How you knows what happen to you zere are some streets you walks on here, zey weel cut off your hand to get your purse. You weel ruin all! You worries me to death. *¡Caramba! ¡Merde! ¡Mein Gott!* After all I do-eeng for-a you!"

Later that evening, I visited a Chilean landholder, who had ranches north of Santiago. She told me a lot about the bloody, intrigue-riddled early days of bile. Even the last three decades have been a vicious circle of difficulties there. She said, "So many of the *fundos,* or great plantations, are worked by diseased, illiterate, poverty-stricken *rotos* — How can they have modern agricultural methods? They hardly know anything of scientific draining, fertilizing and planting. The plows are pulled by lumbering oxen, and the wheat threshed by the unwieldy horse-drawn trilla, with its spike-bottom. So how can they produce enough to give everyone a balanced diet? In 1931, the year l married, the infant mortality rate was one in four!"

And she told me how President Ibañez had then tried to relocate the unemployed nitrate workers in the Araucanian Indian territory and it failed. The Depression lowered trade to a minimum, and the hot-headed students rioted in the streets, along with the unemployed. President Ibañez fled over the Andes, prices leapt, the army and navy revolted, unbacked issues of paper pesos poured forth, nitrate ex pats sank to one-twentieth of what they had been.

The Chilean landowner went on, "How each discovery or invention bodes ill as well as good for someone! Our economy was based on nitrate-production from mines, so the discovery of how to extract it from the air was disastrous for us."

"Didn't things improve under President Alessandri?" I asked. "Yes, but after World War II, there were increased international and national tensions. Ibañez became our president again this year."

Yet, President Ibañez could not solve Chile's mammoth problems. The official exchange value of the peso then was 151 to the dollar, the actual black market rate being 300. Now in 1959, it was 1,000 to the dollar.

And what is the future for this country bigger than France and England combined? This long wrinkled ribbon, 2,600 miles in length, rarely more than 100 miles wide — constantly inundated with rain in the forested south, an arid desert in the north—and predictably fertile only in the center—and with less people in it than New York City?

Several times, in Santiago, I visited the Club Catalán all the members of which came from Catalonia in Spain. Of course they dreamed of the day Catalonia would obtain independence from Spain, sang Catalán songs, revered the Catalán flag they had behind a glass case in the banquet room, and spoke only in Catalán, a language quite distinct from Spanish, but which sounded to me like French words pronounced in the Spanish way.

The triangular territory of Catalonia stretches right up to the Pyrenees, and was, for long periods of its history, ruled by France.

The Cataláns, who are industrious, efficient, energetic, sharp witted, and proud, look down, by virtue of these qualities, on the rest of Spain. Northern rather than Southern in their outlook, they appeared to deplore the "siesta-mentality," and felt the rest of Spain held them back.

"Perhaps you are justified," I told one Catalán as he finished a dish of *zarzuela de mariscos,* and started eating the Barcelona sausage, *butifarra a la Catalána.* "But what would happen if every people went back to where they originally came from, hundreds or thousands of years ago? The whole world would have to migrate!"

Suppressed annoyance clouded his blue eyes. He said, "Do not ridicule us. We have a common cultural heritage, to be proud of."

"But the idea can be carried too far. Many places are poor or one-sided in natural resources, or the type of crops that can be grown, and they cannot have a viable economy above the simple tribal, nomadic or agricultural level unless they are part of some large unit. Common cultural heritage, religion or language, is not always enough. A country may not be successfully independent on the modern civilized level."

"And how many countries are modern and civilized? The capitals of Europe and America are the worst jungles of all—hotbeds of crime and corruption teeming with lonely, selfish, scheming savage egoists," he said.

"I don't apologize for the neurotic disposition of the supposedly civilized man," I exclaimed with feeling.

"Don't you? Don't you?" he murmured with a cunning look that made his sharp features seem like a small arrogant inquisitor.

"No! I don't apologize for anything. Once I read the *Brothers Karamazov.* I was fourteen then, introverted, impressionable. Father Zossima said there, on his deathbed, 'Each man is responsible for all men and for everything.' For years I, too, felt responsible for all men and for everything, felt drenched with guilt. But not anymore."

"How do you know? What has once been in you will always be in you. The anxieties one has suffered do not pass," he said, with an excited look.

I felt that he was accusing me. "You are accusing me?"

The Catalán replied with a curt, bitter warmth, "I am punishing you because you want me to." I rose from the dull greenish table and walked out of the room.

When I reached the street, the cold gusty air swept around me with a funeral breath. I walked on, hoping somehow the darkness would discipline me. I heard the bell of a nearby cathedral. It drew me in with hypnotic certainty.

I walked to the cathedral, climbed the stone steps that the masses of Santiago had so often ascended, and suddenly, with a feeling of agony, I wanted to weep for them, for their hunger, wasted blood, rags and hopelessness, and for myself. Within, the church glowed with a spiritual ecstasy that lifted me away from rage, confusion and insatiable inadequacy.

The next problem that arose concerned my broadcast for Anaconda Copper. The program materialized, vanished, a dozen times before it actually happened. No sooner was it completed than a new crisis arose. Señor Paquirito wanted me to stay in Chile.

"What for you wants to go back to America to play een Boston? I haffa concert for you November *cuatro!* Zey could not make eet a her for zey theenks two days ees not *bastante* to make publicity-ees bad mens zose! You weel make money een Boston? So what? *Mécanique* American weeth no *heart!*"

"But, they've paid me in advance for the concert," I said.

"Oof! What I cares? Eefa you wants more money, make all Latin America weeth me an' my *guitarrista*, an' we weel ride on a burro an' make music ehverywhere village by village town by town, we weel do all Chile, all Brazil, *todo el continente!*" he shouted in an enormous burst of enthusiasm. "You have forced me to come to Chile! An' I am so kind, like a *santo* you mus' be more sweet weeth me — I do not tell you, zey are going to make tremendous law-suit against you, an' I halia not breathe a word, you always says I talks too much. an' yet I am always silent I am mos' silentest man een zee WOORLD!"

Chile was a hard country to leave.

I spent seven hours going from office to office, government building to government building, the day prior to my departure, to get the necessary exit permits.

I FORGOT ALL THE COMPLEX, fearsome problems of Latin America when I returned to the United States, and only remembered the gorgeous, fascinating cities, the charm and admiration for classic music as a great romantic profession, the fact that classic artists were mobbed and adored in South America like jazz entertainers are in North America.

As I tramped the drab, soot-dirtied, muddy, snow-smeared streets of New York, chill and forbidding. I dreamed of Buenos Aires. When I saw the ugly outlines of Carnegie Hall. I longed for the breathtaking beauty of the Teatro Opera and the Teatro Colon. Even the lighting effects used for recitals in Chile and Argentina were soft, intimate and romantic, in contrast to the harsh, stark lights on the Town Hall or Carnegie stages in New York. I winced when Americans asked me, "Why don't you play rock-and-roll?" and yearned for South America, where devoting one's life to fine music is considered admirable, not queer, even if one never makes a financial success at it.

Señor Paquirito wrote me a dozen letters urging me to return.

He said he had "All Brazil, all Uruguay, all Argentina! Another letter asked me to "send a Negro conductor, too!"

The last suggested that I also send Horowitz, Nathan Milstein, Anton Rubenstein and Godowsky, quite unaware that the last two were decades well as Myra Hess, Eartha Kitt, and the entire cast of "Porgy and Bess."

I did not find time to reply to that letter.

He sent me a cable to arrive on April 1 in Rio de Janeiro.

WHEN I ARRIVED AT THE AIRPORT, he said that everything had been arranged and had been tremendous, but "so-an-so — ees a bad man zat!" had spoiled it all, and it was all canceled — "¡es fracasado todo!"

As soon as I was established at the Copacabana Hotel, it all got re-arranged again. I was to have five concerts, in Rio, Sao Paulo, and Santos.

I practiced each day in the luxurious casino at the Copacabana. As I worked at one of the two black concert grand pianos, Señor Paquirito would tell me long tales of the vast sums he had lost gambling there.

One night, Dante Viggiani, a wealthy impresario, gave a party for me at his elegant home. The walls were covered with old Italian paintings. Italian antiques were everywhere.

A young man with a pale, ascetic face spoke to me throughout the evening. He had a strange mystic, yet penetrating serenity, and looked through one, as though through a glass.

"I know exactly what you are thinking," he told me, "What?"

"You are worried about your health."

"Why, that's right. My blood count must be low. I've felt queer, weary and sluggish ever since I arrived."

''Be careful of what you eat. Disease rates are high here."

"Well, I try not to drink the milk. I mix milk powder with the water out of the bathroom tap, and drink it."

"You mustn't do *that!* The orange color of the water comes from mud and mineral deposits."

"What else do you see?" I asked curiously.

"You will not enjoy your stay in Brazil. As soon as you leave you will have spectacular success. Then you will barely escape death, and will have to return abruptly to the United States before your tour is ended. The same thing will happen on your next tour of South America."

"Oh! Tell me more. Go on!" I urged him, fascinated. "You are not married," he said, intensely.

"No."

"How old are you? Twenty-one?"

"Yes."

"You will marry between 1961 and 1963. He will not be from the Western Hemisphere. He will have a strange background, and be unusual in appearance—a writer or an artist—someone you do not even think of now. It will amaze everybody and startle the world."

"You see all this? How? Tell me some more!"

"No, it's grown foggy. I don't see any more. We will correspond after you leave Brazil," he murmured, his eyes shifting from their piercing, quasi-fanatic gaze, to an abstract, suffering one, that made one think of an El Greco painting.

After that night, I never saw or heard from him again.

The next day, I received a phone call in my small, conservatively furnished room at the Copacabana. It was from an English journalist who said he had met my father when he was in Rio in 1948. He invited me to visit him. His flat was in the Copacabana district, not far from my hotel. I agreed.

Nicholas Chesterling was standing in front of his apartment house when I arrived. It was a modern grey-white stone building with a grocery store on one side. We walked into the box-like hall, and took the lift to the third floor.

His drawing-room was very large, and was furnished with an astonishing variety of things from around the world, in every style.

Harpoons hung next to rifles, Masai spears, elephant tusks and Chinese silk paintings on the pale grey walls. There were five enormous stuffed animal heads: two antelopes, a tiger, a yak and a rhinoceros. In a Dutch cabinet, fronted with glass, were intricately carved monkeys and Buddhas from India, a gold and pearl bracelet from Borneo, Ubangi earrings from Equatorial Africa, white jade statuettes, black pearls from Alaska, bamboo boxes from Burma, a Florentine bottle for love-philters, elephant toe bracelets from the Haute Volta, Spanish combs, Liberian tribal toothpicks, a bone box from Mexico, one inch by half an inch that contained a complete set of dominoes, and a Moroccan chess set.

In one corner stood a huge Polynesian totem, in another, a many-armed stone Siamese statue.

He explained their histories to me.

Nicholas Chesterling and I sat down on a Sudanese stool, and he on a Swedish modern clam-shaped chair, and I observed him closely, intently.

Blue eyes, partly-bald head, brown eyebrows, definite chin — nothing was ugly or repellent, but he revealed nothing. I felt I would not recognize him if I met him in the street. The Roman nose did not suggest pride, avarice, or sensuality, it suggested nothing.

He was six feet tall, and wore white trousers and an open collared white shirt.

"What part of England do you come from?" I asked him. "London."

"It's funny, you don't have an English accent at all, you sound more like an Eastern European."

"Really? I've traveled there."

"You seem to have traveled to a lot of places, judging by this collection."

He began to ply me with questions about my tours, especially those in Scandinavia, Haiti and Cuba. He questioned me closely about the Batista regime, and my impressions of Havana. Under his skillful manipulation, I talked and talked. I poured forth opinions and recollections.

He drew me out about my father's writings and associates until I expostulated, "Why don't you write and ask him? He can tell you better than I!" And, with a distant vagueness, he replied, "But I have so little time for letters."

"By the way, where did you meet my father when he was here?"

"The Copacabana."

"He didn't stop there — he meant to, but was told they were 'full'."

"I meant at a restaurant in the Copacabana district."

"Did you write an article about him? You did? My father's friends sent him lots of articles, but I don't remember one by you," I murmured suspiciously.

"I use several pen-names. Let me show you my scrap-books." He showed me a large black book, crammed with photos of himself in every conceivable costume.

Soon he took out two ivory lions from the Dutch cabinet, and said, "These are from the Sudan, the Fung Province."

One was a present for me, and he asked me to take the other to Argentina. "To whom?" I asked.

"An old friend of mine. He will contact you. It's an exquisite example. Look at the elaborate detail work. You won't find another like it. Such a lovely piece — I don't dare send it through customs — someone might steal it! You will take it? How kind. I'll wrap it in this gold paper. Forgive me! I haven't given you any refreshments. Would you like tea?" he asked me in a cool, speculative voice.

"No. No. I didn't have lunch, I was practicing a piece by Villa-Lobos, and I forgot…well, some fruit would be nice. Oh, please don't bother to go out to buy it!"

He left.

I walked to the barred window that overlooked the street, and gazed down as he came out of the house, and turned right to enter the grocery store. Two men came out of the shadows and, one on either side of him, led him abruptly to a grey car. The three entered, the door slammed, the car drove off.

It seemed peculiar.

It had all happened so quickly. He hadn't said anything about going somewhere before he returned. He said he would be back in five minutes with the fruit. I waited. I looked idly at some of his other scrap-books—photographs were there showing him in Spain during the Civil War, in Russia with some top Soviet officials, in Finland, in Mongolia, in Paris. He did not return. The minutes dragged past. Two hours passed. It had grown dark outside. The phone rang. I answered, and no one was on the other end. That happened three times. I got exasperated, annoyed and a little frightened. I was dying of thirst.

I needed to go to the bathroom. I walked through the flat, looking. There were nine rooms. One seemed crammed with a great deal of ammunition. I found a kitchen. It had a service exit that led to a winding staircase. I went back to the living room. I decided to leave. I took the two ivory lions. I wrote a brief note to Mr. Chesterling, asking him to write me at the Hotel in Montevideo. I tried to open the door. It would not open. It was firmly locked from the outside. I walked back to the kitchen, went out the service exit and down the stairway. At the second-floor landing, a woman was bending over, putting a garbage can outside her door. She stared at me. I asked her if she knew Mr. Chesterling. She looked blank. She said the third-floor flat belonged to Mr. Chelnicki. Puzzled, I walked on down to the street service exit, around the corner from the other entrance.

As I came out onto the street, it seemed to me I saw the same car in which Mr. Chesterling had left, being parked in front of the house. He was not in the car. Two other men got out and entered the apartment house. I walked the other way, and went back to my hotel.

That evening I tried to phone Mr. Chesterling.

No one by that name in the phone book. The next day I flew to Sao Paulo for two concerts in the shining modern hall of Cultura Artistica. The auditorium was packed each time. I flew back to Rio feeling terribly sick. Señor Paquirito had found a tiny café where the meals were only forty cruzeiros each, equaling fifty cents American money, and insisted, with an air of triumphant ingenuity, that I eat all meals there.

Whether the queer-tasting food there had poisoned me, or whether the glass of bottled orange juice I had taken in Mr. Chesterling's kitchen had something wrong with it, I did not know. But I felt horrible, was nauseated, had a burning fever, and felt as if my whole body were crawling with leeches.

I wanted to cancel my recital that afternoon in Rio. Señor Paquirito would not hear of it. "Malingerer! How cans you be seeck? Never been my life has I been seeck, how cans you be seeck? Ees dredful! You cans not cancel concert! Ten thousand people weel be there—ten thousan', twenty thousan', mos' fullest concert een zee WOORLD! Ees all plot to ruin *mi reputación* as *impressario!*"

"But I'm too sick to play," I said.

"Oof! You keel me. You are zee mos' baddest wooman I never meet een my life! You mus' play. Or I keel myself. Anyhow, you are alway s fan-tas-ti-co!"

Limply, I dressed for the concert. Backstage, at the theatre, he almost pushed me out on the stage. Dizzily, head reeling, I played.

The reviews the next day terrified me.

Señor Paquirito had not told anyone I was sick. Though he was limitlessly voluble about everything else, he had maintained tomblike silence "like a *santo*," on that point.

"But why didn't you let me cancel the concert?" I said excitedly.

"Oof! Forgeeve! I haf notta did especially! I haf notta theenk!"

After playing the Saint-Saens Concerto in G minor with symphony orchestra in Rio, I left at once for Santos. I had been unable to reach Mr. Chesterling.

Santos was steaming hot. The humidity hung thickly in the air. It was a torture to play the concert on the dampness-swollen piano. The hotel was a marvelous palace in Conquistador style. As I packed to fly to Uruguay, I looked closely at the two ivory lions. Each was six inches in length, and three inches high, but one was far, far heavier than the other. Together, they were likely to make me overweight. I would almost have thought the heavier one had something concealed in the base. I fiddled with it, seeing if there were a secret catch, but I could not open it.

I took them with me to Montevideo.

THE AIR WAS COOL AND BRISK THERE. Everything went splendidly. The reviews were wonderful after my concert at the Sodre. I was invited to return to perform with Fabian Sevitzky with the Sodre Symphony. Uruguayan artists began to seek out Señor Paquirito, begging him to present them, too, in recitals.

He left for Buenos Aires, and I stayed behind to do an American music broadcast. As I packed to leave by sea plane for Argentina, I noticed that both ivory lions seemed to have been misplaced. They were gone. I looked everywhere.

They had vanished. I took the plane, wondering vaguely why I had not heard from Mr. Chesterling. As I entered Customs at the airport, a man asked me if I would take a small package for him in my purse, as he was overweight. I refused. I saw him give it to someone else. Once on the airplane, I saw this person hand it to another, who gave it to another. It changed hands five times. As we lined up to leave the plane, I saw the last person slip it back into the pocket of the first man. He was searched at the Buenos Aires Airport the package was impounded, and he was led off by some uniformed officials whom I assumed to be police.

I DROVE FROM THE AIRPORT to the luxurious Alvear Palace Hotel.

Everett Lee, the American Negro conductor and I gave two Festivals of George Gershwin's orchestral works at the Teatro Colon. Four thousand people packed the hall for each concert, and the seats had been sold out four hours after they were put on sale.

We left for Cordoba to present the same program, accompanied by Señor Paquirito, and María Luisa Desio, a music fan.

María Luisa, the most beautiful girl I had ever seen in my life, looked like a Botticelli Venus. Her hair was like night on the Paraná River, she had classic features, a glorious figure. Superbly dressed, and highly cultivated, she played the piano herself, and it was an exciting event to her to hear the five rehearsals we had with the Cordoba orchestra, and see the background of how music was made.

She was sweet, with gracious manners. She got the newspapers from Montevideo for me, containing the reviews of my orchestral concert with Fabian Sevitsky and the Sodre Symphony, and translated them. *"Mire Ud., Felipa,"* she said, *"El Dia"* wrote, "'Seldom have we heard an American pianist with so much artistic temperament-brilliant, passionate, yet pure, austere, Schuyler has at her command all the resources of the piano, her concert was one of those rare occasions where one hears music recreated. Great!'"

The Cordoba performance was scheduled for 9:30 p.m. on June 12. At 10:30 p.m. it had not begun. There was buzzing, angry talk in the audience. People had been making speeches. Someone waved the Argentine flag. Another man rushed backstage to Mr. Lee, and said. "You've got to play the National Anthem. There will be fighting in the audience, if you don't." Mr. Lee had never seen the music before, but he read the score, learned it in five minutes, and went out and conducted it with the orchestra. At 11:00 p.m. the concert began. It ended at one in the morning.

We signed hundreds of autographs. The audience went home. No one had thought of offering to drive us back to the hotel. We waited for a taxi. Finally, we walked back, twenty-five blocks, to the hotel!

A car shortage had been a by-product of the Perón administration. It was rumored there were less cars in the country in 1955 than twenty-five years before. The results were chaotic in the taxi-business. Though Buenos Aires had two subway systems and what seemed like hundreds of bus and trolley lines, a taxi was like a needle in a haystack. In the provinces they were even rarer.

When María, Señor Paquirito and I left next evening for Rosario, we waited an hour for a taxi. In desperation, fifteen minutes before train time, Señor Paquirito rushed and found a horse and buggy in which we dashed breathlessly to the station, leaping on the train just as it was pulling out.

A surprise awaited us in Rosario. We got a note, saying my concert would have to be postponed twenty-four hours owing to the strike.

The next day throughout Argentina there was a strike. When they strike in Argentina, everything stops: restaurants, business, groceries, transportation, shops, and hotels. The manager of our hotel had to come down and run the elevator for us himself.

Señor Paquirito left for Buenos Aires just before my concert the next night. María Luisa and I stayed on in Rosario. She woke me at dawn the morning after my recital, and said, "I've a feeling we should get out of here quickly."

We took the 7:00 a.m. train, the troops marched into Rosario two hours after we left. We were on our way to Buenos Aires. It took eight hours.

Señor Desio had risked his life to come to the station in Buenos Aires, to meet us. We jumped in his car. Bombs were dropping, flames and the acrid smell of smoke putrefied the air. Soldiers rushed through the streets. Blood and broken glass were everywhere. The city was choked with destruction, from the yawning gulfs of battered houses, to the bleeding corpses in the gutters, and the pitifully young soldiers in ill-fitting greenish-grey uniforms. We heard machine guns and rifles firing, shattered walls and woodwork lay on the ground, the avenues were packed with fleeing women and children.

Revolution had come out into the streets, the crowded places. Like a savage army of driver ants, the conspirators had stubbornly swept from every corner, every alley to fight, fight for church, country and liberty, to eat away at and devour the Perón administration.

It was awesome, and it made one tremble. Why was death, cruelty and suffering always necessary to pave the way for liberty, and, so often, unsuccessfully? I could not answer the question within myself, and I wanted to run away, run from the blood, the burning, the wreckage, the hunger, the soldiers, and the disemboweled buildings, the rumble and roar of gunfire, and the debris of corpses, ruins and hopes.

The uprising was unsuccessful. The lives had been shed in vain. Perón remained in power. I left Buenos Aires as quickly as I could. The revolt three months later smashed the Perónistas, sent him into exile.

I RETURNED TO ARGENTINA three years later.

The country had three years of liberty now, a liberty riddled by uncertainties. Buenos Aires had changed profoundly. It was no longer a gay city, a pall of worry and disillusion seemed to hang over it. There were cracks in the formerly imposing walls, buildings were not kept up as well as they had been. Everyone looked sad. No one smiled in Argentina. Everyone seemed to be wearing suits three years old. There were strikes every few days, or threats of strikes. Prices soared daily. The peso's value plunged down and down. The beautiful pictures of Perón and Evita, that had formerly been wherever eyes could see, were gone. Yawning spaces leered on walls, where they had been ripped off, empty holes loomed in lobbies, where their statues had been snatched away.

Many of my old friends had vanished. I learned not to ask for people.

I was lonely.

I visited Carlos Ritter, an American millionaire who lived in an Asian apartment there, and Rosa Koppmann, a graduate of the Czarist St. Petersburg Conservatory, who gave me wonderful pointers on Russian music.

I played to a packed house at the Teatro Colon.

Ambassador Nufer was gone. He was dead. This saddened me greatly. Mr. Beaulac, the new ambassador, gave a beautiful party in my honor.

I felt dissatisfied, depressed. Then, I received two letters from Prime Minister Kwame Nkrumah of Ghana, asking me to be in New York when he arrived.

Also, I received an anonymous letter at my hotel, threatening me. The winter had somehow misconstrued the spectacular success I had during the Perón regime to mean that I was a follower of Perón.

It seemed like a bad omen. I canceled my last concert and returned to New York.

AFTER MY TRIP BACK TO NEW YORK, where I saw the visiting Prime Minister of Ghana on several occasions, I felt a longing to return to South America, to lose myself in its remarkably beautiful cities, and steep myself in its passion and violence.

A few weeks later I was in Venezuela.

Caracas is brilliant, but the place that drew me most with its haunting romantic atmosphere was Maracaibo, founded in 1571.

In the midst of the vast Lake Maracaibo area, which since 1917 has been the greatest oil producer in the continent it is not too far from the Dutch islands of

Aruba and Curaçao, where the oil refineries are, but how different Maracaibo is from San Niccola or Willemstad.

As I left the Maracaibo airport to go into the city, laden with the heavy handbags I always seem to travel with, a handsome young man ran up to me, holding a wallet in his hand. "This is yours, is it not, senorita? *No es verdad? Ud. lo ha echado por accidente, yo creo.*" It was mine, and it contained three hundred dollars. It had dropped from a gap in the bottom of my overladen handbag, which I had sewn up three times, but always seemed to burst again.

He had a refined yet voluptuous face, which seemed to brood with every emotion save that of tenacity, where pleasure, cruelty, idealism, sensuality, sadism and generosity, were mingled—where the sombre, the vicious, the spiritual and the poetic, had each their force, their exhalation and their domain.

I liked him. More than that, I felt drawn to him-and though I had never seen him before, I felt that I had known him always.

It gave me a swift, weak yet bewildering pleasure when Antonio Matiz introduced himself, asked me if I knew anyone in Maracaibo, and offered to show me the city. He had a car outside that seemed half a block long. It was turquoise, with luxurious gold upholstery.

We drove in it past villas and hovels, past the national college and the nautical school, past the municipal hall, the prison, the library the legislative chambers and the hospital, a beautiful park and half a dozen churches. After two hours of driving, he took me to a social club in a residential suburb along the lake shore toward the south. It was a dusty rose pink in color, with a wall around it and elaborate heavy iron grill-work round the doors and windows, and was in old Spanish colonial style.

A steward let us in, and we walked over the black and white marble floors. The rooms had the sad cloistral calm of luxurious simplicity. We finally sat down in a large room with rose silk brocade curtains around tall, narrow windows. Everything here glittered with gold, a tawny fierce yellow gold—shamefully luxuriant, as though recalling the days of decadent Castilian monarchs long before Bolívar. There was an enormous clock on the mantelpiece resplendent with gold figures depicting the tale of Jason's quest for the Golden Fleece.

Ming vases stood on pedestals of gold-encrusted red marble. On an ebony commode with marquetry of brass, tortoise-shell, mother-of-pearl and ivory, sat a golden cornucopia bedecked with nymphs and satyrs. Over a Florentine coffer with stucco arabesque ornamentation hung a gold-framed painting of the Rape of Europa. There was an ebony armoire with tortoise shell panels and ormolu mountings, and Venetian folding chairs of gilt and carved walnut—Louis XV gilt armchairs with red silk damask upholstery, and tulipwood *escritoires* bearing gold statuettes.

Between the dimly luminous, inquisitorial windows hung gold-framed portraits of severe gaunt cruel-lipped men in black, in costumes of several centuries.

"Those are some of my ancestors," Antonio said wryly. "I hate looking at them. It makes me feel uncomfortable-as though I should have done more for my country. My great-grandfather fought with Bolívar, and what have I done? Nothing! ¡Nada! ¡Nada! I have been chasing the woomans! I should have been part of the uprising that ousted Jiménez in January. If I had been part of that attempted coup last month, it might not have failed. I detest myself! Yo me detesto."

"Well, it's still not too late to start a revolution if you really want to."

"Perhaps it is hopeless. But I love my patria. I adore my pais! All the corrupt politicians, army officers and businessmen should be executed—cleanse the country in a bath of blood, and start anew. The Jiménez regime was hopeless, but things are not any better now, different people have the power, that's all. If I had been worthy of mi sangre I would have taken part in the July coup, helped it to succeed, and then seized and wrested the power for myself, and done away with the others, then I could have ruled idealistically!" he said, fiercely.

"But how can you rule idealistically, when you have to depend on so many other people? The world today."

"It is the fault of the United States that the world is the way it is today!"

"Isn't that an exaggeration?" I argued.

Antonio said heatedly, "It is not! The yanquis meddle too much in foreign affairs, and do not give enough money to South America! They take and they do not give! And they set an example of materialism. All the rich here want to live like Americans so they get richer from the oil revenues, and the poor get poorer. You cannot imagine the squalor of the poor! If I were in office, I would give free education, free housing, and free medical care to all the poor."

I said slowly, leaning forward in the gilt armchair, "That's wonderful! But how are you going to get in office?"

"Money! The money I have squandered on woomans could have made ten revolutions. When I was twenty-one, I went to Europe, and I spent half a million dollars in a year! Then I come back to my parents, and I say, 'Forgeeve me!' And they say, "We forgeeve you. You are our son, nuestro hijo, again!'"

The tall, narrow windows grew darker, as though reflecting the cruelty of Antonio's ancestors, and I asked, "What will you do now?"

Antonio's well-groomed hands clenched the walnut arms of the Venetian chair with bitterness, and he said, "I don't know! I don't know where to start. I have wasted my life on trivialities. Is that all I am good for, to be a playboy, like Pignatari? Always the playboy." He glowered darkly for a few minutes, while the gold-resplendent clock chimed four. Then he added, "I must go home, to change my clothes for dinner — always I change the clothes three times a day. I cannot *bear* for things not be clean — it hurts me even to read a newspaper — it makes the hands dirty, I cannot bear for the hands to get dirty."

"But how can you be a revolutionary then? That involves a lot of dirty work," I said, watching the dusky shadows creep across the tulip-wood escritoire to my right.

"*¡Madre de Dias!* I must do what God wishes. Perhaps I will make love to you instead. Christ said, 'Love one another,' We will travel around the world together, and I will cover you with diamonds and rubies, and we will love, and go from country to country, starting revolutions," he murmured, ardently, leaning forward so that his sharp Spanish features and wavy black air were outlined in subtle contours against the Ming vase behind him.

"We can leave tonight. First, I will take you to Paris, and buy you a new wardrobe. Then, we will get a consignment of guns in Germany, and fly around the world, and then come to Panama. I have a friend with a fishing fleet there — we will invade Panama. I hate the regime there. I burn with violent hatred of it. With a force of a few dozen men, we can take over. Then, with Panama as a base, we will invade Colombia and Venezuela, and create the Gran Colombia of which Bolívar dreamed!"

"But that's far-fetched!"

"It is *not!*"

"It is. Revolutions have to be planned. You can't start upheavals just like that!"

"I will! You can't stop me. I will bathe the streets in blood, *en sangre.*"

"I can't be a party to that."

"Don't you want to be a heroine? You will be Joan of Arc, and I will be Genghis Khan and we will sweep like a holocaust across the continent," he shouted with passionate intensity. "I have decided. You come with me tonight to Paris — or we part, and you never see me again — I go alone. *Es destino.*"

The steward brought in some hot coffee, and a plate of cookies and sweetmeats. Antonio said, "You torment me! You know I have the ulcers. Take it away. You know I cannot eat *anything.* I am dying. You keel me."

"Couldn't you give me more time to make up my mind?" I asked.

"No! I am sincere! I cannot wait. I go tonight. My country, *mi país*, needs me to set it afire! *Madre de Dias,* have you no heart? You are the calculation like all yanquis! Let your head go your heart must rule. Our love will lead the poor to arise! You will be Evita and I will be Perón. *¡Es maravilloso!* I go now to change the suit."

He left the room abruptly. I heard his car drive away outside. I waited. I waited and waited. An hour passed. The clock struck five. It struck six. At six-thirty I left.

I took a taxi to the airport—where I found there was a plane to Caracas the next morning. I spent the night at a hotel. I left the following day.

THREE MONTHS LATER, in New York City, I went to a party at the United Nations Delegates lounge. "Felipa!" someone exclaimed, as soon as I entered. "It is you! I have searched all New York, all the continent for you!"

It was Antonio, looking handsome but weary. He wore a superbly fitting black suit. "Where did you disappear to that night?" I asked dryly.

"But you were not there when I returned! I combed Maracaibo looking for you. I don't find you. I nearly keel myself. Is *desastre todo.*"

"I waited two and a half hours!"

"But I had to bath and change the suit! A Spanish gentleman does not dress just like that! I am not *mecanico* like yanquis. I adore you! We leave for Paris in three days!" he said, with autocratic insistence.

"I can't go. I have to leave for the Dominican Republic for two concerts"

"You cancel them. I hate Trujillo. That dictator..." he sneered.

"I won't cancel them. I can't disappoint the public. "

"You cannot go where they harbored Jiménez."

"But I thought you wanted to be a dictator, *too*. What happened to your revolution?" I inquired.

"Revolution? I do not revolt, and shed blood of my *pais*. I detest Venezuela. They don't *appreciate* me. I shall live in Paris, and devote myself to the womans. You come with me?"

"No! I have to go to the Dominican Republic!"

"*¡Adios!* You are traitor. I love you for three months, and you are *traidora*. Never I trust womans again. *Madre de Dios,* I keel you. No, I keel myself."

His contradictory, refined yet sensual face, moved with fleeting expressions of rage and idealism, capriciousness, cruelty and wounded arrogant pride. He turned on his heel, and furiously walked out.

I did not see him again, in New York. ✠

CHAPTER 8

Mad Love in London
1953, 1956, 1957, 1958, 1959

THERE'S A SPECIAL SOMETHING about its atmosphere, a stateliness, a tradition. A feeling that Dickens was here, Meredith was here, Wilde, Hogarth and Charles II were here.

Even its slums look better to me than New York's.

In 1956, after my Wigmore Hall debut, I stayed at the Musical Club in Kensington. Pianists, violinists, singers, and writers, lived in this wonderfully original place presided over by Adela Armstrong, a former pupil of Beringer.

They were mostly unsuccessful, and the great high rooms with their large bow windows were generally cold and cluttered, but there was an atmosphere of artistic warmth, fellowship, and integrity that made up for material shortcomings.

They made one feel that people were better than things, art more important than worldly success, the Davidsbündler more worthy than the Philistines.

The neighborhood was discreetly genteel in the style of a century ago. The houses all had four stories, and immense windows peering like sleepy eyes from the lofty white exteriors.

The Club made London seem warm and friendly. Enjoyable concerts were often given in its salon. Throughout the house, one could hear excited conversations about art.

A sharp contrast to the Club was 45 Berkeley Square, once the dwelling of Clive of India, now the residence of Dr. Frank Buchman. A luxurious mansion, dignified, richly furnished with art objects and antiques, it is a fitting place for the gatherings from every nation, race, and creed that meet there to discuss Moral Rearmament, and implement its inspiring spread throughout the world.

Many times I have played there, in the long, luxuriously furnished second-floor drawing room-its walls covered with rose satin brocade, its floor with thick carpets, its antique tables with priceless Ming vases.

The audience would be diversified and international, and it was always a great inspiration to play before selfless men and women who dedicate their lives to something bigger than self, to the cause of setting an example of idealistic international humanism based on standards that exclude no group, but, rather, include the hearts of all men.

This, to me, was London at its very best.

Leona Exton was one of the young people who had given up frivolity and superficial pleasures to try to help others find a happier life, through MRA, in accordance with absolute standards.

An attractive girl who could have been the belle of any ball she chose, she had found that relinquishing frivolity had not narrowed her life, but broadened it, giving her the freedom to love humanity as a whole, and be an inspiration to others when they were bogged down by the confusion that follows egoism and self-indulgences.

Living with her parents, a gentle, kindly, old-world couple, at 117 Eaton Square, a beautiful five-story Regency mansion, that seemed to reflect the stately atmosphere of Jane Austen, she sincerely tried to spread good-will without consciousness of petty barriers of race, country, or religion, expressing a feeling of world-love as she mingled with Asians, Africans, and men and women from every country around the earth.

These genteel, artistic, or internationalistic gatherings made one forget the prevailing atmosphere of narrowness and prejudice when it came to actual economic competition with London working-men and professional people.

As I never remained very long, I never suffered from the stings of British insularity myself, but many West Indian, Asian, and African friends told me at length of their woes and bitterness.

A Hindu girl student told me, "I hate the British. They brought us roads, schools, hospitals, and abolished cruel customs but we did not love them for it, for they made us feel *inferior!*"

Rudolph Dunbar, the symphony conductor from British Guiana, said, "The Nottinghill Gate race riots were but the exterior eruption of a long-standing hostile prejudice. This is the hardest country in the world for a Negro classical musician!"

A West Indian intellectual said, "A colored man can't get a high executive post here, no matter *how* well-qualified. It's hard enough for an Englishman to get in, they make it impossible for a colored man. The intellectual and upper class accept a great artist like Marcus Otumfuo, but competition is so keen among the lower classes that they resent any foreigner who might take ' One thing away from them. The Negro has not enough numerical force to constitute a pressure group."

A West Indian woman declared to me, "But so many of the West Indians who come here are unskilled—they don't know how to do anything well, so they get into trouble."

A West Indian writer's English wife said, "Of course there are no barbarous laws against interracial intermarriage as there are in America. I know scores of West Indians and Africans married to an English girl. There is no legislative discrimination. England is not that backward. But this is a white man's country, and the black man who tries to rise is stopped short at a certain point. They'll be smooth, amiable about it, but they won't let him rise."

A Trinidadian woman said, "Oh, I have a job, but it took me ages to get this flat. Why won't West Indians cooperate, work together more? They're too divided, busy intriguing against each other."

An East African girl student said, "My husband and I have been looking for a flat for so long..."

Love, in London is a variable thing.

The swirling fog, the damp, rain, cold, snow, blizzards, inhibit the expression of feeling, and check the inclinations that might blossom and flower in a more temperate climate.

One English writer, who fell in love with me, said, "I can't do anything else well, I've failed at everything, so I thought I'd become a writer because that's easy."

A few months later, he was saying, "I'm working on my *second* book now. The other was rejected by twenty-four publisher,s and I don't care at *all*. Not at *all*." Then he grew thinner, winced on seeing me, and would say dryly, "I see the Schuyler success story moves on."

Soon, this friendship grew strained, and vanished, overshadowed by the powerful figure of Marcus Otumfuo, the brilliant, though erratic, genius from Nigeria, whose paintings shot forth diabolic and obsessive tentacles, that transfixed, appalled, and hypnotized one with violent colors, demoniac figures, and satanic, spellbinding mystery.

We had met once in New York, in 1949, when he had startled me by saying, "I'm marrying Miss H. next week—I need someone to do my housework, and, besides, there's a girl in England who simply *won't* understand that I cawn't pawsib-bly marry her."

Apparently, this union had never been made conclusive, or had since been canceled for, at the close of 1957, after an eight year silence, I received a passionate letter from him, proposing marriage.

As I was in New York, and he was in London, he urged me to cross the Atlantic at once, so that he could give a reception in my honor introducing me to London society, and marry me at St. George's Church soon after.

I was too confused, startled, to have any idea of what I really wanted to do, but my friends overwhelmed me with insistence that I accept that "marvelous," "romantic," or "thrilling" offer, with all its endless possibilities of pictorial representation and publicity, so that I was swayed. My next tour made London a convenient stop. I left New York by boat for Southampton.

All might have gone forth according to plan, and Otumfuo's desires, had I not met a strange and unusual man on shipboard.

He was tall and ironic-looking, with a witty penetrating expression. His questioning, near-handsome face was sensual, but with a sardonic sharpness, although he saw through everything, himself as well, and would be equally at home behind a typewriter or a mechanic gun.

He was a writer from Israel, and his name was Menahem Ariram.

He caused considerable doubts to grow within me.

He would say, "You can't marry an African — he would be constantly unfaithful without even the grace to be hypocritical about it. He will have learned a Western skill, but that will not have altered his attitude toward women, which is formed in one's early years, and does not change. How many tribal wives do you think he has had and discarded? How many children he has not told you about? Also, he will think of you as a servant, not an equal. Should he treat you fairly well, which I doubt, his relatives will not like you, for they will dislike his marrying outside the tribe, for tribalism rigid, retrograde, backwards, brutal, conservative, and closed. A tribe is something you're born into — you, your parents, your grandparents. It's a club into which there are no entrance admissions. If you're in it, it's hard to get out, if you're out, you *can't* get in. They would object to everything about you-your customs, intellect, profession, nationality, the fact that you've travelled around the world alone. I've known Englishwomen who married African, and, in every case, her friends and family accepted the match better than did his. You can't mix the jet age with the canoe age."

"But my friends think it will be marvelous for me to be married to another artist."

"However, he is in the visual arts which greatly differ from the auditory ones. Only Europe has developed music from a minor art to a major one, so only in Europe will you find your music really loved, and you valued because you play it-in Europe, and, to a limited extent among those of European descent elsewhere. While Africans will attend your concerts once or twice out of curiosity, they won't really understand them or give you the respect to which you, as a Western girl, are accustomed. He probably made this proposal, not through romantic attachment, but because of all the fame he's had in London recently. He needs a wife suitable to introduce to British aristocracy, and thus impress the only people who can afford to buy his paintings. Is he a Muslim?"

"I don't know. What difference does it make?"

"A lot."

"You're prejudiced."

"No. I refer to the Muslim attitude toward women, stemming from the Koranic statement that a woman is only worth half of a man."

"I would not mind that."

"Yes you would. Also, the Islamic world is now in a stage of exceedingly intense nationalism, generated by a long period of subjection to others, and reinforced by historic traditions of military prowess. These feelings are less acute in Persia and Turkey because these countries have been independent for many centuries. Elsewhere in the Muslim world, the newness of independence, or coming independence, serves to bring forth all the long-suppressed dreams of grandeur-usually bereft of tangible foundation. By-products of these dreams of grandeur and ultra-nationalism that hanker back to the glorious bellicose past, will certainly include hatred of the West, contempt for females, and an essential unwillingness to understand classical music, the three things you stand for. But they are extremists, and extremism does not really aid the process of causing to disappear certain historical inequalities between different parts of the globe. The Muslim's martial history has acted in a way to pervert their nationalism of today. They find it difficult to think in terms of equality—they must do so in terms of superiority."

"Why?"

"This is partly a product of lacking self-confidence—extremism often covers up gnawing doubts about oneself. I think the Muslims know deep in their hearts that their heroic postures are largely wishful thinking. Unfortunately, their reaction, possibly subconscious, is too often to shout even louder, boast still more extravagantly, and generally assume attitudes of superiority."

The week passed swiftly in repeated conversations and debates on this ageless and irresolvable question, and though I outwardly spoke with affirmative certainty that this major move I was planning was right, inwardly I grew more and more convinced that I really did not want to do it at all.

The Atlantic was beautiful, now still and glassy, now white and delicately sad, now bristling, violent, doleful, with the black-green murky water heaving and roaring in mysterious iniquity. The storm grew ferocious on the last day, throbbing convulsively as the violet sky was slashed with knife-like lightning.

The ship could not dock. After a day's delay, the passengers were brought to shore on a trawler, whose open deck was lashed by sharp spray. Seagulls swarmed malevolently in the whistling wind, swooping against the doleful grey sky.

The Customs in Southampton was a chaotic bedlam. We were told the weather had been ferocious in London, too, where the worst railway accident in sixty years had just occurred. The journey to London was swift, but somber. The vast hulking shapes that swept past us formless fields, morbid, solemn farmhouses, gloomy, tomblike stations, did not lighten my sense of melancholy and indecision.

Dead, ugly blocks of flats grew more frequent. We were nearing London.

It was terribly cold on arrival. There was a plaintive, lonely atmosphere about the gaunt platform.

Marcus Otumfuo emerged from the somber shadows. Wearing a black overcoat that covered his giant frame like a cloak of lynx-skins, he seemed quite formidable, with his bristly black beard, and his set, proud, and determined face.

His words were quite different from his appearance.

"Where have you been? Where? I have met six trains. I was frantic. For two days I have waited! I have been so worried you cannot imagine it, I have left my work to come here, you cannot know how much work? Not those bags? They are impossible! Your bags are too big for my car! Too big. Take a taxi to Kensington. I'll trot along after a while. Must rush back to the flat now, there's a piece of Mary Magdalen's foot I must redo. I've just seen it, just *seen* it. Oh God, I could paint anything, everything. I could paint that post over there! Why ask me when I can come to your Club? How do I know? Everyone who knows me knows that if I *eventually* arrive, it is a great thing! Feeling terrible tonight, you can't imagine. I have ulcer, heart trouble, liver trouble, kidney trouble," he rushed off vaguely into the shadows.

I went, with the bags, by taxi to the Musical Club.

Mrs. Armstrong received me warmly, as usual, and prepared tea for myself and Otumfuo. We waited. Hours later, he appeared in the doorway of my room, weaving triumphantly.

"I seduce you now," he said.

"No, Marc. Have some tea?"

"No, gin!"

"Should you drink gin if you have heart trouble?"

"Heart trouble? I don't have heart trouble. I come to show you my latest press notices. What do you mean you want to ask me some questions? Why should you ask me questions? Of course I have children. Three! Oh, they are wonderful, oh, they are splendid—all different colors! Each one's mother was different, you see!"

The next night was Otumfuo's reception in my honor. It was a great success, and he was urbane and resplendent in perfectly fitting white tie and tails. Save for his wild, uncombed hair, he was a model of sartorial suaveness. I wore a silver lame gown with a long train.

One would never have guessed the chaos that had preceded the affair.

When we arrived at the house, a reconverted mews, where the party would be held, we had found it thick with dirt. Dust lay in heaps, like an invasion of dead locusts, throughout.

The piano, an aged rosewood Broadwood, had rusted strings. As I practiced, Otumfuo went out to the kitchen, with the Honorable Margaret Fleecewood, a long, raw-boned, yellow-haired woman who looked like a sharpened pencil, to fix sandwiches. He emerged every so often to blow some dust from one bookcase to another, wrinkle his eagle's-beak nose, shake his long panther-like head, and shout, "Cawn't you play a little softer? I cawn't stand that racket!"

When it grew so dark that I could not see the yellowed piano keys, I turned on a lamp that was fixed in the grimy wall.

It stayed on, flickering, for four minutes, then there was an explosive sound, and it snapped off, spluttering.

Marcus stormed in, shouting, "She did it! Philippa did it! I didn't do it! *She* did it!"

He grabbed hold of the lamp, jerked it off the wall. The candle he was holding fell on to the carpet, igniting it. The flames crackled and soared swiftly, catching onto the dry, dusty curtain, sweeping up to the top like a swift scarlet serpent in the jungle.

Miss Fleecewood rushed in with a tureen full of water, threw it on the curtain. We all dashed in and out with bowls and buckets full of water, throwing them on the windows and walls with more enthusiasm than accuracy.

Soon, the fire was extinguished, the room was cleaner than it had been in months, and we, sodden and limp, were able to upbraid, and accuse each other of the fire with abandon.

I left, slammed the door, and walked back to the Club. A letter awaited me there, from a friend in America:

Dear Philippa:

How wonderfully, wonderfully happy you must be! This romantic encounter must be thrilling! Walking under the moonlight talking about Rembrandt and Michelangelo, Chopin and Mendelssohn! What an inspiration it must be to be in the company of a great genius like Otumfuo. I know he just adores you. What an inspiration this must be for your playing. I know he must sit, enraptured, for hours, listening to you. Has he painted you yet? Make the most of the radiant beauty of these golden hours, and all the wonderful ones to come....

I threw it into the gas-grate.

To cover up my hair, which was still wet, I put on a silver lame cap. With a fox-fur cape over the silver lame gown, I took a taxi to my reception.

Otumfuo glared at me when I arrived. Some of the guests were already there.

"Take that hat off, "he said, with a bellicose look."

"I like it."

"It's dreadful. I don't like it."

"I want to wear it."

We stared at each other, in fury. I took it off.

The place looked quite cheerful now. The lights had somehow mysteriously gotten fixed, and there were three lamps in the middle of the floor, spaced strategically so their shadows would hide the dust.

The party went forward with grave, stately dignity.

Afterwards, Jacob Turhinson, the sculptor, invited Otumfuo and myself to lunch with him the next day.

I took an hour to dress the next morning, and waited until one-thirty for Marcus to arrive. At two-thirty, he phoned, "Luncheon? What luncheon? Why I cawn't possibly go out to lunch! I have influenza, ulcers, and spinal meningitis! Besides, I have to prepare for my exhibit that opens tomorrow. Oh, I'll ring up Turhinson and put him off. No, cawn't possibly see you for days."

At nine that evening, Otumfuo strode in my door and muttered, "Come right on downstairs now, don't keep me waiting a minute. We're going to Miss Fleecewood's now. Don't keep me waiting! Exhibit? What exhibit? Oh, it doesn't open until next week. No, I'm not ill. Don't be so nosy. No, I did not have *time* to ring Turhinson. Oh, he must have known I couldn't paw-sib-bly come. Come on!"

We raced down the steps, and jumped in his car. It would not start. He opened the hood, fiddled with the insides, it still would not start. On Addison Road, we took a taxi.

We got out in Hyde Park.

Marcus had remembered the address wrong. We had to walk twelve blocks. We entered an elegant block of flats, rang a second floor bell.

After ten minutes, the door cracked opened and Miss Fleecewood,'s head, covered with curl-papers, peeped out. "Why darlings! I didn't expect you. I thought you were coming tomorrow night—come in—marvelous to see you two love birds."

There were pink satin drapes, couches covered with pink velvet, in the luxurious flat. She was wearing a long pink negligee over leopard-skin toreador pants. The curlers almost hid her yellow hair.

"I want you to see some of Tummy's works, darling!" she shouted. "I've got a whole room full of them!" She led me into another room, switched on the light, crying, "Yes, this whole huge *room* is full of dear Tummy's perfectly marvelous wonderful *paintings!* Look!" The enormous room held a magnificent display. Bright colors leapt to the eye everywhere. Jungle greens, macaw purples, blood reds, tiger yellows, burning oranges, serpent browns. It was splendid, tremendous, breathtaking, primitive, violent, diabolic, and wild. Each picture seemed to reach down from the wall with tentacles and hypnotize you with devilish glee. It was demoniac, horrible, transcendent, petrifying and wondrous. I had never seen such powerful paintings. They stunned me, I could not move. "Darling! Darling! Darling! Aren't they wonderful!" screamed Miss Fleecewood. "Don't they make you just *adore* dearest Tummy? Of course you mustn't marry him, it would *ruin* you. He has three mistresses anyway. But you must *adore* him! Look at the wall behind you!"

I looked, and was overwhelmed. Now I was prepared to admit he was the greatest painter on earth. On the wall was a fourteen-foot square mural a solidly packed, swarming picture, full of hundreds of animals and birds, masks, drums and people. On the front of it, walking down a road, balancing fruit-loads on their heads, were a dozen naked boys, without G-strings "Don't you just love those dear sweet cute itsy bitsy naked *boys?*" cooed Miss Fleecewood.

"Oh, yes," I said vaguely.

"Dear Tummy loves them so. Loves to point to them and say, 'That's life! Life!' I'll quote you the poem I wrote about them:

'Liars, heat and driver ants,
Stink and dust and elephants
And little boys without any pants
That is Africa for me!'"

Back in the drawing room, Marcus was lying asleep on the pink velvet sofa. I crept out.

Two days later, Otumfuo phoned to say, "I cannot see you, God. I have work to do. Years and years of work. I am ill. God. I have ulcers. And spinal meningitis."

That evening, there was a loud thump on the door. Otumfuo walked in, looking haggard.

"What's the matter?"

"Sick? I'm not sick. I'm dying. They've just taken it. It! Oh God, you know what I mean. My painting of Mary Magdalena, taken it to the Gallery, and it's not finished! The foot. The foot's not right! I told them to postpone the showing and they wouldn't. I detest the British, they have no souls. I will not live here anymore. I shall go to Milan. To Paris, to Port Harcourt. God, have to go now. Be back to see you at eight. Of course I'll be on time. I'm *always* on time!"

At nine-thirty, he returned.

"I seduce you now!" he said, dramatically.

"No!"

"You marry me tomorrow," he muttered.

"No. You don't need me."

"I need someone to do my housework very badly."

"You could mention love."

"Nigerian man never says: 'I love you' to his wife."

"No! I'm flying to Istanbul tomorrow. No, I won't cancel it. The boys are expecting me, and I won't let them down."

"Boys? What boys?" he asked, with a blazing, terrible look.

"Twelve hundred boys of Robert College."

"What! No! Twelve hundred boys. I won't permit it! It's unthinkable. I kill you. No! No!"

This argument, and the resulting denunciations and anger, were sufficient to draw our friendship to a close.

But growing more and more interested in Africa, I developed a mystique about it.

I explained this to Nicholas Princeton, a West Indian friend living in London, "I apologized and rationalized over Africa's bloody history, forgot that the slave trade in Africa continued long after it had been abolished in the West, smoothed over in my mind the reality that the slaves shipped to the New World had been sold by African and Arab chieftains and traders to the white slavers who otherwise could not have gotten them in any great quantity."

"But has the slave trade ended in Africa?" he said, as we drank tea in his tepidly under-heated London flat.

"Has it? Once I knew a French woman Senator, Madame Jane Vialle, herself of mixed French-African ancestry, who told me, before her death in a plane crash, that she planned to bring up in the United Nations the fact that Arab slave traders were still stealing girls in Africa and selling them to harems and brothels in the Arab world, prices for girls rising to as much as $1,500 in Saudi Arabia."

"What is your definition of slavery? Is it broad or limited?" he asked.

"I would consider myself a slave if I lived in a society where I had to follow a fixed pattern of rules laid down a hundred or hundreds of years before, and which I as an individual could not alter."

"That is true," he said, putting another shilling in the gas meter to attempt to prolong the feeble warmth.

"That is one reason independence of the nation does not necessarily bring true liberty of independent action for the individuals that make up that nation. It may not comfort you to have the same 'heritage' as your neighbor if you are both starving—along-ingrained pattern of tribalism resents independence of the individual. And independence of the individual, the right to do as I choose, so long as I do not injure another, it is the only type of liberty that really counts," I said.

"Perhaps you are right. What do you think of Nkrumah, in Ghana?"

"Few realize he did a daring thing in marrying an Egyptian girl who was not only not of his tribe, but also of different country, religion, race, color, background and culture from himself. Few African leaders are that brave. European royalty has usually married royalty of other countries. African royalty, almost without exception, has not."

"I gather you are a universalist and against all types of prejudice."

"It is class culture, civilization and philosophy that matter. It is man's ideas that make the man."

Now I shall write about an African Muslim I met in London, Mustapha Jannat Al-Kamar. At first, full of my glowing convictions that the soil of Africa my mother, I was enthusiastic about him, not realizing that like many Africans, he was dual, with a dualism that could perhaps only fully be explained by Dostoyevsky.

Mustapha wore Western suits, and said he was Westernized. Yet, surprisingly, he did not want to introduce me to any of his friends. This was because, in his country, women are locked up.

His own sister never left the house unless her husband or brother-in-law escorted her. She would have been ruined had her face been seen. If her husband brought friends home, she had to wait in a back room until they left. She could not greet them. If her husband came from a trip, he went to see his friends first, his wife last.

One day, Mustapha took me to see a friend of his in the hospital. I thought I was going in too. When we reached the door, I was told to stand outside and wait. I, being female, would have polluted the room's air had I entered.

Mustapha's conversation, on the rare occasions that he made any, was mostly; "America is dreadful," mixed with, "God, I hate the British!"

Sometimes, I said, "But aren't you grateful to the British at all?"

"Why should I be?"

"They stamped out the slave trade in your country, built schools, hospitals, gave it accurate boundaries, intelligent administration."

"You British! I hate you British!"

"But I'm not British!"

His deep dark eyes flashed. He continued to harangue me. "Everything in the outside world is inferior to everything in my country," he snarled.

He constantly lambasted America. "How can you defend America? America is dreadful, horrible!"

"Have you been there?"

"No! I do not have to be there. I know that it is horrible!"

"How? Prejudice? But you're so full of prejudices yourself. You out-Faubus Faubus. And, anyhow, you've never had any contact with Americans."

"The American soldiers landed in Lebanon! They landed in Lebanon!" he yelled.

"But they didn't do anything when they got there, didn't kill people or take over the country. Some Lebanese told me they were glad the Americans came, that their coming prevented a massacre."

"How *can* you defend America?"

"But look what happened in Iraq."

"It was wonderful in Iraq! It was splendid in Iraq! You say they killed the King? But he killed hundreds! Hundreds!"

"If you have proof of this, tell me. Maybe I could make it into an article, so the American public would see the other side"

He always clammed up tightly, with a vague and distant look, at the mention of an article.

Our friendship did not last long.

After meeting others like him, I grew to appreciate the West much more.

Yet, Africa itself is a great teacher, for everything is there, every color, every contrast, every cruelty, nuance, surprise.

Once, Whitman said, "Do I contradict myself? Very well, then I contradict myself. I am large! I contain multitudes!"

Africa is like that. ⊞

CHAPTER 9

A Curious Race

Holland, Germany
1953, 1955, 1956, 1958, 1959

MY MOST VIVID IMAGES of the Netherlands are associated with Ernst Krauss. There was a gentle beauty about his spirit, a true integrity of soul I had never before seen in an impresario. He was a great man. And he showed me how an impresario could also be a poet, and a great gentleman.

He was always beaming, jovial, gay, and a true, generous, faithful friend.

He was tall, with a noble, kindly face, and distinguished white beard.

He had been Pavlova's manager, and was in his late sixties when l first knew him. He has been one of the greatest inspirations in my life. His spirit still lives within me, I still think of him in the present. For me he will never die.

His wife was kindly and inspiring, too.

They lived in a tall narrow house in J. W. Brouwersplein, just behind the Concertgebouw in Amsterdam, Holland.

They sent artists on tours throughout Northern Europe.

They were always honest, always sincere, always undeviating in their integrity.

They proved that you can be successful without tricks, sneaky dealings or lies.

They proved that sincerity can win in the long run.

In 1953, they presented me at Concertgebouw. Afterwards, Mr. Krauss took me up to Roermond, Holland, a small Dutch town whose spirit belies the false impression so many have of the Dutch as a ponderous, heavy, dour people. My recital took place on the anniversary of the town's founding. The mayor and chief politicians were there. Everyone made speeches after my performance, and then we had a gay banquet. Everyone was laughing, jubilant, merry-making, cheering, drinking toasts, and telling jovial stories.

I also loved playing in Zaandam, a small town where some old men still wore sabots, and nothing seemed to have changed for a hundred years.

The recital was held in an old Dutch reform church, whose floor was covered with spotless white sand. Each seat had a tiny charcoal stove beneath it. The entire audience rose and bowed to me after each piece.

I gave many concerts in Holland in the following years, in Amsterdam, Rotterdam, the Hague, and other cities, and over radio and television.

It was wonderful to see Mr. Krauss after each performance, always jovial, always kind, always encouraging.

Then Mr. Krauss died, in June 1958. I was heartbroken.

When I returned to Holland in March 1959, Lineke Snijders van Eyk and John de Crane had taken over Mr. Krauss' business.

Lineke was a glowing blonde, with beautiful blue-grey eyes. John, handsome and dark, had formerly been an actor in the Swedish films. They made a happy, delightful pair, both young and full of idealism and hope. John said, "I think it's just wonderful being an impresario. It's so exciting, such fun. Something new happens every minute! If only I could partly equal Mr. Krauss, I would be so happy. I want so badly to do everything as he would have done."

John de Crane drove me, in his bright red car, to the modern buildings of NKRV radio, Hilversum, where Hugo de Groot was waiting for me to begin the orchestral rehearsal.

He had banged his knee against a table that morning, and was limping. When he saw that I had the flu, he said, cheerily, "Hallo! Seems we're both in a fix. But since I have not to dance, and you have not to sing, we can make good music together!" The rehearsal went wonderfully.

What made me happiest was when John came back after the performance that evening, and said, "It was splendid. How I wish Mr. Krauss could have been here to hear you. He would have been so proud of you."

And that gave me more pleasure than anything else he might have said, for somehow, I had felt Mr. Krauss' spirit was there.

I NEVER FELT THE KINSHIP FOR GERMANY that I did for Holland. I flew to Hamburg first in October 1953.

When my SAS plane was grounded with engine trouble that nearly caused a crash, I was forced to spend a night in the rain-swept city.

I stayed at the Vier Jahrezeiten Hotel, where I had an elegant room with exquisite etchings on the grey walls, and stately furniture with petit point inlay.

I met an American journalist there, and we explored the cold wet city together. The misty rain had a sweet smell, as though of death. The moist air clung to our nostrils, the wet streets were soaked, the gutters drenched with splashing floods.

We went into a nightclub, where the atmosphere was stale, but dry and warm. The harsh music of American jazz made the air seem electric and exciting. Morton Karensky began to tell me about the revolution he had covered in Latin America.

"The disparateness of the intrinsic elements in so many Latin American countries makes the quasi-democracy they attempt to practice farcical in many instances, turbulent in others. Venezuela once had fifty-two revolutions in seventy years, Peru had forty in fifty years, Bolivia over fifty governmental changes in little more than a century. Movements of revolt are most likely to succeed when four factors are cohesively present. First, discontent riddling society throughout owing to important dissatisfactions. Second, a tightly-knit group of revolutionists ready to fight for their aims. And third, propagandists to stimulate and render articulate the grievances and resentments, while proposing that a new order will solve these problems: the lack of strength in the existing government to smash the revolt at its commencement-" he said, his grey eyes looking sharply at me through his black-rimmed spectacles.

He told me a queer tale about a revolution in which he had participated in Colombia. Wanting to show that he could do something besides pound a typewriter, he had actually lived with the rebels, carried messages for them, helped to dynamite some buildings and shoot a few unimportant people.

He hoped to conquer the twentieth century malaise of confusion and lack of belief by plunging into action, no matter how destructive. He was sent into Bogotá to kill a certain man he had never seen, in such a way as to cast the blame on the political party in power. His nerve did not fail him, and, after much bribery, trickery and elaborate plots, he achieved his goal. He had lost touch with the rebel forces during the last few days of fulfilling his plan.

After the death, he was shocked to find that it had not been desirable or necessary. Two days beforehand, the head of the ruling political party had decided to pacify the leader of the rebel forces by offering him a job in the government, which he had accepted, and then disbanded his revolutionary activities.

The murder was now an unwanted faux pas, and Morton Karensky had to leave the country rapidly via fishing boat to Panama, where he took a tramp steamer to Haiti.

There, he had gone into the interior, and lived for a while in the hut of a voodoo priest, hoping to lose his doubts in the simplicity of nature, and his lack of faith in the diabolical worship of the serpent god. Then he discovered that nature was not simple, but cruel and unpredictable. The country people were not innocent, but calculating, tricky and cunning, and that mysteries of voodoo worship were no better than the witch cults of renaissance Europe, and far less convincing, for modern knowledge enabled one to see through them.

He left the countryside for Port-au-Prince, where he found insincere superficiality, and imitation of Paris. Everyone he met as intently eager to plot revolution, but no one had a clear plan of what to do with the country when all the government had been exiled or annihilated.

Now, after being fleeced, or tricked, in British Guiana, Venezuela, Cuba and Chile, he had come to Europe to complete a book about the evils he had seen.

TWO YEARS LATER, when I returned to Germany, en route from Iceland to Egypt, I remembered this evening. Hamburg seemed empty now. In Frankfort, I gave a Brahms concert over the waves of the futuristic Hessischer Rundfunk, one of the most beautiful radio stations I have ever seen. It was almost too remote in its modernism for me to feel at ease. In Munich, I played Beethoven over the Bayerischer Rundfunk, which was smaller, older, more crowded.

On the night train back to Amsterdam, I met a violinist whose left hand had been injured during the war, and as a result, went from being a concert artist to playing in nightclubs. He asked me for a loan of 500 marks, which I declined to extend.

Each year, from 1953 onwards, when I visited Holland, the people looked better dressed, and more prosperous. The girls were pretty in a healthy way that made the English girls look wan and rachitic. In August of 1959, Amsterdam was sultry, quite different from the cold drizzle of Belgium to the south.

Lineke and her husband, Theodore Snijders, took me to see a curious bicycle race, in an immense stadium built when the Olympic Games were held in Amsterdam several decades ago.

It was a third full. The race had just begun, but no one seemed to be taking the least interest in it though this was a World's Championship. In the sloping arena, the racers were competing, two by two, but the queer thing was that they were going as slowly as possible.

It was amazing.

Each two racers would circle the arena three times.

The first was crucial, for in it, each racer must try to go slower than and keep behind the other.

This could be long and drawn out.

Sometimes the cyclists would remain motionless, like statues, for ages.

Theo whispered to me, "This is important. Do you know two racers remained motionless once, on the same spot, for one hour and fifty-two minutes?"

"That must have been thrilling for the audience," I replied.

After the slow race, there would be a very swift fast race, and then they would go around the arena once more, slowing down. Three hours passed.

Now a new variation occurred. Motorcycles appeared. All the winners of the bicycle competition appeared in the arena on their metal steeds. They were really letting themselves go now. Motorcycles and bicycles pressed forth in confused, yet cunning array. The motive was for each bicyclist to race just exactly behind a motorcycle, so that the wind from behind the motorcycle would carry him along in a kind of suction, so that he almost flew along, going twice as fast as he could otherwise. Yet it would be a disaster if he did not race just exactly behind the motorcycle. A spare motorcycle and cyclist stood breathlessly poised on the grass at the sidelines, just in case.

Now they dashed round and round and round. It seemed quite without beginning or end, and I could not keep track of anything. It was quite impossible to tell who was ahead of whom. "Do you know who's first?" Theo asked me excitedly. "It's the man in the brown jacket, isn't it?" I replied, with bated breath.

"Oh, no!" Theo replied, "he's last! It's the man who looks last who's first!" Somehow, this confused me. They kept on going round and round. After two hours, Lineke and I tripped away, leaving Theo to stay to the bitter end.

When I visited them again at noon the next day, I asked Theo eagerly, "Who won?" He did not quite know.

Now Theo and Lineke took me on a boat trip through the shimmering canals of Amsterdam. It was really beautiful. Then we saw the Rijks Museum. What an artistic feast it was! And the last painting we saw was Rembrandt's splendid, "Night Watchman."

Then we had dinner at an Indonesian restaurant, where the food was exotic and highly-spiced, and saw a wonderful collection of Walt Disney films in a modernistic theatre. Then we returned to the Snijder flat in Van Breestraat.

Theo, who at twenty-seven was an earnest, intelligent young man, plied me with questions about the outside world. They often thought of emigrating, it seemed-what country in the world, since I voyaged to so many, would I most recommend to them? Amazed, I replied, "But you're in one of the world's best countries already, how could you think of wanting to leave? You can't imagine how inferior most places are to Holland! You say you'd like to see the world, too? There are plenty of places it's nice to see and hell to live in!"

"What would you think of our going to Argentina?"

"I know some Swiss who are in business there—but it's been awfully difficult for them—the peso is constantly being devalued, it's worth one-half to one-third as much now as when I first went there."

"Well, maybe some other country in Latin America?" Theo suggested.

"There's terrific inflation in Chile, too. Brazil is prosperous in some regions, but communications are so poor that the riches of one area are not distributed around the country."

Lineke said, "But I'd like some warmth. It rains so much here."

"Rio has such a humid warmth disease rates are high. You won't find anything approaching the cleanliness you are used to in Holland. The food has not the quality you are used to here."

Then Theo asked, "What about Japan?"

"It's very cold there in winter. And the overcrowding is terrific. Of course, through legalized abortion, the birth rate has been reduced. Hong Kong is a wonderful city in the visual aspect, but the refugee problem is increasing and apparently insoluble, and Red China could grab Hong Kong at any moment. The Near East has the problems of backwardness and perpetual instability."

"But how about Africa? After all, it's the only underpopulated continent, and it has splendid, unexhausted natural resources," said Theo.

'The marvelous thing about Africa is that it is still so greatly as God made it. But tremendous disruptions are taking place, and will increase. The balance of power is like a basketball in a wild game there."

"I was offered a post in Surinam," recalled Theo.

"The people are nice there, but there are armies of insects: red ants, huge cockroaches."

"What are they?" asked Lineke.

"You don't know what a cockroach is?" I asked, startled.

"No?"

"But you *must* know what a cockroach is!

Theo said, "You must mean *kakkerlak*. I've seen the word in the dictionary. What does it look like?"

"You mean neither of you has seen one?" I described it.

"We have plenty of them in New York!"

"Then I guess we'd better not emigrate to America," Lineke said timidly, smoothing the folds of her yellow cotton dress, and looking as though I had said something very astounding. "Maybe we had better stay here. There was a chance for one of us to go over a few years ago, but we didn't want to be separated. We married for love, you know, and we're even more in love than three years ago."

"Do you think Europeans feel about love differently from Americans?" I asked.

"Each one is different, but in general, the European man thinks of his bride as a woman completely devoted to his wellbeing. This is no problem for her, since she loves him so much, and the things he expects from her are exactly the things he would love most of all to do. Don't marry anyone unless you think you will never want anybody else than the one you're in love with. You must have a strong love, for in a good marriage each partner is able to place himself completely in the mind of the other, so you stop looking at things only from your own point of view and with your own eyes, but you also see everything as your partner sees them. And then you have a real everlasting link that will never tear, since you don't simply understand the other, but sort of *are* the other. And you could not turn away from part of yourself! If you love very deeply, this mind-link should start forming even during the time of thrilling infatuation, and grow slowly during the years. That is real love."

As she spoke, I watched her dark gold hair framed resplendently in the flickering light, and the gently sweet look of understanding affection she exchanged with Theo, and I felt that here in Holland, for the first time in all the lands I had visited, someone had been able to explain love to me.

In the spring of 1960, they wrote me that they had bought a house in Amsterdam, and were having a baby! ⊞

CHAPTER 10

I Play for Queen Elisabeth
Belgium: 1953, 1956, 1958, 1959

T O ME, BRUSSELS IS THE MOST CAPTIVATING city in Northern Europe. The Belgians excel in creating the effect of visual style and loveliness, and this talent pervades everything they do, whether it is the architecture of a street, the design and effect of a government brochure on the Congo, or the harmonious planning of the Tervuren Museum.

The Belgians have a genius in their instinct for beauty. Brussels' combination of medieval, Renaissance and modern buildings fascinates the romantic.

In 1953, I made my Brussels debut at the Palais de BeauxArts. The concert was presented by Paul Fabo, and his assistant, Gustave Rougon. I met André Gascht for the first time, and from then on, whenever I performed in Holland, Paul and André would drive over from Belgium to hear me.

André was born in Arles, Belgium, on June 1, 1921. He is one of Belgium's most noted poets. A government official ever since the war's end, he is the son of an outstanding General, a leader in intellectual and artistic circles, and an amateur art collector.

Of all the young men I have ever met, I think he is the nicest because his character is sincere, honest, yet poetic. He has a puckish, yet mystic, good humor, and is wittily amusing, without ever being cruel. In six years I have never known him to tell a lie, and he is always exactly the same.

There is little of Brussels, or, indeed, Belgium, that André has not shown me, but my most treasured recollection is of seeing the Forêt de Soignes with him.

This marvelous forest is within the city limits, but one feels within another world as soon as one crosses its magical threshold. The trees branch upwards like a cloistered cathedral, the ground is moss-covered and all is peaceful and silent.

No signs of human habitation poison the spiritual atmosphere of the woods. Here, one can feel truly alone with God.

Another memory that I love to recall, is the Tervuren Museum. It combines a natural history section on Congo fauna and flora with a wondrous display of Congo carving, craft and sculpture. Whether it is the Belgian genius for artistic selection and planning, or whether the Congo simply produces the greatest art in Negro Africa, I do not know, but the effect is overwhelming.

André and I walked from exhibit to exhibit, viewing an appallingly ferocious circumcision mask, now the ghastly costume of a leopard-cult murder, to a queer antelope-horn trumpet, now an enormous drum as large as a lion.

We made jokes or stared in awe at each one, until finally we were too tired to see any more. Then we left the Museum, and went through a beautiful deserted garden behind it to a small restaurant. But there was no one at all there but two cats. The cats sat on our laps and kept us company while we quoted poetry to them.

In September 1958, André invited me to come to Brussels to see the world's fair. It was a heavenly experience, like a dream or a fairy-tale.

André met me at the railroad station, along with Paul Fabo, Roger and Katrina Nonkel. We went to a café to eat and talk.

Paul Fabo was a rare, delightful personality. He was born in Dahomey, West Africa, educated in France, and for some years was an actor before becoming a journalist. He was black as the night on the Congo River, with broad, benevolent features and a jovial disposition, he was always happy, always laughing, always gay, and beamed with joyful good will and bonhomie. Never have I seen such enchanting good humor in any man.

Roger Nonkel was a typically solid, dependable Flemish civil servant, a fine example of the best type of Belgian administrator. He had brown hair and eyes, and a sober reliable face. One feels one could always trust him. He had lived with his Polish wife Katrina, for many years in Lusambo, Kasai, in the Belgian Congo. Katrina was quite pretty, with aristocratic features and golden hair. She was shivering in her camel's hair overcoat. "It's cold!

"I can't get used to it after Lusambo, where the temperature is almost always in the eighties.

"When do you come to Elizabethville? January? I'll be back in the Congo then. I'll try to attend your concert. You'll be playing at that splendid modern theatre that was built on the site of the former airfield—it's the best in Central Africa. The stage is reversible. The University in E'ville is very nice, you know, it's growing quite rapidly—it's completely integrated—one out of every six students is African."

She drank some tea, and then noticing that I was admiring her gold bracelet with charms dangling from it, she added, "This bracelet? I got it before my marriage, when I was living in Johannesburg."

Then, Roger Nonkel told me about Kasai province, which touches Kivu, Katanga, Leopoldville, Équateur and Province Orient, and showed me photographs of the great troupes of 120 dancers and musicians from the Congo and Ruanda-Urundi that had come to perform at the Exposition. He added, "Ruanda-Urundi's music differs from Central African Bantu music. Ruanda-Urundi's Tutsi-music has a five-tone scale similar to Uganda's. Antelope-horns, usually with side-mouthpieces, are used throughout the Congo, as are zithers, lutes, lyres, curved harps, and drums. Xylophones exist in Leopoldville Province's Gingu Territory. The Konda tribe, near Lake Leopold II, developed polyphony in vocal music."

"How many tribes does the Congo have?" I asked.

"No one can say exactly, for ethnographs differ on the definition of 'tribe'—one calls 'tribe' what another calls 'clan.' Each tribe is divided in many small subdivisions, and every ethnic into several tribes. Some writers call each small subdivision a tribe, others only acknowledge the great ethnic tribes."

"It's all rather confusing, isn't it?"

"Now, the Mongo ethnic is supposed to contain the following main tribes: Kundu, Batetela, Bankutshu, and Bahamba—but the trouble starts when one tries to count the smaller branches. The Batetela have three main branches: the Watambulu, the Ngandu and the Djovu. If we call them 'tribes,' we must eliminate the name of 'Batetela' among the Mongo tribes, and replace it with three other names: Watambulu, Ngandu, and Djovu."

"I see the question is far from easy!" I said, laughing.

"That's right. No one can answer it. But as a rough guess, I would say between two and three hundred tribes."

Soon, we all departed.

André Gascht went home to his apartment in Woluve St. Lambert.

Paul Fabo went back to the Rue de Ruysbroek, to the office of *Africa and the World*, the weekly newspaper he had been editing since 1949.

Roger, Katrina, and I left for Ghent. When we arrived, over an hour later, I noted that the street signs were all in Flemish. We were now in the heart of Flanders.

Even in the rest of Belgium, Flemish is used as well as French on all signs, posters and public advertisements.

Many people still speak the Walloon tongue (somewhat similar to Provençal), and a German dialect spoken in the Grand Duchy of Luxembourg and one Belgian province.

Roger and Katrina drove me to Einde Were 43, to the home of his aunt.

After dinner, Roger took out his scrapbook and showed me a photograph of a Mangbetu woman with an elongated head.

"I read that original dwellers, indigenous like our American Indians, were the Batwa or Batshwa," I said.

"Yes. The four main groups of Congolese: Batwa, Sudanee, Bantu and Hamites, are as far apart from each other as the Latin, Germanic and Slav peoples are in Europe."

"The Batwa are the pygmies, aren't they?"

"Oh, yes. They lived in Central Africa long before the invasion of the three other groups. The last pure ones are said to measure only 120 centimeters. I've never seen one, but I met many of mixed race measure about 140 centimeters, or four and one half feet."

"Are they all over the Congo?"

"In a way. They are living in the deep forest, where they are hunters and good ones. They have no knowledge of agriculture, and exchange meat for vegetables with the other peoples. Then there are the Bantu, who sometimes are divided into Bantu and Semi-Bantu. They are about 90 percent of the Congo population. 'BANTU' means 'the men,' and it comes from the root 'NTU' meaning 'man.' 'BA' is the prefix of the plural. That is why we don't write 'batetelas,' only 'Batetela' for it is already plural."

"One man from that tribe is called 'Mutetela,' for 'MU' is the prefix of the singular. For instance, the plural of 'Muntu,' 'man,' is 'Bantu' the plural of 'Muindu.' 'Black' is 'Baindu,' the plural of 'Mudjali' is 'Badjali' that of "Muluki,' 'rower,' is ' Baluki' that of 'Mukasi,' 'strong' is 'Bakasi.' The last of the four great groups are the Hamites, or Nilotic types. You would better know them by the name of Watusi, or 'Watutsi.' They are very slim, tall, averaging two meters, or six feet seven, with long legs. The few that live in the Congo are mostly along the lakes of the volcanic northeastern part. The majority of the Watutsi live in Ruanda."

"How many languages are there in the Congo?" I asked.

"Congo dialects are imperfect with limited vocabulary. There are several hundred dialects, more than tribes, because in some tribes they may speak several dialects derived from the same original but still different. The Congo dialects should be divided in two groups, the original local dialects and the vehicular dialects."

"Is an original dialect one that has received little or no external influence?" I inquired, taking the large black scrapbook, and leafing through the pages. Some of the photographs were extraordinary.

"Naturally, the most important dialects are 'Lomongo,' of the Mongo people, 'Tshiluba' of the Baluba people, and 'Kicongo' of the Bakongo people."

Katrina, who was drinking some coffee, interjected, "The vehicular dialects are simplified tongues using a mixture of words from different original languages for the purpose of communication between tribes. You might call them 'pidgins.' Lingala, which we both speak and which is the official language of the Army and of the Western Congo, has some European influence, for instance, in words like *mesa* from Portuguese word for 'table,' *bolangiti* from the English word 'blanket,' and *pasopo* from the Flemish 'pas op' which means 'look out.' Lingala is the most used dialect on the radio."

Roger added, "There's also Kiswahili, the official language of East Africa, which shows a strong Arab influence, and Kituba, which is a mixture of Tshiluba and Lingala. The Sango, on the other hand, which is a commercial language of the Ubangi river people, is derived from the Sudanese tongue, Ngandi, and has practically no European influence. Of course, the more prosperous urban people speak French."

I drank some milk, and Roger stirred cream in his coffee, saying, "If this were the Congo, I would be putting avocado in my coffee. I would mash the avocado until it has the consistency of heavy cream."

Early the next morning, we visited a wonderful medieval church. As we gazed at the paintings and stained glass windows, I asked Roger, "I know there are three and one half million Catholics in the Congo, and nearly a million Protestants, but I would like to know about the Pagan animists. Do they have a God that is like Jesus, a God of Love and Compassion?"

"No. God, to them, is just Power. Not fundamentally bad but so powerful that it is better to conciliate Him. He is invoked in some prayers and in the oath, but, except for that, there are no ceremonials. The latter are performed only for the benefit of 'spirits' or to conciliate dead ancestors."

"Then religion is not active to these animists in our meaning of 'doing a fraternal or human act for reasons of religious creed'?" I asked, pausing to look at a splendid white marble bas-relief over a seventeenth century tomb.

"No. And, with regards to the animist pagan religions, discussion still rages as to whether you can call them religions in the exact Western sense of a doctrine and dogma in full coordination, having full assent of all. What they have, are beliefs and rites with which they strive to conciliate the supernatural forces and form a defense against them. Though they may have one great God called 'Zambi' in Lingala, 'Mangu' in Kiswahili, 'Maweji' in Tshiluba and so forth, there are hosts of spirits, and each little community may have a different inspiration in worship."

When we left the church, we walked for a long time through the tranquil streets. We often passed houses with "1667," "1608," "1690," etc., written over the doors, to show the year the house was built. Our discussion of the Congo tribes finally got around to female circumcision.

I asked Roger, "Is it true that female circumcision is still practiced by the Congo tribes that are of Sudanese origin?"

"Yes. It seems difficult to extirpate the custom, even among Christian families. It's age old with them. The tribes do not seem to have any explanation for it, merely saying that 'it has always been done that way.' Possibly, the custom began to diminish woman's pleasure during sexual relations so she would stay faithful to her husband, even if he were an old man, and not look for a lover. For you must remember that before the Europeans reached there, power was in the hands of clan heads, and most of the women, by polygamous unions, were concentrated in the hands of a few. Even in 1936, I met a chief who still had 300 wives."

"I read that some old chiefs collected women the way others collected stamps, building up their collection piece by piece during a lifetime, or just taking over a whole share by inheritance," I said.

"Yes. And, naturally, young bachelors would be pursuing the young wives. Of course, chastisement for adultery was usually cruel, but I suppose they felt that even painful punishment was not frightening enough, if once they knew what love was like."

He went on.

"So, I guess, they imposed excision so that, not knowing pleasure, the women would feel no temptation to commit adultery. But there is the danger, sometimes, of hemorrhage from bleeding, and witch doctors not being able to control it. Why do the women submit? I suppose the women have no personality and submit without discussion to whatever the men impose," he added.

"A conversation on that subject would either bring no answer, or the statement, 'Our ancestors have always done it that way.' The men say they do not see why they should stop it for, 'what was good for the ancestors is good for them.' They would not dare to criticize the ancestors because the clan is a unit to which belong the dead, the living and the as yet unborn."

"Have you ever seen a female circumcision ceremony?" I asked. "Is it rare for them to allow a European to attend?"

"Very rare. However, about ten years ago, I succeeded in winning the confidence of some of the Bwaka enough so that I was permitted to witness the secret ceremony. It took place in a small glade in the midst of the deep forest. The young girls who were to be treated, were kept apart, dressed as men, for they were considered as being asexuated until they were excised. In the glade were the witch doctor and his assistants. Then a young girl came up, accompanied by her parents or some intimate friends."

"How old was she?" I asked.

"About fifteen. She wore a man's shirt and some breeches. Then she undressed, was seated, nude, on the knees of a man who was himself seated on a primitive chair. Her back was to him, and, her legs dangled over his. Members of her family kept her legs open, while the man on whose legs she sat took her round the breasts with one arm and pulled her slightly backwards. The other hand was kept free. The witch doctor now took a knife with a short blade that slightly had the shape of a crescent. With his other hand he threw some ngula powder on the spot he intended to work on."

"What is ngula powder?"

"Dark red, it is said to have astringent power that helps to bring forth coagulation of the blood. It is made by scraping the wood of a tree named 'ngula,' which is also one of the best woods used for cabinet making."

"Does the operation take a long time?" I asked.

"Well, the action was quick. The witch doctor took the vagina lip in one hand, and cut it off in a saw-like movement, then repeated the gesture with the second lip"

"Does the girl cry very much?"

"The assistant on whose knees the girl was sitting put his free hand over her mouth to stifle the cry. Afterwards, the wound was sprinkled again with ngula powder, and another I could not identify. The girl was released, and walked away with a trail of blood flowing down. She was supposed to do a few dance steps to indicate her stoicism. Then she retired to the guardianship of her family."

It had begun to rain heavily. We went to a nearby Brasserie. The place was so crowded that the food took a long time to come so I asked more questions.

"Are women still heavily tattooed among the Bantu tribes? I have seen some photographs where it was most elaborate."

"Twenty years ago, erotic tattooing was still practiced by the Baluba and Batetela women, on their chests, back and especially abdomens. The wrinkles impressed during cicatrization were supposed to be rather exciting. But now this custom has been stamped out, particularly by the efforts of the missionaries. Yet it would be hard to find a middle-aged woman who does not bear these marks," he said.

"The Baluba are Bantu people, aren't they? Do they also practice female circumcision?"

"No. The Bantu don't. Neither do the pygmies. Now the Baluba have a custom that is quite the opposite—an artificial selling of that region with herbs, prickling or injection," Roger added.

"I've heard there is a very unusual religion called Kiban-guisme."

"Yes, it is a mixture of Protestantism and paganism, but it is not officially recognized. Its creator was a certain Simon Kibangu, who died as a Catholic, so you see it is quite unclear. Already there are dissidents, and side-growths, such as Ngounzisme."

"Now, to return to those who practice pure animism, the dead members of the clan play a big role in the life of those who are rather afraid to do something the dead do not approve of. If a person is thought to have the 'evil eye,' and is denounced by a sorcerer, he must prove his innocence by a poison-proof; that he must drink a poisonous concoction in the presence of witnesses, and if it doesn't affect him, he is considered innocent. You asked me about illegitimate children? Well, to my knowledge, the Africans welcome children, and long for them, legitimate or otherwise. If the child is illegitimate, it will belong to the mother's clan, whereas, if legitimate, it belongs to the father's clan," Roger said.

The next morning, Roger and Katrina, and their two children, drove back with me to Brussels. It took nearly two hours, owing to the heavy early morning traffic.

En route, I said to Roger, "I was just fascinated listening to you! You should write a book!"

"Well, as a matter of fact I am!" he said, laughing, "but it's about the race problem in America!"

"I am sure it will be a success. You have a remarkable memory! From what I read about the Congo, the Belgians have made it a very efficient state. I'm looking forward to my visit!"

"Good. We have a little present for you here, to watch over you until you arrive." He took an ivory bracelet-amulet from his inner pocket. "You notice that each segment is a carved oval that has a face at each end, it's supposed to protect and make you beware of two-faced people!" he laughed as he presented it.

Katrina and Roger embraced me when we arrived at my hotel in Brussels. I was sorry to see them drive away.

In two hours, André came to my hotel to take me to the Fair.

He was wearing a grey tweed suit and grey raincoat which made his hair seem more blond than ever. We took a tram. It was terribly crowded. 1 grew dizzy, so André led me off into the fresh air. We sat on the steps of a house that had "1692" written over the door. We started to talk, and I asked him about his poetry, "André, I read your books, *La Saison Triste,* and *Le Poids du Monde,* and 1 thought they were splendid. What are you writing now? Won't you quote some of it for me? Your poetry's wonderful."

"Oh, that is too many eulogies for a simple person."

"You're too modest, André. Please."

"Well, since you insist, I will quote you some of my 'Psalms of the Night'."

> I dare not trust you, God of evil,
> Who strangles joys and teaches pleasures,
> In grim refuge of bitter measures,
> That thirst for sacrifice for the devil.
>
> You have fed youth's heart on dust and cinders,
> Sadness mingled with corruption,
> And shown it death and strange disruption,
> To the beasts of torment it surrenders.
>
> I dare not trust you, God of error,
> You have refused to me all light and day,
> Till my empty soul has no place to stay,
> Till it faints with vertigo and terror.
>
> You torture me with voluptuous flame,
> Of heaven you speak to me with laughter,
> And shadows then torment me after
> My hope is ravished since you came.

But my favorite poem by André, is this excerpt from a poem written in honor of the forest, a year later:

> In the dawn of one's fortieth year,
> When the blood becomes less alive
> One is ready to follow, more certainly,
> The chance that presents itself.
> Here it surges, at the edge of the forest
> Where you wander—
> The ardent, fiery young girl

Who speaks hidden words to you.
She will show you the pure waters
Whose promise shines in you.
And the torrid season that lasts
When all forests grow cold.
She is the most living part of you—
And your only reality.
Offer yourself to her
And you will live in joy.

We took a taxi to the Fair, then rode through the magnificent exposition on a little train. The giant Atomium towered over everything. Then we walked back in the other direction to visit the Russian and American pavilions, neither of which appealed to me.

The American one had an attractive exterior, all shiny glass, round airiness. Inside it was too empty, an uninteresting disappointment. The distasteful collection of modem paintings looked like they had been painted by a chimpanzee. We left, going out past the enchanting fountain.

The Russian pavilion was tasteless, overstocked, like a nouveau riche woman putting on all her clothes and jewelry at once, just to show she had them. Great machines stuck up from amidst the trivia, like cacti in a desert, the implication being that no one else had thought of these quite ordinary machines. It was gloomy, humorless, and pedantic, with an elephantine earnestness.

We walked swiftly through the tasteful, elegant, dark British pavilion. Outside, in its garden, was a pitifully inadequate representation of the African countries in the British Commonwealth.

Only the Belgian government, at the Fair, gave a just showing of African art and culture.

France gave a better showing of African culture than the British had, but lagged far behind the Belgians in this respect. Though four million square miles of Africa was in some way related to the French Community, I only saw a small room on Algeria and another on French West Africa in the French pavilion. Otherwise, the French pavilion was wonderful—heavenly, stylish and chic.

I liked the Belgian Congo pavilions the best. What a magnificent display of Congo art! Stunning wood-carvings, frightening masks, hypnotic bas-reliefs, amazingly original paintings, splashed with violently screaming, yet magically seductive colors. It was the most exciting, moving and original art at the Fair.

I loved the quaint, exotic, original pavilions of some of the smaller countries.

Turkey, with its ancient mosaics! Mexico with stone Toltec statues! The United Arab Republic with its ivory-inlaid Asian art-works! Siam with its gilded pagoda!

It was a crime for so much exquisite beauty to disappear in a month, for the bright shining buildings were soon to be destroyed!

On the following March 11, I was back in Europe. Despite a bad bout of flu, I was preparing to play the Gershwin Concerto over Hilversum radio.

Then, I received a letter from André, mysteriously hinting that I should "come at once" to Brussels.

I flew on March 12. From the airport, I took the train into the air terminal. André, clad in a grey suit and raincoat, was waiting there. He had a droll, cryptic expression. He said mysteriously, "You have a rendezvous this afternoon that is most important for you. Who is it with? Ah, with a certain lady."

"Your mother?"

"No! The Queen!"

"The Queen?"

"Yes. Her Majesty, Queen Elisabeth of Belgium. Dr. Albert Schweitzer wrote her from Lambarene urging that she hear you play while you were in Europe. She asked Countess Carton-Wiart, her lady-in-waiting, to find you, and everyone has been looking for you for ten days. You must be at Stuyvenberg Castle at four this afternoon." André put down the Flemish newspaper he had been reading, and smiled at me.

It was one in the afternoon. Anxiously, I waited. Held up by motor trouble. Mr. Fabo arrived in half an hour. "I can't wear these clothes," I said.

"I'll take you to the flat of Joseph Esser, author of *Legende Africaine*. You can change there," he replied.

It had begun to drizzle. The streets were packed with cars. We drove slowly. We neared the Rue de Ruysbroek. This street housed Mr. Fabo's journal, *Africa and the World*. The street had a compelling, strange atmosphere, as though Jan van Ruysbroek, the medieval mystic and ecstatic teacher, still haunted the way which bore his name, as though still seeking God in the depths of his own soul, he were looking down from the spiritual ladder of Christian attainment on the cadential, daring, downward-plunging street, and musing back to the dark blind days six centuries before when he had been vicar of the towering Cathedral of Saint Gudule.

Mrs. Esser helped me dress at her apartment. She said my orange leather coat, limp from three months of hard travel through thirty-three lands, and the hottest, humid, coldest and driest of weathers, was "impossible," and lent me her own costly sable coat to wear.

Mr. Fabo drove me to Stuyvenberg Castle. I was strangely calm.

Her majesty, Queen Elisabeth of Belgium, is one of the world's greatest patrons of music, the close friend of the world's most eminent artists, and the sponsor of the internationally renowned music competition, the most important of its kind anywhere, which takes place annually on the grounds of Stuyvenberg Castle. It has catapulted many a musician into instant fame.

This would probably be the most important performance of my life. What should I play? Before I could think, our car stopped in front of a white stone building.

Inside, we were greeted by Countess Carton-Wiart, and Baron and Baroness Kerchove. Soon, my old friends Gilbert Chase, the brilliant American musicologist, and his Danish-born wife, whom I had known well in Argentina, arrived.

We all waited in the luxuriously-furnished drawing room.

Soon, Her Majesty the Queen came in.

She was charming, elegant, with a dignified regal grace that belied her years. She wore a pale rose-grey silk suit, her grey hair was in flawlessly perfect waves.

We all entered a large music room, with its black concert grand Steinway piano.

The first work I played was the thirty-five minute "Pictures at an Exhibition" by Moussorgsky. This is the piano piece I most enjoy performing because of its wild savagery, and religious exaltation. Her Majesty honored me by praising my rendition. Then, I played for three hours, going from the shimmering quasi-Asian works of Griffes, to the romanticism of Chopin, from the glitter of Schubert, to the Celtic melancholy of John Field, from the snowy clarity of Beethoven's "Waldstein Sonata," to the enchantment of Ravel's "Jeux d'Eau," the Attic delicacy of his "Sonatine," and the cruel, sardonic " Albo rada del Gracioso," from Aguirre, to Japanese "Cherry Blossoms," and Gershwin's rhapsodic blues, and two of my own compositions, "Manhattan Nocturne" and "Rumpelstiltskin." Her Majesty urged me to play more and more, praising what I did with a warmth that made me feel inspired and most deeply grateful.

Three hours passed.

When I had played the equal of two concert programs, Her Majesty exclaimed, "Oh, you must be tired! It was magnificent! I did not realize how the time had passed."

Refreshments were brought us to. Her Majesty poured tea.

Then we posed for photographs in the garden. Her Majesty, wearing no coat, seemed not affected by the cold, though I trembled despite the sables.

When Mr. Fabo and I departed, Queen Elisabeth kissed me on both cheeks, and wished me good luck. I truly felt it had been the crowning experience of my life, as though all else had merely been leading up to this wonderful occasion.

NOT UNTIL JULY 1959, did I return to Brussels. It was drizzly and cold. My summer clothes were inadequate. When André took me to Bruges on August 2 to celebrate my birthday, I shivered and my teeth chattered, so that he had to lend me his suit jacket to put on.

But Bruges was a wonderful city, where one could retreat into the Middle Ages and Renaissance without the slightest intrusion.

The canals were tranquil, covered with the serene beauty of gliding swans.

On our way back from Bruges to Brussels, with Paul Fabo, we stopped off at a restaurant where an artist painted pictures with sand.

One room was laid out with an immense canvas. Little dishes of pink, blue, red, etc. stood in front of the canvas. The walls were covered with portraits done that way. On Tuesday, August 11, I was received again at Stuyvenberg Castle by Her Majesty, Queen Elisabeth of Belgium.

For once, the sun shone brightly, bathing the green gardens behind the white stone building with a splendid light. It was one of those rare days when everything seemed perfect. Her Majesty wore a wide white garden hat, a white suit, and a white silk coat. Countess Carton-Wiart and Baron and Baroness Kerchove were there, too. I wore a blue satin brocade Asian suit, a red silk coat from Hong Kong, and a blue flowered hat.

Her Majesty and I spoke about Dr. Schweitzer, and about this book. The Queen insisted that I eat an ice and sent a waiter to fetch it.

With regret I left the lovely garden.

The Queen had been so gracious and charming to me, that I felt lost in the glow of contentment.

Soon after, I received a letter from Roger Nankel in the Belgian Congo:

> In September 1960, we expect to have our first native government.
>
> Independence will be reached probably between 1962 and 1964, depending on the decisions taken by the Belgian and Congo governments.
>
> So you see great changes are expected.

Great changes, indeed, that, had they been able to look 130 years into the future, would have startled the fiery Brussels opera goers of 1830, when they ran forth into the streets from a performance of "La Muette" shouting, '*Imitons les Parisiens!*' and began the revolution that won Belgium's own freedom and independence from the Dutch.

I thought of this as I walked, on the Rue Brassart, to the Club Baninga, where the Congolese gather in Brussels. When I finally found it, there was a small unpretentious sign hanging over a dim doorway.

I entered. No one was there. I gazed at the bar, the wall behind which was plastered with photographs of African scenes and Hollywood movie stars. I gazed at the dark rose walls, at the tables standing around in the dusk, trying to find some answer to the questions in my mind. Then a dark, handsome Congolese, escorting a curvaceous Belgian girl, came in. More Congolese, well-dressed, their somber faces remote and reflective, entered, accompanying chic, striking Belgian girls, whose faces showed far more intensity and excitement then the Africans' did.

The music began. First, hot, sensual Cuban rhythms, then the deep, sensuous exotic beat of Congo music, that somehow made all the Latin melodies seem forced, artificial and commercial.

The Congo music was natural, rising from the sod of the tangled primeval forests, from the jungle lakes, the muttering volcanoes, the cataracts, the savannahs and the gigantic Ruwenzori peaks, from the trunks of huge elephants, the bellies of crocodiles, the hoofs of red buffaloes. It was gentle as the equatorial calm, and violent as the tropical tornadoes. Often, it was sweet, with a childlike purity, a transparent innocence.

The music of the Americas has lost this innocence. I mused it has become lascivious and corrupt, or hard and vulgar, or abstract and sterile. But in Central Africa, there is still this innocence.

The earth is largely as God made it there. The vastness of its ancient species moving to nature's laws. Artistically, this created an innocence that welled forth beyond the tangled rules of civilization, and reached the spirit precious, lonely, mournful, yet jubilant and exalted.

On my last night in Brussels, I smiled and felt happy, eager for joy and laughter. I felt I had discovered something miraculous; or perhaps rediscovered something that I had long, long known.

In December 1959, events sped up. The Congolese demanded immediate freedom. The Belgians surprised the world by sending King Baudouin to the Congo where he promised complete cooperation with their wishes. June 30, 1960, was set as the Great Day of Liberation. I had already received an invitation to return. I looked forward with intense excitement to seeing the Drama of Independence unfold for what would become the largest nation area in Africa. ⊞

CHAPTER 11

The Land of Death Cathedrals, Snow, and Swedish Officers

Iceland, Sweden, Denmark, Norway, Finland:
1953, 1955, 1956

CELAND THAT MASS OF VOLCANIC rocks, glaciers, deserts, lava streams is one of the earth's most bleakly volcanic lands.

It is riddled with thousands of craters, gigantic fissures, lakes due to glacial erosion. Slopes of table-land are swept by clouds of drifts, pumice dust, and rains of volcanic ash. A field of unbroken lava at Odaöahraun, called the Lava of Evil Deeds, covers 1,300 square miles. Earthquakes are frequent.

Heather tracts melt into birch woods. The wildlife ranges from reindeer and white foxes, to seals and eider ducks.

I left Reykjavik, the capital, where natural hot water from the volcanic springs is pumped into the houses, on the night of October 12, 1955. Our small car belonged to the American Embassy. With me were an American girl, and Cristin, the chauffeur, who was handsome and solid, with yellow-white hair like the faint glimmer of the Arctic sun.

Our destination was Akureyri, on the opposite side of the island.

At nine that evening, our car lunged through the pools of dirty, muddy slush outside the hotel. I had no aversion to the trip, but felt stimulated by the adventurous sensation of excitement. Since the Icelandic government had praised its "highway system" warmly in publicity brochures, I looked forward to a pleasant trip, and was dressed in a fragile hand-knit suit.

We left the stark buildings of Reykjavik. The lightning slashed across the purple sky. The thunder boomed like the voice of God on the Day of Judgment. The diabolical winds swooped and thrust like swords in a battle. The rain pelted like bird shot. A bad goat path. That was what the "wonderful highway system" had become. Our car leapt, trembled, jumped and heaved over stones, mud, and ditches.

We passed geysers. We climbed up rocky, jagged cliffs.

The screaming of the storm drowned our voices.

We got to Thingvellir. We were too weary to press on any farther. There was a modern rest-house there staffed by two servants. We slept a few hours, had some tiny, cold shrimps for breakfast, and drove on.

The glassy dawn sky hovered like a stigma of death over the shroud-like earth. We drove slowly, feeling our way like moles. A few bleak houses stood like propped-up corpses on the frozen ground.

We passed holes dug in the hard black funeral earth. People lived in them like vampires in their tombs. It was cold as a crypt. The wind howled a requiem as we lurched round skull-like hills, a few bony trees, and ghostly plateaus. We shivered. Vast glacial lakes sped past us.

The white sky darkened to pall-gray. A sickly yellow haze spread over everything. A few scattered desolate houses began to appear like frozen eyes peering over the surface of the earth. Church bells tolled from far away, then nearer, nearer, nearer, until our ears were deafened by the tolling.

We were in Akureyri.

My concert took place in a cold, dimly-lit hall. But the house was full, the people were cordial and hearty, the applause was heated. But it was an anti-climax, as were my concerts in Keflavik, and will always be overshadowed by memories of that wild ride over the frozen hills.

Iceland, to me, will always be the Land of Death.

I MADE MY STOCKHOLM DEBUT at the Konserthuset on October 20, 1953. Stockholm seemed a cold city, aloof, distant, and rejecting. My plain narrow room at the Hotel Nobel was always under heated. One had to pay extra for baths, of course. Everyone was impersonal, and took not the slightest interest in me.

From sheer loneliness one night, I wandered into a coffee house and just sat there. A glum man with wild hair and a scarred face came in and sat next to me. He started writing Chinese poetry on the menu. He turned to me leeringly and said, "I am a poet. But one cannot be a poet here. Not in this country. In Sweden one must always be drank. Drank!"

Lars Malmstrom, a journalist who was big and jovial, entertained me one evening at his home. Two days later, when I sprained my ankle on a slimy cobble stone he carried me to the hospital. He was the nicest person I met in Sweden.

Copenhagen was gay by contrast. I got ovations at my two recitals at the Odd-Fellows Palaeet. *The Social-Demokraten* wrote, "Superlative.... The Crown-Princess of the piano." *Landog Folk* said, "A splendid American pianist with sonorous tone and big technique." *The Politiken Review* remarked, "Vivid playing, musical mind, artistic sense, wonderful technique."

I loved the sparkling atmosphere. The rich good food. The sight of hundreds of bicycle riders pedaling to work each morning.

TRONDHJEM, NORWAY, had an austere grave dignity. It was dominated by the noble edifice of the Nidaros Cathedral. The church was once the meeting place for Nordic pilgrims from far and wide, and the center of the worship of St. Olav. Within its walls kings were crowned and interred.

In 995, the hero king Olav Tryggvason brought the Christian faith to Norway, founded the town of Nidaros, and erected a church. Both decayed after his death. Then King Olav Haraldsson took power and was killed in 1030, at Stiklestad, by his own people. His corpse was buried in a sandy bank. Soon, from this, there sprang a fair fountain, that wrought miracles and healed sickness.

It is written that a wooden chapel was built on this spot, the altar placed over the heart of the king. Then a stone church was erected by Olav Kyrre. By 1300 it had become a splendid cathedral.

In 1328 it was burnt, and again in 1432 and 1531, in 1708 and 1719. Restoration began in 1869. I gazed with awe at the magnificent stone carvings within, and thought:

"Faith created this. A faith unquestioning, undoubting, unoccupied with the taint of analysis, skepticism, doubt. It soars towards heaven. It does not wonder whether there is a heaven, or jeopardize its eternal soul with rationalization. It loves, sacrifices, acts with fervor. It believes equally in God and in the Devil, in miracles. prayer and in sin. It has not spoiled the purity of its ideals with modern indecision and gross materialism."

I went to a music museum where they had old, old musical instruments. The directress congratulated me on my concert of the night before, and asked for my photograph. I am told it still stands there, exhibited beside medieval tromba marinas, serpents and lutes.

The twelve-hour journey by third-class train back to Oslo was freezing.

Ambassador Strong had a reception waiting for me at his residence when I arrived. I gave two recitals at the University Aula in Oslo, and received rave reviews.

Kurt Londén was waiting at the airport when I arrived in Iklinofors. He had a hearty Falstaffian manner about him, a great booming personality that sent forth sparks of joviality. He was always laughing, always making jokes. One could hear his delightful, rumbling laughter a block away.

He was big and white, like the snow on lofty mountain-peaks.

He presented me in two recitals, on the radio and at the Kauppakorkeakouloussa.

The *Hufvudstadsbladet* wrote, "This young pianist with the Dutch name and the jade complexion, was a fascinating new acquaintance for the public. A distinguished talent, she plays with infectious gladness, feline power, and glorious rhythms." The *Helsingin Sanomat* said, "A truly great talent. She caused a furore. A star pianist."

On November 15, I played in Tammerfors, under the baton of Eero Kosenen. The orchestra and I played the "Saint-Saens Concerto No. 2." The Finland *Aamulehti* wrote, "A new young star who rises above the other American pianists we hear. She played with passion, maturity, poetry, gaiety, and continuous faithful virtuosity perfectly climaxed."

Finland was strangely different from the rest of Scandinavia. In Norway, Sweden, Denmark, English is taught as the second language in the schools, and almost anyone one meets on the streets speaks English. In Finland, Swedish was taught as the second language, and rare was the person who spoke English.

One was ever conscious of the proximity of Russia. On the train back to Helsingfors, I sat next to a prominent Finnish Communist.

First he told me about the long-standing hostility between the true Finns and the Swedish Finns. Then we started to discuss literature. He was thoroughly acquainted with American books of importance. We spoke of *The Naked and the Dead*. I said I had not enjoyed it, I had found it too brutal. But he said, "But life is all brutality. That is all life is. There is nothing but sex and death. Nothing."

Once, in Helsingfors, I went to the Kauppakorkeakoulussa to practice. When I arrived, l was told, "I know we gave you this time, but we must cancel it. The Russian Embassy just sent some artists over, and said we must turn the hall over to them. It is sudden, but we must. We cannot afford to offend them."

Mr. Londén took me to the airport the morning of my departure. They would not let me leave. I did not have a labor permit. Mr. Londén had sent one, months before, to my Swedish manager, who had forgotten to give it to me. There was much commotion and argument. Mr. Londén finally telephoned some Helsinki officials, and I soon was given permission to depart.

Returning to Stockholm I could not find a hotel room.

I had not thought of phoning in from the airport, because I had met Lionel Hampton and his band there, and they had amused and distracted me with tales of their latest tour, their troubles when instruments had been left behind on airplanes, and comments on my "real crazy" clothes.

Once in the cold, austere city I visited my manager, and telephoned a Greek friend. He arranged for me to stay overnight in the home of an acquaintance from France.

It was a black night when I arrived at the grim six-story stone house.

It took an effort to walk to the top floor.

The icy room was filled with cigarette smoke when I arrived. About ten people were there, the Greek, the French acquaintance, two Poles, a Ukrainian, a Lithuanian and some Russians. They were drinking wine and vodka, and talking in low voices. Most of them were refugees.

As I slowly appraised them, wondering what chaotic pattern of events had brought them there, the Frenchman rose, and went to the kitchen, returning with two kerosene stoves which he lit. Now it was a little warmer, not much.

The men had kept on their fur hats, the two women wore heavy sweaters, and I kept on my overcoat. They drank more and more, getting more confidential, bellicose, and lachrymose. The Polish woman, who came from Nieswiez, told me about her horrible experiences during World War II, and about her dead fiancé, a Polish officer who had been shot in the back of the head and murdered by the Russians, along with thousands of his compatriots in 1940, in the Katyn Forest Massacre.

Her story affected me with sensations of guilt and misery, as though I personally were responsible for all she had suffered, and deserved punishment for it — my head ached, and an icy sweat dripped down my forehead. I gripped the edge of the chair with a feeling of anguish.

The drinking went on and on. How was it possible for people to drink so much? One of the Russian men brought out a balalaika and began to play it, not very well. Then someone turned on the short-wave set, and we heard the start of a broadcast from France. It flickered and choked with static. Soon it was drowned out by the Russian with the balalaika, who began to sing coarsely, with a vulgar and infinitely sad attempt at gaiety.

I thought of what they had escaped, the death, the wreckage and the disaster, and I wondered if their flight to the supposed world of freedom had brought them anything but a greater disillusionment, for perhaps they had only left the barbarity of the East to find the corruption of the West, and no ideal to cling to, and nothing to look forward to anywhere, and no answer, no, not one, to the tormenting spiritual questions found. Perhaps nothing looming in the future but a grey continuation of the ceaseless material struggle to keep the physical body from being in too great a discomfort. Perhaps they felt their blood-shedding, maiming and hunger had been in vain, and that of their comrades, relatives and enemies too, had all been in vain—that it was all useless and in vain, and nothing would be solved ever. After all, evil was irremediable.

I went to bed in a cold room, a few doors away, which was three-hundred years old, slightly younger than the rest of the house. Disheveled, worn out, I fell on the bed in my overcoat, and slept until dawn. I awoke, and left the room. No one was outside. The flat was completely empty. There were no traces of the gathering the previous night, and it seemed as though no one had ever actually been there at all.

I walked down the six flights of steps to the cold, vacant street where, some blocks away, I found a taxi stand. I arrived at the airport in time to take an SAS plane on to Copenhagen and Hamburg.

IN 1955, I HAD AN EXTENSIVE TOUR of Scandinavia, which unfortunately, had to be canceled so that I could return to Argentina. I agreed to come the following year, after leaving Southern Europe.

On January 17, 1956, I flew from Madrid to Stockholm.

I was so sleepy on arrival, that I went off and left all my bags at the airport. Later, I dashed back in a taxi to get them and from there rushed to the railway station. I arrived in Linkoeping on January 18 at 3:00 in the morning.

At noon, I gave a Mozart concert at a high school. That night, l played at a Swedish military base, where the soldiers—burly, hearty and handsome—carried me around in triumph on their shoulders afterwards, and the buff, gay, blond officers toasted me with champagne until midnight. The next day, I gave a recital in Mottala, playing the "Beethoven Appassionata," the "Ravel Sonatine," on other pieces. It was deadly cold, but dry. Returning to Linkoeping, for another recital on January 20, which the *Oestgoetha Correspondenten,* Sweden's oldest newspaper, gave me a gold medal. I took a third-class coach to the Swedish border on January 21.

When I disembarked, it was snowing. The snow was a yard deep on tracks and platforms. l found no one who spoke English, or who would help me with my three suitcases. The ghastly cold made my feet stiff. Running from track to track, I fell repeatedly from the weight of the bags.

Where was the train? The midnight blackness hung gloomily. Racing after one train, I slipped, knocking my head hard.

I missed it, but it had been the wrong train, anyhow. The right one chugged in, an hour late. I dragged the bags on. A conductor emerged, and told me I was not in the *right* car, and that I must get off, walk three cars down, and get in the *right* car. He refused to let me walk through the train. He did not help me with my bags. The train moved. I threw the bags off, jumped down, ran with the bags in a wild dash to the fourth car, and hurled my bags through the open door to the iron platform, and leapt in myself.

At dawn when the train arrived in Oslo, Gerd Gamborg, a pretty petite blonde with glorious golden hair, and three beautiful daughters took me to her home to rest.

I played in the University Aula that night, over radio the next day, the next in Porsgrunn. There, while I played Bach, a newspaper photographer leapt on the stage, ran over to me, thrust a big camera in my face, and started shooting flash-bulb pictures. The audience booed.

I cast a murderous glance at him, someone else jumped on the stage and pulled him off, and I went right on playing Bach.

I was feted by the concert society that night. They drank endless toasts to me, shouting, *"Skol! Skol! Skol!"*

THE NEXT MORNING, AT DAWN, I left by third-class train for Oslo. The train was very late. In Oslo, I found my plane was very late too. It was supposed to leave at four that afternoon. It left at 8:30 p.m.

At 7:00 p.m., Gerd Gamborg took me to the airport. I had to take the orchestral parts of the Gershwin "Concerto in F" with me to Helsinki. They were very heavy. I decided to put them in my sweater, so as not to pay excess baggage. On our way out in the taxi, they slipped down, and stuck in my skirt. They stood way out, so under my bulky coat, it looked as though I was eight months pregnant. When I got on the plane, everyone was most sympathetic about my "condition."

The plane arrived in Stockholm fifteen minutes after my flight to Helsinki was supposed to have departed. A thick blizzard raged.

Whipped by the lashing winds and stinging snow, I raced across the airfield to the Helsinki plane, which had, thank God, been kept waiting for me.

I reread the letter my Swedish manager had given me, and was glad to see that my next concert was not for two days, and I would have a day of rest. But I arrived in Helsinki to find Mr. Landen pacing up and down anxiously.

"Your concert is tomorrow at noon! Didn't Helmer Enwall tell you? The orchestral rehearsals start at nine o'clock in the morning!" he cried.

I had not eaten in twenty hours when I arrived one in the morning at the hotel. Yet, the performance next day was a great success.

Afterwards, a gay, sparkling party was given to me at the home of a prominent conductor. Bon mots abounded, and all the musicians told the naughtiest stories in their repertoire. Everyone was hearty. I decided it was essential to be hearty in Scandinavia. In that cold and dark country, with the seasons so violently exaggerated, one must either drink, commit suicide, go mad or be hearty.

Upon returning to the hotel room, I found a letter from Norway awaiting me. Trembling in the freezing, incredible cold, I opened it. From Gerd in Oslo, it enclosed a review which said I was, "Warm, passionate, fiery, burning!"

Shivering with chill, I donned three pairs of stockings, three sweaters and my heaviest coat, piled four blankets on me, lay on the marble-like bed, and went to sleep. ⊞

CHAPTER 12

Triumph in Paris Hunger in Madrid, An Angry Young Man
France, Spain, Italy: 1955, 1956, 1958, 1959

PARIS, THOUGH THE QUEEN OF CITIES, did not impress me favorably on my first visit. Drab, dull, dismal, gloomy — it swamped me with its dark sinister immensity, so narrow, close, and old — like a shadow reflected from another era.

It was November 1955.

I had just come from the brilliantly clear dry openness of the Near East.

Señor Paquirito had arranged my Paris debut for December, at the Palais Chaillot, with Albert Wolff and the Pasdeloup Symphony.

Having sailed across the stormy Atlantic from Buenos Aires, just to hear my concert, he cabled me one afternoon to meet him at the American Embassy.

When I rushed into the Embassy, the receptionist asked me, "How do you like Paris?"

"Too gloomy."

"Oh we all think that when we first come, but after a while you get to just love it."

As glowingly enthusiastic as ever, Señor Paquirito now dashed up to me, and said, "Wonder-fool to see you, wonder-fool! I haf dislocate my shoulder on zee boat, comeeng, bot ees steel *fantastico!* Zee tour in Spain? What for you asks? Of course ees all arranged. Ees *magnífico*. Spain weel be foolup everywhere!"

What was really "full up" was the Palais Chaillot concert.

Despite the packed house, and the expert accompaniment of Albert Wolff and the orchestra, my mind was troubled as I played the "Rhapsody" and "Concerto in F."

At each pause, my mind would range back to the threatening letters that a music company had been writing me, and to the difficulties I had preparing for the concert.

Finding a piano for practice had been difficult. Some days, as l worked on my keyboard at the Hotel Garnier. But it had rained constantly, the sky was gloomy, no outside light could penetrate my room's murky greyness. When one turned off one dun electric light, all the others went off, so I could scarcely see. Also, it was too cold. A sign on the door forbade cooking, washing anything, or using any electrical appliances, so I could not bring me a heater.

The manager of the hotel, hearing of my difficulty, gave me the key to a wonderful apartment where I might go to practice on a piano Schubert had once played on. But as the weather grew colder, there was no heat at all, and I was afraid to bring in an electric heater for fear it might explode the ancient electrical connections.

Then Vera Moore, an outstanding English musician, let me come to her house, but she had to use her piano most of the time for pupils' lessons. Madame Wagner let me use her piano sometimes. Occasionally, I practiced at the Luxembourg Palace on Madame Gaston Monnerville's piano.

Gaston Monnerville, President of the French Senate and the second most powerful man in France, is a Negro from French Ghana, and is happily married to a white Frenchwoman.

His having retained this formidable position throughout thirteen years of shifting French administrations, he shows his brilliant astuteness. As a private individual, he is also highly-cultured, wise, intellectual, courteous, charming, and a wonderful friend.

He, and Madame Monnerville, live at Luxembourg Palace with their son, Jacques, in the splendid suite in which Napoleon I and Josephine once dwelt. In fact, Mr. Monnerville uses the same desk that Napoleon once used. This suite is magnificent, the walls covered with seventeenth century tapestries by Gobelin, made with gold thread.

Lions snarl, lovers embrace, costumes gleam, and fruits shine from these glorious tapestries with the same brilliance as though they had been woven last year. There are also splendid paintings and statuary, exquisite carpets, and Madame Monnerville's adorable collection of parakeets from French West Africa.

Madame Monnerville, who is a very sweet, gracious, and warm person, also paints brilliantly herself, and showed me many of her beautiful works on my visits there. She is a great music lover too, and has several pianos. I always play for her whenever I come to Paris. Madame Monnerville had a wonderful reception for me, just before my concert at the Palais Chaillot, with two hundred guests of the Paris elite.

Albert Wolff had requested me to bring my copies of the orchestral parts of the Gershwin "Concerto" and "Rhapsody" for the orchestra to use. I did. About a week before the concert, I started getting insulting letters from the Salabert Music Company, charging that my bringing the music had kept the Pasdeloup society from having to pay money to them to get the parts, and therefore I must give them $150.

These letters started coming every day, twice a day. They threatened to stop the concert. I was terrified. Madame B, an agent in Paris, told me, "Now, of course you mus' geeve zem zee money, you mus' always geeve zee money." Mr. Monnerville told me this was nonsense, and suggested that I get a lawyer.

I asked Señor Paquirito to speak to them, but he ran off down the street, shouting, "I don' wants responsibeelity! Never een my life I has responsibeelity!"

My acquaintance evinced immense disinterest in advising me, and melted away. The concert took place. No one stopped it. But the letters started again. I wired my mother. The cable cost $20. She wired back that this was ridiculous, that she had spoken to the Harms Company in New York who said I had a personal right to use my own music. Finally, I think, the Harms Company sent a letter to Paris, and the whole thing quieted down, vanished, and Señor Paquirito and I departed for Spain.

WHEN WE LEFT PARIS by second-class train for Madrid, on December 23, I had no foreboding of the turbulent events ahead. He had assured me that a Spanish manager had arranged a "wonder-fool" tour for me. Though I urged him to confirm it by phone or cable, he said that was not necessary.

En route to the railway station, he suddenly remembered he had left his briefcase at his hotel, so we had to turn back in the taxi, dash recklessly there through dense masses of Paris traffic, grab the briefcase, and speed back to the station.

At the gate, he refused to have his suitcases put in the train's baggage car. A half-hour of furious argument with the baggage-master resulted, Paquirito shouting loudly, "Spaneesh ees zee bes' een zee world! *Ehverything* zat was ever invented een zee world came from Spain! Columbus was born een Spain!" Finally, two of his bags were bound with steel, put in the baggage car, and we boarded the train.

The rain, streaming down gloomily, streaked the grey windows, as we sat in hostile silence in the otherwise empty compartment, while the train swept over the ghostly fields of France.

Numb with resentful apprehension, I sat, unable to read or think. Señor Paquirito had insisted I buy first class tickets from Irvún to Madrid. "We mus' not arrive on third-class, like peasants—ze station weel be fool of journalists to meet us!" That had cost a lot. Then, the night before departure, he had collected my fee from the Pasdeloup society, taking it to pay his hotel bill. Later he gave me the minute remainder, not nearly enough to pay the bill at my hotel. I had to use all my own money, was left with almost nothing. Had I not thought audiences were awaiting in Spain, I would have canceled the trip.

At Irún, he lost the baggage checks and half of each of our tickets. The difficulties this caused made me angrier when we pulled into Madrid. No one was there to meet us. Two days later, he found the manager. He knew nothing of our concerts. Like a strange tropical plant shooting up, a new tour was soon arranged.

He found he could get concerts for Mr. Lee, too. ANTA, in New York, agreed to send Lee over. I had been economical on the appropriation ANTA allotted me for my Near East tour, and $350 was left. ANTA had planned to send me that money to use on my Spain tour. Then my mother agreed for my $350 to be used to buy part of Lee's ticket, so he would be able to come. The letter informing me of this was delayed. I only got it after he was on his way.

The first concert, with the Madrid Symphony, was a Gershwin Festival. The night before, I was in bed. Señor Paquirito phoned me. He shouted breathlessly, "*¡Es desastre todo!* Ees all deesaster! He faint een last rehearsal. Zey carry heem to hotel. Spaneesh doctor come, ees zee greates' een zee world, all Spaneesh doctors are greatest een zee world. He say Lee haf hundred an' forty temperature. Poor boy. What you says I should go see heem for? I am Spaneesh gentleman, I cans not go like zat. I needs an hour to bath an' hour to feex zee hair, an hour to dress. What for you talks about you haf spen' five hundred dollars? What ees money? You are so *mecanique*. All Americans are *mecanique*. You are *mercenaire*. What matters eef you lose money? I am zee mos lose man een zee WORLD! I am like a *santo!*"

I hung up the phone, threw on my clothes in five minutes, took my electric heater, honey, lemons, and vitamins, ran out of the hotel and took a taxi to Mr. Lee's hotel.

Once there, I dashed up the steps to his room. I plugged in the heater. I spoon-fed him lemonade and vitamins. After several hours, I left.

The next morning, Señor Paquirito told me, "Weel be concert! He recover. How seely ees zee vitameens! Zee Spaneesh doc; come zees morneeng, see all your vitameens, he throw zem zee toilet, ha-ha!"

The concert was at noon. I dressed elaborately in my ace gown. I taxied to the Metropolitan Theatre, I had not seen it before. It was filthy, incredibly encrusted with years of dirt. The house was packed. The concert only began forty minutes late. The reviews which appeared the following two days were fine. Then, I had to leave for Scandinavia.

Señor Paquirito was furious. His waved brown hair trembled with anger as he shouted, "What for you goes to Sweden? So what eef you has arranged zee concerts seence two years? You mus' cancel all. You mus' stay here or Mr. Lee weel have no concerts. Cancel all or I keels myself!"

I lost my temper. Later that night, I went to pay my hotel and found Señor Paquirito had put all his expenses onto mine so it was three times what I had expected. When I got to Sweden, I had to have my manager there, Helmer Enwall, send back money to Madrid to pay for the rest of his bill, so he could go to Barcelona and Valencia, and recreate the orchestral concerts that had mysteriously vanished.

In Norway, I received a letter.

Señor Paquirito told me in it how wonderfully he had now arranged everything. Could I stop off in Paris on the way back to Spain, and rent some orchestral music not in the Madrid Symphony's Library?

I rerouted my air ticket to return to Spain via Paris, a more expensive route, so I could obtain the music. At one stop en route, I made a long distance phone call to Madrid, and found they did not need the music at all. Now it was too late to change my ticket. But at least I congratulated myself on having had the bright idea to send most of my money back to New York from Scandinavia. My money could not vanish if I did not have it with me. Arriving in Madrid, I found the recitals I had been told I would have immediately on my return had evaporated.

Anne Brown, the American singer for whom the role 'Bess' was created by George Gershwin, arrived and gave an orchestral concert with Mr. Lee and myself and the Madrid Symphony. The house was almost full, but I got no fee. I was told it "had been used elsewhere."

I was starving. My stomach seemed like a bottomless abyss. I lost 10 pounds. I thought of nothing but my hunger. I dreamed and day-dreamed of food.

When I went to Barcelona, where I had been preceded by Anne Brown and Mr. Lee, Señor Paquirito did not meet my plane.

Going to his hotel room, I knocked on his door.

Opening slowly, he peered out. Oddly, one side of his hair was straight and grey, the other side a rich shiny wet brown, and he held an open brown bottle in one hand.

"What's that?" I asked, "Hair dye?"

"*Signorina!* How cans you say such a theeng? You eensults me. I am greates' *empressario* een zee world! Ees not kind zat! Why you deesturbs me? Yes, you weel have concert tonight. Playing Grieg weeth zee orchestra. What I care you has lost seven hundred dollars? I has los' a thousand, ten thousand, thirty thousand, hundred thousand! I am mos' lose man een zee WORLD! I am proud of my eentegrity! Even when I am young an' am a crazy dancer, I has eentegrity! Always I travels weeth seexteen suitcases, an' *princesas* een my entourage—*marquesas, condesas, duquesas, princesas!* Was *maravilloso!*" he shouted dramatically, gesticulating so that the dye began to dribble on the beige carpet.

"What princesses? Where?" I asked, repeating it cruelly.

"Why, why, why? What you means *what princesas?* All zee *princesas* een zee world! What I care you don't eat. You gets theen, you looks better!"

I felt weak at the concert that night. It was supposed to begin at 9:30 p.m. It started an hour late. The orchestra was exceptionally good. I wore a turquoise tulle gown which l had worn for my recitals the previous month in Leon and Madrid. It hung loosely on me now. As a singer and actress, Miss Brown was every much the diva. The hall was beautiful, there was a large crowd, I got an ovation after my performance of the Grieg Concerto with the orchestra. I was too hungry to notice.

The next morning at dawn, l simply left. I was tired of the Spain venture. I went to the airport in a taxi. One dollar remained in my purse, after I paid for it.

Having worn all my clothes, one on top of the other, as I had no money to pay for excess baggage, l looked as if I weighed 200 pounds. It was wonderful to reach Paris.

From Paris, I flew back to New York.

IN FEBRUARY 1958, I REVISITED PARIS. I lived at a small hotel on the corner of the Rue Vauguard the Hotel Trianon. It was the same one where the heroine, played by Brigitte Bardot, lived in the film, *Love is my Profession.* On this trip, the mystery of Paris, the secret poetry, the entrancing, rain-swept magnetism of her dim streets, enraptured me. I felt like a leaf fluttering between the centuries, without anchor, timeless.

I saw the Monnervilles at Luxembourg Palace many times, and I made new friends.

One cold, rainy evening, l visited Countess Francoise Goguet. She lived with her family in a small street near the Gare St. Lazare. The Goguet apartment was large, and filled with *objets d'art,* a grand piano, a pipe-organ and hundreds of books. I went there many times, and her hospitality was always magnificent. Her husband is a retired Naval Officer, whose hobby is exotic cuisine. His sauces are veritable epic poems. One of her daughters, Jacqueline, is the only female carillon-player in France.

Countess Francoise Goguet became my godmother in November 1958. When I returned to Paris in February 1959, she saw me off at the railroad station, on the occasion of my departure for Milan. The journey took twelve hours.

I had hoped to have a compartment entirely to myself. But just as I was settled on the hard leather seat, a large man in striped pants and a cutaway, dashed in from the hall outside like someone rushing from a house afire.

The train began, rumbling to move, as he dropped exhaustedly on the seat opposite me. He wiped his face with a large pocket handkerchief.

"My name is Godefroi Galant," he said, looking me up and down, like a sausage manufacturer looking at a pig. "I am the Poet Laureate of France!"

"How nice!" I said, reaching in my briefcase and taking out some of my publicity. "I'm a concert pianist. Would you like to see one of my programs?"

I handed him some of my publicity. He gave me some of his, which he had apparently been holding in his hand all along, for just that purpose. I gave him some more of mine. He thrust some more of his at me. I gave him more of mine. He gave me more of his. It was like a game of cards.

"I will arrange a tour for you in Soviet Russia!" he exclaimed.

"Fine! When?"

"Oh, the next time I go there for the General."

"Which General?"

"*The* General."

"What General is that?"

"General de Gaulle, of course!"

"Oh, I didn't know you were a diplomat."

"*Naturally* I am a diplomat."

"Then you must know a lot of people I know. Monsieur Gaston Monnerville, the President of the French Senate, perhaps?"

"Well, I haven't had *time* to see him recently."

"Marie-Hélène LeFaucheux, formerly the vice-president of the National Assembly, maybe?"

"Well, you see, I am so busy."

"How about Christian Jayle, the President of the National Assembly of the Congo?"

"Oh, I never go to parties. I am a savage. I hate civilization. Only once a year do I go to parties."

"That's strange."

"I am strange. Do you know, I am a composer, also, I have written fifteen piano concertos. You can copy them down for me. I am the *second* Beethoven!"

I raised my eyebrows and said coldly, "Indeed?"

"I play brilliantly, but I only play my own works. Of course, I never practice. I have a tape recording of myself playing my latest one with an orchestra. It's in my flat in Milan. You can listen to it and copy it down. That is, if you are sure you know how to do it *right*. It has never been written down. It has only been played by ear. One, two, three! One, two, three!" He leapt up now, and started to gesticulate frantically, like a conductor, shaking the tails of his cutaway, and waggling his head, so that his wispy yellow hair trembled with agitation.

"Oh, you're going to Milan?" I interjected, startled. "I'm on my way there now, to play at the USIS Theatre on March 4."

"You are? Do you speak Italian?" he shouted, pacing up and down the floor of the tiny compartment like a caged cheetah, his enormous hands held behind him in the 'Napoleon-pose'."

"Some. I can read it easily."

"I speak it flawlessly. *Arrivederci! Arrivederci! Ne! mezzo del cammin di nostra vita! Mi ritrovai per una selva oscura!* I speak twenty-seven languages!" Standing on tip-toes, he began energetically to trace the number "27," over and over in the air. He grinned wider and wider, stretching his pale bloodless lips like elastic, until I thought they would split. His watery blue bulbous eyes stared at me fixedly.

"Ah, excuse me! I have to go to the ladies' room," I said hastily, rising, deftly slipping a mystery story I had been reading into my hand, and going out into the hall. I walked, as fast as I could, to the lavatory. I stood up there for an hour, reading *The Hollow Man*.

When I returned to my compartment, the attendant had made up two beds, one on either side. Mr. Godefroi Galant was not in evidence. I crawled in one of the beds. It was so freezing cold, that I soon emerged, put my overcoat on, and crawled back in. The sheet and thin blanket were too short, so my feet stuck out. Nevertheless, I went to sleep.

In the middle of the night, as the train was hurtling wildly through the French countryside, I began to dream that someone was pinching me, and nibbling the calf of my leg.

Sleepily, I shook my leg, and opened my eyes.

Godefroi was perched on the edge of the other bed, looking nonchalant.

Wearily, I closed my eyes and slept again. This time I dreamed that a leopard was biting my knee. I woke up instantly, and sat up. Godefroi stood in the middle of the floor, gazing distantly out the window at the dim farmhouses.

My brain felt drugged. I could not keep awake. I sank into slumber. I dreamed that a pair of hands were around my neck, choking me. I woke up. The room was completely dark now. Someone had closed the curtains tightly over the windows and doors. The blackness was bottomless. I felt a hot breath on my cheek. My throat seemed to have a tremendous weight on it. I could not breathe. I could not scream. Everything seemed red inside of my head. I felt I was sinking into a bottomless well.

Suddenly, the train lurched violently, and chugged to a stop. Excited voices were heard outside. Footsteps were heard in the corridor. A far-off voice said, "Passports! Passports!" A harsh voice next to me said, *"Merde!"* and abruptly, the pressure was released from my throat. In a minute, the compartment-door opened, Godefroi stood briefly on the threshold, his bulky profile illuminated in the dim hall light, then the door slammed violently, and he was gone.

I lay there for a minute, stunned. Then I got up, fumbled for the lights. I raised the window curtains, and turned the ceiling light on.

There was a loud knock on the door. It opened. A man in a uniform came in asking me in German and in French if I had anything to declare to the Swiss Customs. I said no. My throat felt so sore I could hardly speak. As soon as he and the other officials had departed, I went back to the lavatory. I spent the rest of the night there until dawn came.

When we arrived in Milan, there was still no sign of Godefroi. Apparently, he had left the train at the border.

I was met at the station by someone connected with the American Embassy. He drove me to see Mr. Krauss of the United States Information Service, and Mr. Luigi Lapegna, my manager.

I had several newspaper interviews that day. My throat felt so raw, it was more and more uncomfortable for me to talk.

The next evening, I gave my concert at the USIS Theatre.

It went well, and the next morning I was offered a fourteen-city tour of Italy in 1960.

At noon, a journalist named Signore Cavaliere Cabildo came and took me sightseeing. We visited the Sforza castle and other places of interest. Signore Cabildo helped me select a pair of Italian shoes. They were exquisite wine satin wisps, but they hurt dreadfully after I had walked a block in them.

I returned to the hotel. Signore Cabildo departed.

My phone rang as soon as I got to my room.

"Lincoln King speaking," the voice on the other end of the line said. I've been trying to get you all day. I'm downstairs now, and want to see you about something very important."

"Do I know you, Mr. King? You see, I'm really not feeling very well right now."

"Oh, you're against me because I'm black, are you?"

"Well, I don't know you? I don't care what color you are!"

"You'll have to prove that by seeing me. I met you after a concert you gave as a child prodigy in Atlanta fifteen years ago but I guess you don't believe in paying attention to your fans," he said belligerently.

"It's not that! Well, I'll come downstairs, but for just a few minutes."

Reluctantly, I took the lift back down to the lobby.

Lincoln King was standing in front of the lift door when I stepped out. He was a dark nutria-brown color, with thick black hair and very white teeth. His face was creased in anger, as though he had been resentful for a long time, and he wore a flawlessly cut, very expensive-looking black suit.

He led me over to some seats in the lobby, and we sat down.

"Well, I knew you'd be a real sweetie and come down," he said, though he still did not look pleased.

"Yes. What did you want to ask me?"

"I want all your contacts so I can put them in use for myself. I especially want a list of all your managers in Europe, and letters of introduction to all the Prime Ministers and Kings you know in Africa. And then, I'd like to ask you for a contribution, too. I've just composed an opera, and I need some donations to help with the copying of the scores and parts. I'll only ask you for $100."

"Well I'll have to think about it. What is your opera about?" I asked.

"It's a broad fantasy of mingled concepts. All the great Negro leaders of history appear in it, and have philosophical discussions with each other about the race problem in the Deep South. I myself play the parts of Menelik I, Samuel Coleridge Taylor, Dumas, Frederick Douglass and Marcus Garvey. Will you contribute the $100?"

"It's a little difficult. I don't have any money for that purpose with me now. Why don't you ask someone wealthy?"

"You're wealthy enough!"

"No I'm not. The concert field has its limitations."

"Why don't you try the field of *commercial prostitution* then?" he shouted.

"What?"

"Prostitution! If others do it, why can't you?"

"Hush! I don't *want* to!"

"Well I've had to do it! I've been forced to! I've not been lucky like you. Come outside now, and we'll walk around, and I'll tell you what my life has been like since you are so scared that these white people will hear some of the realities of life."

"But I don't want to go out! I was out all afternoon. My feet hurt. These shoes don't fit," I said.

"You ought to be glad you've got shoes! I didn't always have shoes. I guess it's just because I'm black that you don't want to be seen on the street with me!"

"No! You misinterpret me!"

I argued a few minutes, but finally weakly allowed him to lead me out on the street. It looked like rain. The well-dressed Milanese crowds, better-garbed than those of Paris, were hurrying through the streets. We turned a corner. We walked past several solid grey stone buildings.

Lincoln King said angrily, "I wanted to be a pianist, too, like you. But I was illegitimate. That doesn't mean my mother wasn't a good woman. She was as good as your mother! It's the good girls who get in trouble. My father just walked off, a month before I was born. My mother had to raise me all alone. We lived on a farm in Georgia, near Nicholls. I guess you never heard of Nicholls, Georgia?"

"No."

"Well, I have Nicholls in my bones. I loathed it. I hated everyone and everything there. We were sharecroppers. I had to pick cotton! Then we moved into Nicholls, and my mother did housework, and they had beautiful pianos in some of those houses and I would have loved to have played them, but I couldn't. I read about you when you were a child, and I envied you. God, how I wanted to be where you were, but I couldn't. I was just a little nigger boy in the South with no father and no money!"

"Well, I'm sorry you've had such a hard time" I said debating to myself which one of the shoes hurt most, the left or the right.

"Oh, you're sorry? Well, I'll tell you—I hated you. I hated you for years, and your father, too. I don't like his articles. I've been waiting for fifteen years to meet you, and tell you how much I hate you!"

"But, why? I haven't done anything to you."

"You existed. I tried to follow in your footsteps, but I had no money. I had to sleep with someone to get the money for my first lessons. Then I went into the Navy. Nineteen years old, and thrust into the Navy. It was hell. I met my wife then, she was a WAVE. I knew I wanted to be a musician after the war so I saved my money. I made $1,100 dollars a month pimping on the West Coast."

"Why didn't you save it? Then you might have some, now," I said, acidly. It was starting to rain.

"Oh, so you're against me? Like all the others. I made $10,000 smuggling silk and then I came to New York. I studied for two years, and then it was gone. I had to work as a stevedore for a summer, but it ruined my hands, so I started to live with women for their money. I'd long since divorced my wife—she was one of those dirty Negroes—she looked down on me."

"Maybe, she didn't like your manners," I murmured. He did not listen.

"I lived with lots of women for their money—black, white, brown, yellow! Any woman! Any woman! I'd do anything for money. I finished my piano studies, and then I found I couldn't get a hearing. My debut cost $2,000 dollars and nothing came of it. The music business is a racket. Almost all the concerts m the U.S. are controlled by trusts that have a flagrant monopoly. It's a crime, the rat-race they've made out of music. These corporations push the artists they want, and leave the rest out on a limb, no matter how good they are."

The rain was pouring now. We took shelter under the awning of a sweet-shop. I said, "I know the music business is hard. It's been difficult for me, too. I wonder why so many young people flock to such an indescribably hard field. Why don't they become doctors or scientists or engineers, instead? Why rush to a path that is horribly overcrowded, and almost hopelessly impossible?"

"By the way, I'll give you my frank opinion of your concert last night. I liked your Mussorgsky and Ravel, but not your first encore. Stay away from the classics. Do you play Beethoven? You do? You shouldn't," he said, angrily.

"I *like* Beethoven."

"He holds too much suffering for you. God, how he suffered. He was a homosexual, you know."

"No, he wasn't."

"He was."

"He was *not,*" I said.

"Yes, he was."

"How do you know? He looked manly."

"I look manly, too, and I'm a homosexual."

"I thought you said you'd had so many women?"

"I'm both. I'll do *anything* for money. The man I'm living with now is paying for all my lessons. He's decided that I should be a singer. I have a wonderful voice. I'm a baritone. He'll see that I get to La Scala when I'm ready."

"Well, I wish you lots of luck. Would you mind if we go now?"

"Yes, I'd mind!"

"I have an appointment."

"Ha! Well give me the $100 before you go."

"No."

"But you promised it to me!"

"I didn't."

"Yes you did," he said furiously. "I'll write and tell your mother you promised me, and I was counting on it, and you let me down!"

I said, "No, goodbye!" and ran down the street, leaving him standing, glaring, under the sweet shop awning. I did not return to the hotel, but took a taxi to the USIS. Mr. Krauss was having a party there. After it was over, he took me to a luxurious apartment where a soirée was being given by an Italian lady, Fabian Sevitsky, whom I had last seen when he directed my "Sodre Symphony" debut in Montevideo, was there, charming as ever, eyes twinkling as he told me amusing anecdotes.

I rode back to Paris on the train, freezing cold, with five other people on the hard uncomfortable beds in the compartment. André Liotard, the explorer, met me at the Gare du Nord, and Georges Apedo-Amah took me to a superb lunch at The Sign of the Club-Foot Queen, the restaurant Anatole France made famous. Then, I grew terribly ill with a throat infection. Yet, this time, I loved Paris. I had gotten the "Paris fever," at last. ⊞

CHAPTER 13

Assault at the Pyramids Around Turkey
On a Scooter, A Concert for Men Only

Egypt, Sudan, Lebanon, Turkey, Jordan:
1955, 1958,

I KNEW THE ISLAMIC WORLD was rich in poetry. Reading the unexpurgated Arabian had filled me with rapt visions of romantic lovers, jeweled palaces, fantastic tale tellers, exotic verse.

The luxurious Abbasside days of Haroun Al-Rashid, genii, and the silver streaking splendor of giant rocs, intrigued me.

When I flew to Egypt in October 1955, I expected miracles to happen.

The trip began badly. After Nice, the plane jolted horribly as the lighting slashed the dark, formless clouds and the rain beat on the ghostly windows. It aroused the most morbid fancies into one, and they were not dispelled when we arrived, at last, at the cheerless Heliopolis airport that serves Cairo.

There was nothing romantic about the bus drive into Cairo.

A bedraggled taxi took me to the Semiramis Hotel. The dark-skinned bell-boys wore baggy red trousers and embroidered red and gold jackets. The desk was much lighter in color.

The next when I awoke in my grey and depressing room, I ordered breakfast, which took nearly two hours to arrive. Then, it was unappetizing, for the green oranges were hard as golf-balls, and the yellow yogurt tasted like rancid camel's milk.

I went out to lunch, to the home of some friends of a vague Hungarian acquaintance of mine. The disintegrating, moldy apartment house, though fairly new, had the secretive air, and musty, crumbly look of so much of Cairo.

My host, Sayed Jamhuryat, was slight, wiry, with a narrow face that seemed all nose. The water he gave me to drink was unboiled, a fact he did not deem necessary to tell me until I had three glasses.

Back at the hotel, I was sicker than ever.

I wandered through the sumptuous dining and reception rooms of the hotel, until I met an Egyptian I had once known in New York. Hussein Bakry Saad, was extremely undersized, thin in his vaguely cut brown suit, and had a hooked nose, brown eyes and pale skin.

Not being a Muslim, he had acid remarks to make about the followers of Islam. "Don't believe Muslims when they say they have no race prejudice. A good white Lebanese family would not let them marry a Sudanese. And the dark-skinned Sudanese are prejudiced against the lighter-skinned one of Egyptian origin. I applied for a job in a Khartoum firm once, and was told contemptuously, 'We do not want you! You are too pale! You are a red man!'"

Sipping from a cup of thick strong coffee, he paused, and continued, "And Islam is riddled with sects, schisms, divisions. While North and Northeast Africa have known Islam for over millennium, West and South Guinea, the Volta and the Southern Sudan were not influenced by it until the nineteenth century. In West Africa, the Islamic veneer is frequently a thin overlay over a more or less animistic base, so it is hard to tell whether people are animistic Muslims, or Muslimistic animists."

"Is it true that Islam offers conflict than Christianity with African modes of thought?" I asked.

He nodded, "Africans are often confused by spiritual standards. Christianity is an obstacle to such key facets of African life as polygamy, the bride-price, and the low position of women. Christianity, in general, opposes female circumcision. Islam is sweeping over Africa like a forest fire. Africa has 2 million Christians, 70 million animists, and 86 million Muslims. There are twenty-two times as many Muslims in Senegal and Mauretania as there are Christians. There are forty-one Muslims for each Christian in Guinea. One-hundred and six Muslims to each Christian in the French Sudan. The ratio is four-hundred and fifty to one in French Niger. Yearly, Muslims increase."

"Why is this? How about the Christian missionaries, who've done so much good?"

"They are too few. What they offer is philosophically strange to the African mind. They are mainly white. Those who proselytize for Islam are mainly colored or black. Also, the primitive animist is full of fears inculcated by the mysterious malice and difficulty of nature around him, fear of the unknown, fears induced by terrifying pagan ceremonies."

"So primitive man is not simple and happy?" I asked.

"He is riddled by terrifying fears. Even a stone, root, or tree incite fears, for it be an evil spirit that must be propitiated. Islam resolves these fears, is simple, direct, easy, and does not demand very profound cogitation. It settles everything. If you perform certain physical acts, then you are good. The soul does not need to be challenged. Islam is taught a legal mode of doing things. Islamic religious and secular law is handed down in writing and is precise."

"What about the spiritually religious aspects as the essence of God and His relationship with man, and man's soul grows within his own personality?"

He ordered another cup of thick brown coffee, lit a Turkish cigarette, and went on, "Those spiritual aspects are and are mostly transmitted orally. Often, in a West African village, one can find an authority on the slightest details or ritual of washing, but can find no one with an exact knowledge of theology. They are more concerned with one's action, than with one's soul-growth in belief. Doing in common with others is more important man one's inner soul. Thus Islam becomes firstly a specialized manner of doing ritual acts, social conventions and refraining from breaking taboos. Often, in West Africa, any ideas about the spirit are to an extent quasi-adapted from previous primitive concepts. There is one tribe where people do not ask, 'Are you a Mahommedan?,' but 'Are you one who performs ritual prayer?' Religion, to an African Muslim, rarely means reflective spiritual development, but, rather, laws of common group-action that rule his life."

"How about Christianity?" I asked.

"Islam soothes the African's fears. Christianity brings new fears; ideal of goodness is so high, how can one reach it? There is guilt over conflict of good and evil. The emphasis on monogamy, the Marian tradition, and dignity of woman, are contrary to what the African male, generally, has been used to."

"What is your religion?"

He lighted another cigarette, settled back in roomy red chair, and "Being liberalized, I do not hold to strict dogmas, but I was born into the Coptic Church, one of Christianity's most ancient forms. Its most significantly different tenet is monophysitism—which says had but one *composite* nature."

"I don't understand."

"Not many do. It repudiates the of Nestorius as strongly as that of Eutyches. The doctrine states Jesus to be one person with one nature formed by indissoluble union between human and divine nature, but that despite this absolute union, the two natures continue to be unconfounded, uncommingled, and distinct, separate yet inseparable. You cannot imagine the blood was once shed over this doctrine. The Copts are now the purest descendants of the ancient Egyptians. Before Islam's coming, Egyptians were almost wholly Christian, divided in two hostile sects—Melkites, and the more numerous monophysites." He went on to tell me at length about Coptic church services.

The next morning, I missed his company when I found out my plane would be over twenty-four hours late. I went to a music store, which also sold bathroom equipment, stoves, refrigerators and vacuums, in a chaotic disarray.

There, I was taken to an upright piano, rickety and untuned in the basement, in a cubicle that smelled of stale urine.

When I finished practicing, I had the sudden inspiration to visit the Sphinx, and Pyramid of Giza.

I took it for granted that it would be illuminated at night, with guards and guides. I hailed a taxi. It was a long drive through the dark city. At one spot, the driver stopped, and a dragoman, whom I had not requested, entered the car.

When we reached the great Pyramid—whose base is 13 acres, and it was not illuminated, except by the dim car lights—we sat alone on the vast expanse of yellow sand, without a trace of guards or guides. I was looking out puzzled, when suddenly, the dragoman grabbed my purse, knocked me out of the car, and the two drove off leaving me stunned by the roadside. I got up.

It was terribly cold and I was very frightened. I reassured myself, recalling all the millions of people who had passed that way since 3700 B.C. Above, the stars blazed coldly, remotely, just as they must have done then.

After an hour of anxious waiting and pacing, I heard a car coming. The driver stopped, surprised. He turned out to be an Englishman. He was most sympathetic and drove me back to Cairo.

I REACHED HELIOPOLIS AIRPORT at 2:00 a.m. Our flight was hours late reaching Khartoum. The heat was broiling a blast furnace there.

A week later, I flew back to Cairo, to spend the night before leaving on a cargo plane for Beirut, at six o'clock in the morning. I awoke at 5:15 a.m.

After taking a taxi halfway to the airport, I found that I had left my passport at the hotel. We raced back, then dashed, tires screaming, to the airport. I arrived, breathlessly, at 5:55 a.m.

The plane was not ready. Two hours later, after immense commotion over my currency declaration that some official had lost, the plane left.

I arrived in Lebanon, to find that six concerts had been arranged for me to play at schools in the next twenty-four hours.

I played four of them, and flew on to Istanbul.

My recital was packed there despite torrential thunder storms.

It was two years before I returned to the Islamic world, still hoping to discover some trace of that romance.

When I arrived in Istanbul in December 1957, Clarin Sommer, Robert College's Music Director, met me at the airport. A tall man, with an earnest, studious, friendly face, he did not seem as if he had been intimidated by Beethoven and Palestrina, nor that he would play football and the harpsichord equally well.

We drove past modern buildings built with American aid, and eventually downtown Istanbul, with its atmosphere of ominous mystery and silent grey houses with sparse narrow windows. The people on the streets were dressed in clothes as fashionable, and modern as those of Paris or Milan, but they seemed depressed, and unhappy, though they would have preferred the fierce days of the Seljukian and Ottoman Empires.

Clarin Sommer, his sandy hair glinting like a shy sunbeam in the twilight, said, "It's a good thing you came now, I'm leaving next year."

"Where will you go?"

"Kidron, Ohio."

"How could you think of leaving this marvelous, history-laden place?"

"It's inconvenient sometimes. You can't always get things."

"But Christian Byzantium was here, Empress Theodora, the Sublime Porte, the Grand Seraglio!"

"But when it comes to having a photograph developed, you have to go to Beirut to get a really good job."

We passed trams clattering noisily on the steep hills, and more slit-like somber grey houses. Soon we reached Robert College, in Rumeli-Hissar Village.

I was given a clinically bare hospital patient's room in the infirmary. Its sharp odor of chemicals and disinfectants reminded me of the chemistry laboratory where I had dressed for my first Istanbul concert, in 1955.

My two concerts in the Assembly were well-attended. The long brown hall was filled with handsome students, proud and hawk-faced, with a classic masculinity.

The next day, I went with several teachers to a performance of Sheridan's "The Rivals," at the girls' college, a short distance away.

The hall was packed with female students when we arrived, all beautiful, one of the most stunning assemblages I have ever seen.

The play commenced, enthusiastically acted, without the faintest conception of style. It was presented as a ponderous and terrifying melodrama.

The next day, Clarin drove me throughout Istanbul, and the surrounding villages on his Vespa motor scooter.

When we reached the fortress of Rumeli-Hissar, built by 6,000 workmen in forty days, after the subjugation of Byzantium in 1453 by Mehmed the Conqueror, I climbed up from the base where restorations were in process, to the highest ramparts of the mammoth stone walls. It was a magnificent edifice. Once chains had been stretched between it and the similar fortress on the opposite side of the Bosphorus, to impede the passage of any ship down the strait until tribute was paid.

The Blue Mosque in Istanbul was splendid too. As it was a State Museum, females might enter. It had immense vaulting arches, elaborate filigree-work, tiles in every subtle, sensuous shade of blue: azure, turquoise, and sapphire. A few worshiping men knelt on carpets, Mecca.

Then we saw the Obelisk brought Egypt by Theodosius, the Sancta Sophia, the Cistern of 1001 Columns, the Imperial Gate, and the Seraglio Museum.

Once 1,600 women had lived in Seraglio, never leaving except for an occasional ride in a closed boat or carriage. If a strange male entered the Seraglio, he was flayed alive, and his hide nailed to the wall. As it was forbidden for a loud noise to be made there, conversation was mostly whispered, and if a slave dared drop a plate during the Sultan's dinner, he was beheaded, for he had made a noise.

Later, I noticed that with many Egyptian and Sudanese friends who had been raised during the period of Turk influence, they spoke so softly I could hardly hear them, and they were always rebuking me for talking too loud.

Before leaving, I had dinner at Clarin Sommer's home: Turkish *kilic,* or grilled swordfish with bay leaves, rice with pine nuts, *borek* pastry with parsley and white cheese. Through the dusky windows, we watched the purple fall of night on ancient Propontis.

ON DECEMBER 19, I FLEW TO BEIRUT, LEBANON, once one of the Phoenician Coast's most ancient settlements, and famous in the fourth-century for its school of law, to which students from throughout the Roman Empire flocked.

It is still an outstanding educational center.

"Lebanon," deriving from the Semitic "laban," meaning "white," has many religious groups: Maronite Christians, Orthodox Catholics, Greek Uniates, Sunnite and Shiite Muslims. The most unique are the Druzes, who believe in one incomprehensible, passionless God, appearing in successive reincarnation; as do people, who, when good, are reborn in increasing perfection, and, when bad, sink to camels or dogs. The Muhwaddin, as they call themselves, use both the Gospels and the Kiran as scriptures, and are non-polygamous. Hakim Biamrillahi founded the creed in the eleventh-century.

After my concert, I stayed at the beautifully furnished modern Alumni Club. Often I visited Nedko Etinoff, of the American University's Music Department, and his Armenian wife, Anniki, who prepared wonderful meals. She introduced me to white Bulgarian cheese, the most luscious cheese in the world, and a thin Lebanese bread made in such immensely long sheets that I thought at first it was a tablecloth.

The fruits and vegetables were splendid, for nothing in the world can compare with the juicy taste of Lebanese fruits. The apples were juicy as grapes, lettuce luscious and savory, carrots delectable, and juicy plums.

Mrs. Etinoff had a gay, jovial personality, and was always laughing. What might seem a catastrophe to others, was taken philosophically by her.

She said many refugees of the Turkish massacre of the Armenians were still living in Beirut, "But, you know, no matter how poor, their places are always spotlessly clean, and they always have a musical instrument. Each house with a musical instrument! They love music! You will find all over Africa, if there are any Armenians in a place, they will come to your concerts en masse."

With a Philippine engineer, Armando Navarrete, I visited the ruins of Byblos on December 21. As we drove through the teeming streets of Beirut with their contrast of modern and ancient, I could not believe that this peaceful setting had been the scene a century ago, of a massacre of the Christians, with thousands slaughtered by the Druzes and other Muslim factions. We left the city and to our left was the transparent Mediterranean, glinting grey and gold in the dazzling sweep of the sun's brilliance. The air was sharp as wine. We passed an old Roman bridge, and then reached Byblos, from which our word "Bible" comes. We saw Phoenician, Assyrian, Greek, Arab and early Christian ruins. On the summit of an old Arab castle, swept by the winds, one could gaze at the crumbled Roman theatre below and the faraway villages, and feel the brevity of man as compared to his antiquity.

Back in Beirut, I saw many breathtaking beauties in the streets. Only some older women were veiled. Of course, in Istanbul, one never saw a veiled woman. What shocked me about Khartoum, the Muslim city I visited next, was that I saw no women at all, veiled or otherwise. Oh, one caught sight of some English, Greek, Syrian and Armenian girls, but not a Sudanese woman!

Only males were in the hotel, streets, restaurants, and at my concert. The nightclub had a few stale weary European hostesses.

There are some pagans in the southern Sudan who are free. And, elsewhere, the Beja tribe, formerly Christian in the Middle Ages, has retained much of a woman's former status.

Being alone among thousands of men is fascinating at first, then appalling, for social situations become formidably difficult.

One party I attended had thirty men, and the only women was an English woman besides myself. She and I sat in a corner attempting to be unnoticeable, while the men told jokes, drank heavily, and danced with each other. I created a scandal at this affair because, having been invited by one man, I had come escorted by another, and, while there, had spoken to a third.

The center of social life in Khartoum, which means "Elephant's Trunk," is the Sudan Cultural Center, where young men spend evenings playing games, chatting, drinking *limon,* and listening to poetry readings.

Many are exceptionally handsome mixtures of Arab, Nubian, and Negro. Some are well-educated, fluent in verbalized self-expression and magnificent "non-truth" tellers. The long tradition of Arab poetry and fantastic tale-telling, gives them a natural tendency to poetically embroider what they say. Perhaps they sometimes feel that beautiful speech is such a great art in itself that it does not have to relate to the dross of reality.

Too, they tend, if educated, to have inferiority complexes about the backwardness of their country and the Arab world in general. When I asked them pertinent questions, they either closed up tighter than clamshells, told marvelous "non-truths," mingled part-truth with part half-truth and utter lie, or alternative truth and lie about the same thing.

Always, they began by telling me how they adored European classic music, particularly my renditions. In the intermediate stage, they still claimed they adored it, but always managed to be absent if I threatened to play some. In the stage, they DID NOT like it AT ALL.

One, Hajj El-Malik, began by gushing to me about his enthusiastic love for America. He wasn't a Communist, not he! Later, it appeared he was a "socialist." Still later, he said in triumph, "Why I can't stand America! I hate the West, everything about the West! I am as red as that apple behind you! Of course I'm Communist!" He spoke with the gentle look of a caged rhinoceros.

Zaid Ahmed was the same. So was Mahmoud Al-Jawhar and Abdel Hisab Badri. They were all the same.

I got to know Muhammad Hussein Keddad well. He was golden-skinned, with wiry black hair. Though his suits never quite seemed to fit him, his ties had a way of looking poetic.

Eloquently, he spoke of his sensitivity, idealism, belief in women's rights. When I knew him better he began to speak fiercely about how, "Our girls do *not* really want freedom! Our girls are good Arab girls!"

As we passed the Nile Bridge one evening, I asked him what was surely a harmless question, "What are your sister's names?"

Wincing, as if he had been struck, and was seeking to flee, he finally muttered, almost inaudibly, "Why should I tell you that?"

"Well, why not?"

"I choose not to. Wherever I am, I must be master! I must be master! You are not circumcised. They are circumcised!"

With angry, bull-dog tenacity, I said, "You'd better tell me. I want to know!"

Silently, he cogitated, then muttered, "Amina, Zobe," but his voice trailed into the sand, and I could not hear the rest.

When we reached the Omar Khayyam Restaurant, we entered an inner room with exotic Arabian Nights carpets, couches, trays and inlaid tables. We ate some steaming *durra*, while he drank the banana beer.

At length I asked, "Do your sisters go to school?"

He said coldly, "They went for four years, but then they were removed so they could stay at home like good Sudanese girls!"

"Don't you plan to train them for a profession?" I asked.

"No! Why should I? A good Sudanese girl stays at home!"

"I guess you do not believe in woman's freedom as in England or Sweden."

"I find woman's freedom in West LOATHSOME!"

The next day, as we passed the juncture of the Blue and White Niles, he told me he had been poor and had to work hard to rise. An hour later, he said he was connected with "the ninety-nine noblest families of the country." An hour afterwards, he informed me, "My brothers are all doctors and lawyers," and elaborated on that impressively.

Yet, as we were about to visit an open-air cinema that evening, he said, "You know, my brothers are all illiterate." As we left the cinema, he told me, "You play for kings and queens, but I am really like a prince! A prince!"

That night we played some chess on a traveling chess set I had bought in London. I won the first game. He did not like that. "Well, only reason you're winning is that your set is so peculiar!"

"How?" I asked.

"Why, you call that piece a Queen. We do not have a Queen on our chess-boards here. That piece we call a Minister. No Queen is on our boards!"

As we returned to the Grand Hotel, passing rows of beautiful sausage-trees, I asked, "How is it so few books on the Sudan have been published in America? I'd love to write something on your country. Would you help? I would be sympathetic." But it seemed he could not demean himself by collaboration with a woman.

Once Sir Hubert Huddleston, a former Sudan Governor-General, wrote, "The lag in the emergence of a healthy and balanced community (in Sudan)...is due in general to the inferior position of women, and in particular to their forcible subjection to the harmful practice of pharaonic circumcision."

In 1951, Michael Langley wrote, in *No Woman's Country*:

> The lives of Sudanese women are grim...they look like dispirited drudges. Marriage in the Sudan was always a wearisome ordeal them...Man's possessive hold, and the dominant status of the male is maintained...Female circumcision is as common in the Northern Sudan as tonsillectomy in Britain...it renders woman's part dead passive...Sudanese girls are mutilated at an age when European girls are trotted off to first communions...the most disagreeable country in the world in which to be born a woman.

There was something about golden sand, turquoise sky, and deep Nile waters, though, that fascinated me.

My recital for "Men only," of course was well attended.

I looked forward to revisiting the city.

AT THE BEGINNING OF 1959, I was on my way back to the Near East and Northeast Africa. Would I get to Beirut in time?

That was the question that kept haunting me throughout that long, agonizing twenty-four hour journey across Asia on January 16.

The BOAC plane had been twenty-four hours late leaving Kuala Lumpur. I was supposed to have had a radio concert with a studio audience on Friday, the 16th. It was too late for that now. I had wired to postpone it Saturday morning. But would I get there?

I fidgeted nervously in my seat.

An Englishman, who was seated next to me, asked, "'What's the matter? Are you upset about something?"

"Yes! My concert!" I explained the whole story.

"Well, it's just bad luck. They'll survive it. Maybe you've had a hex put on you."

"Oh, nonsense!"

"No, it's not nonsense. These things happen. They go on all the time. I could tell you a story about a friend of mine in Singapore that would make your hair stand on end."

"Go ahead and tell me. I'd like to see my stand on end."

"Well, this friend of mine, Arthur Rogerson, worked for a big commercial company in Singapore. He'd been out in the Far East all of his life in India, New Zealand, Hong Kong, and Shanghai. He'd knocked around a lot, and he'd been in some pretty isolated places for a while. He'd picked up some 'undesirable' habits, too. He hadn't seen any reason not to, but they hadn't caused him any trouble because he'd always been very discreet. A close-mouthed chap. It was rare that he would open up and tell you anything."

"Now, he came to Singapore and that's such a congested place that people know a lot about everyone pretty soon. A rumor, just a little small rumor, but an evil, insinuating one wound its way to the knowledge of the heads of his company. They gave him the advice, discretely couched — of course a velvet glove sort of thing — that it would be wise for him to get married, and soon."

"He'd never wanted to lose his freedom, and settle down, but shortly afterwards at a party one evening, he met a Dutch girl, from Sumatra. Jouck van der Speelaans had been born in Indonesia, and lived all her life there, except for one brief period at school in Holland, which she had hated. She loved the color and life of the Orient and was miserable in the rainy cold of Amsterdam. But now her father had been in all the trouble and strife in Indonesia, and she was forced to leave. She had come to Singapore to visit for two weeks and then take the next boat to Holland."

"Since Arthur and Jouck both had a motive in their minds, it didn't take their engagement plans long to develop. He invited her for a drive the morning after they met. Four days later, he proposed, and she accepted. Jouck had desperately wanted to avoid going back to Holland, this seemed like a godsend to her. In two and a half weeks they were married. They went to Rangoon for their honeymoon, and then came back and settled in Arthur's villa in Singapore."

"Arthur kept off his old ways for quite a while, then, little by little, he slipped back. He had an affection for his wife, but she was too new, too recent. He'd had his other pattern of life for too long. He was used to it and, what's more, he liked it."

"Jouck was a little bewildered at first at his gradual disinterest in her, but she didn't know what to make of it. She attributed it to business cares."

"Arthur had now developed quite an attraction for Ali Yusof Kedah, his new houseboy. Ali hesitated some time before giving in to Arthur's desires, but this was not due to any great wrestling with conscience, but rather, it was the crafty longing to Arthur's passion to its height through suspense and uncertainty. Ali did not really care one way or another, it gave him an ego — the satisfaction to be wanted. Anyhow, Ali saw the possibility of getting lots of money out of Arthur, which could pay for the future education of Ali's younger brother, Abdul, so Abdul would not have to be a houseboy like Ali."

"Ali gave in to Arthur, and for a while, all was tranquil. Arthur was happy, Ali was happy and, was no more unhappy than before. She had no idea what was going on."

"After some months, Ali suddenly began to refuse himself to Arthur. He made no explanation, but withdrew into Asian secretiveness and mystery. Arthur was stunned. He was fifty now, an age when one takes things less lightly. He was losing his hair and his figure, and the years of tropical climates had made him somewhat weatherbeaten. Ali was twenty, small, lithe and dark, with fine eyes, and jet black hair, and a smooth amber-colored skin. Arthur could not stand reception. It wounded his ego mortally. It shocked him to the core of his being."

"One night, he tried to assault Ali, but it didn't work. He was too old. After that, he fancied that Ali stared at him with a sly secret contempt."

"Arthur went to a Chinese seer to ask the reason for all this. The seer was bent and old, with a skin like dried parchment and two little beady eyes like old raisins. He drew figures in sand, and threw six ivory sticks with Chinese characters painted on them into the air, and noted the patterns in which they fell. He told Arthur, after the most evasions, that Ali was in love with someone else."

"Then Arthur went to a Malay sorcerer. He had a sorcerer cast a spell to drive Ali away from this new object of his affections. The sorcerer asked for 20 pounds, but assured him that there was no doubt they would work, within a month."

"At first, Arthur counted the days but a new shock came and nearly drove him out of his senses with grief. His wife went on a visit to Penang province, and, a few days after her return, came down with malaria. She'd had it several times before, without too drastic results, but this time she grew sick and, despite medical care, became more violently ill, and died. Despite the harrowing strain of the illness, she still looked young and childlike against the pink pillows of the bed, just after her death. Her blond hair and delicate complexion were like a little girl's."

"Arthur had two more shocks the next morning. The servants seemed to have disappeared. He woke up to an empty house. He had the body moved to a funeral home the night before. Now he was completely alone. He had always said he liked solitude better than anything. Now he had it, but it was desolate and forlorn."

"For lack of anything else to do, he opened the seventeenth century ivory-inlaid secretary his wife had brought with her from Indonesia and began to go through her papers. In a hidden drawer at the back that he had not noticed before, he found a pile of letters. They were appalling."

"Most of them of them were from Ali Yusof Kedah. They were ardent, passionate terms that made clear that Ali and Jouck had a flaming love affair. Arthur had never had the faintest intimation of this. It had commenced at the same time that Arthur and Ali had been in love, and Arthur had been dropped! And Ali had also been getting money out of Jouck, 'for Abdul's education'!

"Arthur was stunned. He was totally crushed. In fact one morning he aged ten years. In a few days he came down with brain fever, and was desperately ill for many months."

I said then, "Yes go on! I want to hear the rest!"

"But that's all," the Englishman said. "It's over."

"But where was the hex?" I asked.

"Don't you see? His own wife died of it."

"What happened to Arthur, then?"

"Oh, don't know I lost track of him," he replied vaguely.

Soon, the lights over the door flashed, "Fasten Seat Belts." The overhead lights came on, glaring strongly. A voice said, "We are preparing to land in Karachi."

We landed. We stayed there about an hour. New passengers boarded, Pakistanis and a few Europeans. The plane rose in the air. After fifteen minutes, another Englishman, about fifty-five, came up the aisle, and stopped by my companion, saying, "Why Alfred! Wonderful to see you. This is a surprise. We were so sorry to hear your wife died." Alfred rose hurriedly, muttered something incomprehensible, and escaped to the men's room. When he emerged, much later, he took another seat, in the rear.

Rough weather came up, shaking the plane to and fro like a dead fish on a storm-tossed sea. It was a clear cold dawn in Beirut.

One of the pilots drove me to the Etinoff's house, through the peaceful, sleepy city whose calm belied the violence of recent months. En route, I gazed at the Arabic script on walls and placards, trying to decipher it. When we reached the street on which the Etinoff's lived, the shutters of the shops were still closed. Mr. and Mrs. Etinoff were standing on their balcony, looking down on the street, waiting for my appearance. As soon as they saw me, Mr. Etinoff came down and brought my bags out of the car and up to their second-story flat.

I came up too, weary, but happy to be with people I had known for four years, and whom I knew to be dependable.

Mr. Etinoff lighted a kerosene stove standing in front of their piano, to make me a little warmer, and asked me about my trip. After I had told them some stories, I asked him, "How are things in your classes at the American University?"

"Oh, fine, fine," he said. "But don't let me keep you talking. You'd better come and eat something. Mr. Garth will be here in a few minutes to take you to record the radio broadcast this evening. They were distressed that you couldn't get here yesterday so they've made a special place for your music this afternoon. You'll be the first American artist they've had over Radio Liban."

Mr. Garth was an American, hearty, portly and amiable. He said, beaming and cheerful, "Well! Isn't it nice to see you. You'll have to go to Jordan this afternoon, you know. You have a sold-out house in Jerusalem tonight!"

"Tonight! But I didn't know anything about it!"

"You didn't? Well, they're all looking forward to your coming."

He took me to an office building to make the recording. First, I had to spend an hour fixing the pedals of the worn ancient piano. The handsome Lebanese engineers accepted this delay with the patience born of four thousand years of recorded history.

It was hard to keep my eyes open while I recorded, for I had been thirty-six hours without sleep or a full meal.

When I finished, I bought an air ticket for Jerusalem at the bright modern offices of Air Jordan.

JERUSALEM WAS BEAUTIFUL. Its ocher sand had serenity, the clear sky the sharp brilliance of a blue diamond.

Camels, horses, donkeys, and sharp-nosed burnous-covered men thronged the dry, dusty streets.

I went directly to the recital hall. It was packed.

The next morning, after a few hours of sleep, I drove to the airport. Then I remembered I had left my passport at the hotel. Someone drove back fast to get it for me. He returned just in time for me to board the plane. I got to Beirut at ten in the morning. I had lunch with the Etinoffs. Then I visited the botanical gardens.

At two that afternoon, I flew to Cairo, where a journalist, Ramez Halawani, drove me through the city. He was the handsomest young man I had ever seen.

Cairo had changed since my last visit.

It looked more hopeful, clean, bright and modern.

Khartoum looked different, too.

I flew to "Elephant's Trunk" the same day, arriving shortly after midnight. It was penetratingly cold there as it had been in Cairo. My teeth shook with chill. This was usually one of the hottest spots on earth. Mohammed, a chief's son, met me there. He had arranged a concert for me. Also, he treated me to wonderful hospitality throughout my stay. There are young men in the Sudan now, educated abroad, who are not part of the old order of inflexible orthodoxy.

But the majority are on the other side so it will be a long time before the old order changes.

This time, I visited Omdurman, quite different from Khartoum. What I saw seemed mostly dried mud buildings.

In the *suq,* or market, marvelous ivory-work, and the heaviest gold jewelry I had ever seen was sold.

Two old women, wearing ancient heavy black veils, scampered through its dusty streets.

At Khartoum's University, I was actually introduced to six girls, but they did not say anything to me. I was told that educational facilities for women were constantly improving, that there were now four girls' schools in the entire country, and twenty-four girl students at the University. And I was thrilled to discover that there were now five public libraries in the Sudan.

Everyone treated me beautifully. I was showered with hospitable invitations.

Yet, people were warmly courteous up to a point, and then it all stopped. The veil was dropped, mysteriousness was resumed, they suddenly vanished. I became so imbued with their psychology that I almost turned into a Sudanese girl myself. One night, going to a party at a diplomat's house, I wore my most concealing dress, and wrapped a long veil around me.

To my surprise, I met another woman there, who had just arrived in Khartoum. After I had talked to her for some time, she said, "I am monopolizing you. Why don't you talk to some of those nice young men over there?"

"Oh, no! I could not do that!" I replied instinctively. "I could not go and sit with the men! They would think I was a harlot!"

Hussein Rashad said to me, "Never in her life has my mother gone to sit with the men! Even if you asked her to sit with the men she would not go!"

"Are you kidding?" she asked, puzzled.

"No. I am not. If I go and talk to those men they will think me a harlot."

"But, you're an American girl! You'd better get out of here before you fade away."

In two days I left for Ruanda-Urundi.

But it was some time before I could get used to seeing Belgian men and women eating together in the restaurant in Usumbura. ✠

CHAPTER 14

Champagne with the Emperor
Ethiopia: 1955, 1957

D URING 1954'S SUMMER, I HAD A SURPRISE.
Emperor Haile Selassie of Ethiopia and entourage visited America.
Among them was the Dejazmach Amaha Aberra.

A Hungarian, Mr. Feuer, who had business interests in Ethiopia, telephoned us to suggest we entertain the Dejazmach—a title that might be translated as "Prince"—at a private banquet with only twelve distinguished, hand-picked guests.

We made elaborate preparations.

The guests were important.

The *viandis* were sumptuous.

Everything was wonderful.

Except the Dejazmach did not arrive.

This is an Ethiopian custom.

At 8:00 p.m. we were cheerful. At 9:00 p.m. we were puzzled. By 10:00 p.m., we were anxious. The lettuce had wilted, the sherbet melted, the salad was stale.

The guests stared poisonously at empty space.

My father feebly told bad jokes at which no one laughed.

My mother hovered at the door.

Mr. Feuer sat, grinning in a corner, as though something were terribly funny.

At midnight, the guests left.

Two days later, the Dejazmach came.

He suavely entered, superbly dressed, smiling slightly to show perfect white teeth. He regretted, he explained, to be a little late, but he had been detained by a sudden business appointment.

With flawless grace, he sat and condescended to be served.

He had an austere profile. He was completely perfect, as we saw him, and His Imperial Majesty's grandson, on other occasions.

The Dejazmach, whose skin had the golden tint of a sunbeam on a Coptic Church spire, with deep brown eyes that were beautiful but not revealing, and a voice that vibrated with rich yet aloof modulations, corresponded with me when he left the U.S.

To my surprise, it was reported in several gossip columns that I was in love with the Dejazmach. One article improved on this by stating I was about to marry His Imperial Majesty's grandson, while another hinted I was about to elope with the Emperor's son. Yet, I had not said a word to anyone about the Dejazmach.

The pale, gnomish Mr. Feuer seemed to have vanished. I could not find him. Wonderingly, I called his office, and was told he was in Addis Ababa, not to return for a year.

A week later, he telephoned me. I asked, "When did you get back?"

"Back? I have not been anywhere," he replied.

The next week, I got a clipping in the mail:

> The Cats say hotcha Prince X is
> goin' it strong for that box-thumping
> chick. No bear she! Dig them dice!

I tried to phone Mr. Feuer, but was not able to reach him for six weeks. Then he called and said, "Ah! Since I spoke to you I have been to Ethiopia five times to inaugurate a new air company."

"Will you take me over on it?"

"Oh, you see, it is only for cargo. I must give my stockholders a sixty percent dividend each month."

His voice held a warm purr.

WHEN I ARRIVED IN ADDIS ABABA in November 1955, Mr. Feuer was at the airport to meet me, with Mr. and Mrs. Ingalls, my hosts.

He gave the airport officials instructions to forward my bag whenever Ethiopian Airlines should discover it in what city they had dumped it.

Then we drove off, and went to the Ingalls home.

Their two blond cocker spaniels and pet spider were at the door waiting to greet us.

Later, I dressed in a gold lame gown for the reception they were giving that night. I was cold. I plugged in my electric heater. It blew all the lights out.

The reception was scheduled for 7:00 p.m. The electricity was not fixed by 8:00 p.m. It did not matter, because the guests did not arrive until nine that evening.

There were many Ethiopians. It was an honor that they came.

Among them was an extremely dignified-looking lady, whom Mr. Feuer told me was Princess Kallamork, a woman general, who had led a section of His Majesty's troops against the Italians during their Ethiopian invasion, and who had later been raised to the rank of Princess by His Majesty as a reward. The Dejazmach came, too. He arrived before midnight.

He sat beside me.

He looked at me.

This was interpreted by everyone as being extra significant.

Great comment arose in Addis Ababa about this.

The next day, there was a luncheon in my honor, at a beautiful outdoor patio at a house I shall not identify. But everyone forgot to come.

Only Mr. Feuer and the Dejazmach were there. We sat under a white umbrella in the garden, with blue delphiniums, and a servant named Guiorguis served us with *enjerra* and *wot* sauce. The *enjerra* was flat grey millet-bread in long thin sheets like sliced sponges. The *wot* was burning pepper-sauce. We also had *chai,* or tea.

Mr. Feuer looked at me with elfin smiles throughout, as though musing on airy intrigues and puckish plots. The Dejazmach spoke briefly about the Monophysitism of his Coptic religion.

Later, Mr. Feuer drove me to the Armenian Club.

En route, he said, "Aha! So the Dejazmach speaks to you? Do you know what that means? Ah, that means a great deal. Aha!"

We passed juniper and eucalyptus trees. The pure mountain air was clear and cold.

Mr. Feuer added quizzically, "Do you know that I am ninth-rate? And therefore must surround myself with first-rate people. Do you see? Do you?"

We stopped, entered a gateway, got out. We climbed to the second floor. The director of the Armenian Club led us to an ancient piano. A gnarled, bowed upright, half-toothless, by which I mean the keys were not there.

"What's this?" I asked.

"Your instrument for tonight's concert. We tried to get a grand, but the last time somebody lent us one, we couldn't get it up the steps. We lifted it by a rope through the window. The rope broke. The piano crashed. It was ruined. So now no one will lend us a grand piano."

There was an overflowing crowd of Armenians at the concert that night.

They gave me blue delphiniums, and an Ethiopian silver bracelet with silver Amharic lettering, at the close.

The next morning I missed my plane to Nairobi.

I was ready to go, but some people came to me and said the plane had been grounded in Asmara so it would not be going anywhere. I had no access to a telephone, or transportation to the city. There were no houses around where anyone spoke English. No taxis cruised in the vicinity. I was isolated and helpless. Stranded.

I missed my concert in Nairobi. I sent them a cable. I wrote letters and letters explaining. They never forgave me there.

The next day, I had a concert at the YMCA, at 8:00 p.m.

That morning, it was hinted to me that His Imperial Majesty would like to see me at noon. At noon it was insinuated that he would see me at 2:00 p.m. At two that afternoon, it was implied that he would see me at 4:00 p.m.

At 4:00 p.m., nothing was said.

At 6:30 p.m., I was told that the Command Performance was definitely scheduled for 8:30 p.m. I must not be a moment late, or it would "Grave Displeasure."

They did not care that I had a sold out house waiting for my concert at 8:00 p.m. This did not concern them.

Ambassador Simonson asked the palace to please allow me to play forty-five minutes for the audience of plebeians. Condescendingly, this was given.

I began my concert at YMCA five minutes early. I played without stops. No intermission. I sped from piece to piece. Then an arm waved violently, like a witch's wand, from the wings. It was Mr. Feuer. Time to go.

The Ambassador got up and made a brief speech to the audience explaining a Command Performance had come. Then, he dashed from the hall. Mrs. Simonson followed. I dashed, Mr. Feuer dashed. Mr. Ingalls dashed. Mr. David, a newspaperman, dashed too.

We raced to the cars. We leapt in. We sped to the Palace. We jumped out.

Into the luxurious halls of the Palace we were led. We waited half an hour in an anteroom. Then we were led to a mysterious closed door. Mr. Feuer, Mr. Ingalls, and Mr. Talbot were told they must stand outside and wait. They could not come in for they had not been invited.

I was wearing a diamond lavallière and a blue chiffon and black chantilly lace gown with skirts.

When I entered, with and the Ambassador and Mrs. Simonson, we curtsied three times to Empress Menen and the Lion of Judah Emperor Haile Selassie, who sat surrounded by many members of the Imperial family, on two high thrones.

The piano was a black Bechstein. Beginning with the "A Minor Bach-Liszt Prelude" and "Fugue," I played for over an hour, after which His Imperial Majesty pinned two medals on me, one silver, one solid gold.

Then sitting on Louis Quinze chairs, I conversed at length about Ethiopian music with the younger members of the Imperial Family. They were warm, cordial, and all were very attractive, with large eyes, golden skin, and classic features. They all wore formal, well-cut evening clothes, as did Their Majesties. Empress Menen wore a maroon silk gown. Emperor Haile Selassie wore several of his medals. The Emperor had sharp, noble features, and an expression of farseeing dignity and grave meditation that was both ancient and modern. Perhaps Menelik I, the son of Solomon and Sheba, had this same austere, aristocratic strength, keen yet refined. It was an expression that mingled the sands of Israel and Southern Arabia, with the mountains and craggy ravines of Ethiopia. The remoteness of Laka Tana and the Blue Nile were there, as was the blazing vastness of the Danakil Desert. The Emperor looked like a man who would never be defeated, who would always remain the master of every situation a wise eagle who flew above the mass of common humanity, yet could descend when he chose.

I felt strangely humble and filled with admiration in his presence.

After the sumptuous champagne banquet, I left.

Mr. Feuer, Mr. Ingalls, and Mr. Talbot were still standing outside, waiting. As we departed, I was handed a discreet envelope with a check from His Majesty.

The Ambassador, Mr. Simonson, and his wife, took me to the airport when I left the next morning. I thought him one of the nicest American Ambassadors I had ever met.

IN DECEMBER 1957, I FLEW BACK to Addis Ababa, and was met at the airport by Mr. Talbot, and Mr. Bishop, director of the YMCA.

My practice keyboard was confiscated at the airport.

Mr. Bishop had to argue three hours to get it back for me. He went to officials, supervisors of officials, and superiors of superiors. He explained that it was my tool.

He insisted desperately that, like a carpenter, I would be helpless without it. He promised them tickets to my concerts if they would relent. Finally, he won.

I celebrated Christmas with Merlin Bishop and his wife.

It was one of the nicest Christmases I have known. We sang carols and hymns and rejoiced. Ethiopia is one of the world's oldest Christian nations. It was converted to Coptic Christianity in 340 A.D. by Saint Frumentius. Menelik II united the divergent sections of the country in the nineteenth-century. Now its territory, including Eritrea, is 398,350 square miles.

Mr. Bishop was a man with the real Christian spirit, who loved people better than things, and believed in unity with all humanity.

He was white, with an amiable face. He was born a poor boy in the deep South, in Georgia, I believe. He had terrible struggles to get an education many more fortunate people take for granted, but he never resented this, or became bitter. Rather, it gave him more sympathy for all humanity.

In an issue of *Ebony Magazine*, I gave my specifications for the "Ideal Man." Many people wrote me and said a man like that couldn't exist. Yes, he can. He is Mr. Bishop. I was describing my impression of Mr. Bishop, and were I to meet a man like him, I would marry him at once. He had spent seven years in Addis Ababa, following twenty-five years as a missionary where he met his wife, who was born there.

My first concert was at the magnificent Haile Selassie I Theatre. All the Armenians were at the concert, but only six Ethiopians came, Dejazmaches, brought by Dejazmach Amaha Aberra.

The next day, Afewerk Teklé, a young man in his early twenties, took me to his home to see his paintings. Ethiopia's most outstanding artist, he was trained in Europe as well as his homeland, and has a spiritual penetration far beyond his years. One picture, the skinless multicolored face of a man, seemed to evoke the moaning anguish of modern humanity.

His other paintings had an El Greco mysticism that translated to the Coptic religiosity of the Amhara. The eyes gazed upwards with a delicate, sad faith, a pellucid mirroring of the tears, doubts and resignation of devotion, luminous sweet innocence mingled with a tormented yearning for regeneration. Suffering was there, and death and gentle grace, and elusive shining happiness in the splendor of God.

I found here the soul of Ethiopia, one of the most religious nations I had ever visited, where mysticism was not tainted by the skepticism of the twentieth century, there were no buts as to whether saints and miracles can or cannot exist, but rather an unstudied crystal-clear acceptance of the wonders and glories of Divine Justice and the Spirit. ⊞

CHAPTER 15
King Mutesa and I
Uganda: 1957, 1958

ON JANUARY 3, 1958, at eleven-thirty that morning, I should have left Khartoum.

But they said, "Plane is seven hours late. Go to bed. We will call you one hour before plane departure, so you will have time to get ready."

I went to bed.

At five-thirty in the morning, there was a pounding on the door. "Plane in ten minutes!" Like a tornado, I rushed around the room, packing. In seven minutes I was en route to the airport.

It was noon when my plane arrived at Entebbe, Uganda.

"You'll have to pay 200 pounds in order to take this into the country!" the Hindu customs official declared as he tried to confiscate my keyboard. He could not believe I was a professional musician. I had to empty my concert programs out of my suitcase to convince him.

Entebbe is 3,761 feet above sea level, so I did not feel the blazing dry heat until I was in the car, en route to Kampala. Then I was driven 84 more miles to Masaka, to the home of Mr. Basudde, a wealthy planter.

Mr. Basudde had a high domed forehead, with cocoa-brown skin. His wife was the prettiest girl I saw in Uganda.

Joseph Kyagambiddwa, their house guest, was a thoroughly trained musician who was trying to record and transcribe Baganda music in its pristine, uncontaminated form, lest European influence corrupt its purity. Chocolate in color, he had an innocent expression that made one feel he really loved his neighbor and believed all men were good.

Joseph Kyagambiddwa and Mr. Basudde drove me, the next morning, to the St. Thomas Aquinas Seminary. The tall, sharp, grass grew over the path leading there, so our car had to mow it down as we went. We arrived late, having taken two hours for fifty miles. The mass had already begun, so we softly entered the church on tip-toes and knelt in the back. The monks and priests were singing a Gregorian chant with a beatific, antique purity, their faces inspired with faith and reverence.

Due to the heat, and my exhaustion, I felt faint before the end and was taken out into a separate small house to recover. One of the brothers stood guard over me there, "I must watch you to be sure nothing happens. The river is only a few yards away, and frequently a hippopotamus will come up here, knock on the doors of the monastery and try to come in."

In half an hour I was taken outside, and I found that all the monks and priests had on a grassy knoll, to sing Baganda music especially for me. Their black faces against their long white robes were serene, devout, and spiritual.

First they sang, "Obusolu Bwa Lubale," or "God's Little Animals." Then they sang, in melodious, rich voices:

> Basiba embuzi mwesimye:
> Ezango zalya akawulula.
> Abantu balamu bankyaye,
> Lubale waggulu alinjagala.
>
> You owners of goats are happy!
> Mine ate poisoned grass!
> Ah, the living people hate me,
> The God above will me.

These songs were sung a capella, and like all Baganda music, were Pentatonic in scale, each tone 1-1/5 tones from the next.

Now Mr. Joseph Kyagambiddwa, a graduate of Manhattanville College of the Sacred Heart in New York, rose to conduct the choir and explained to me, "Now we, dear Miss Philippa Schuyler, will commence, that is, we shall, shall we not, indeed begin to sing more elaborate, more intricate songs, or shall we call them choral odes? Odes, yes, Miss Philippa, odes of expression of ideas more deep, or is profound the word? Historical ideas are heard here, with structure more weightful, more serious, is it not so? Soon, soon we sing for you 'Wanderers,' an odic song of Galla peoples marching down from Ethiopia, southward, to become great Ganda people here. Oh heavens, spectators of centuries, speak and tell us what you saw? Did you see cities become deserts and routed humans flying madly through fierce storms? Oh, scarred valleys, speak to us did you not see oceans of fire, rivers of blood, apes rejoicingly drinking from skulls? Would not take century to tell? So shall we not sing 'Mmomboze'?"

With this word, he played few chords on a small hand organ, to give the brothers the pitch, and they sang:

> Nsanga Ayokya gonja, asigala enkoto gwendya;
> Obugoma nsanga bulēge Ewa Namasolee Lukuli.
> Nantawongerwa katono bwomuwongera ebbuzi eddene,
> Ajula kwesala ekyambe—

"Now," said Mr. Kyagambiddwa, when they finished, "there are other songs, great works of our people, that I have collected for my book, *African Music the Source of the Nile* not so, Miss Philippa? Would we not love to sing them all for you? But the hot sun rises high in the heavens, so one last song we will sing 'Ssanya,' or 'Destructive Famine.' Now, you must know, after the death of the Blessed Martyrs of Uganda, there were, were there not, civil wars? Oh, the revolted against Kabaka Mwanga, the Tyrant, and dethroned him, the Mahommedans rose against the Christians and were defeated, the Catholics and Protestants began to fight each other, the deplorable, oh the deplorable result, Miss Schuyler, was our greatest famine the time of Kagulu, the Black Nero, do we not sing 'Ssānya'?"

Joseph Kyagambiddwa expertly directed the brothers in the haunting, sad melodies of "Destructive Famine." Then, in perfect harmony, they performed work by Palestrina. To close, in my honor, they sang two American Negro Spirituals. After I made a speech thanking them for their wonderful singing, we left.

I glanced behind me with a feeling of poignant sadness at the buildings of the monastery. They seemed to me like some far-off cloisters in medieval Europe not in architecture, but in atmosphere and spirit.

"This is what it was like in the Middle Ages!" I thought to myself. "This shows one better than any historical novel, what it was really like then, when people still had a pure, simple, unchallengeable faith when miracles, and the devil were real to people, when there was atheism, Marxism, over-population, nuclear fission, or synthetic ideas, things and values!"

No sooner had we left the monastery grounds and come out to the road when we saw several hundred Baganda women who had gathered to see me.

They wore bright, exotic, colorful long gowns in red, scarlet, purple, and orange, as brilliant as the plumage of macaws, and they gazed at me, touched my white dress, and said with voices of awe, "Our Miss Philippa! She is so beautiful, is Miss Philippa! Do we not love her? How we love her! And we long to hear her music! Oh, Miss Philippa, we *love* you!" Then, they chanted such beautiful things to me that it truly touched my heart.

As we got into Mr. Basudde's car, and drove off through the elephant grass, Mr. Kyagamoiddwa stroked his green tie and said, "Do you know, it is very important your coming? Now, all the Baganda are saying, 'Is wonderful Miss Philippa. Can a young girl do all that, achieve so many things? God loves her. Perhaps then, we should not despise our girls? Perhaps a girl can learn as can a man, and then should we not teach our girls?"

We drove back to Masaka and stopped at the Mission, where I had the great honor of being received by the Most Reverend Joseph Kiwanuka, Bishop of Masaka. He was kindly, sweet and serene, and I felt humbled before him. "I am coming to your concert this afternoon," he told me, "you know, I love music."

Back at Mr. Basudde's house, I picked up a book to read while I rested before the concert. It was *Facing Mount Kenya* by Jomo Kenyatta. A violent thunderstorm arose, the rain shooting in fierce primeval sheets, slashing in grey swords of fury. But when I arrived at the Hindu movie house, a line of Baganda, Hindus and Europeans, two blocks long, was queued outside, trying to enter.

The theatre manager had canceled one showing of *Insanyat* to give time for my concert, and the theatre was covered with pictures of me next to pictures of monkeys and elephants. The theatre was jam-packed with members of the Baganda, Toro, Anhole and Hima tribes in full regalia. There were some musicians with leopard-skins around their waists, Hindu girls in bright saris, Hindu men in *dhotas,* and veiled Indian Muslims. Bishop Kiwanuka with several brothers from the seminary, and some English people, too. A spinet, an English Challen, lent by a British engineer was pushed out on the stage, and Mr. Kyagambiddwa went out, too, to make a speech.

"Dear people of Baganda," he said, resplendent in a white suit and yellow tie, "is it not an honor to see you? And all our African Indian and English friends too? This day is great, for Miss Philippa is here, oh she is here. Oh, she will play for you soon, yes soon. And from New York she comes, that great city with its skyscrapers has produced Miss Philippa. And what will she play? It is heavenly what she will play. All great masters will she play."

An hour later, I began. There was great applause for Scarlatti, less for Chopin, and enormous clapping for Beethoven, Schubert, and Liszt.

Only the thunderous pounding on the doors by the tribesmen outside (there had been no room for them in the jam-packed theatre), marred the occasion.

After my six encores, Joseph announced that King Mutesa's private musicians would give a special performance there in my honor, the next day.

Joseph and I stayed to see the three-hour Hindu *Insanyat*. Though overacted in the style of fifty years ago, it was freshly original. Hundreds of young dancing girls. The hero, a brilliant chimpanzee, mimed, danced, sang, played flute and drums, solved puzzles, carried notes for lovers, and rescued the prince when the villain hurled him from a turret. Enthralling.

At intermission, I asked the theatre manager for the ladies' room. After startled silence, he put me in care of a guide, who took me a long way from the theatre to a teetering shack. Inside, dug in bare earth floor, was a small hole crawling with insects. The ladies' room.

Joseph, Mr. and Mrs. Basudde and I, dined at the manager's home that evening. All wore Western clothes save Mrs. Basudde, resplendent in a blue and gold Baganda costume. During the first part of rich, highly-seasoned meal, Joseph spoke at length about the twenty-nine clans of Baganda, with totems of birds, fish, beasts and vegetables. Then, to ingratiate myself with my hosts, I talked about my love of Hindu philosophy and culture, especially *Bhagavad Gita*. There a cool silence, and my host said icily, "We're Muslims, you know!"

The next afternoon, when I arrived at the Hindu theatre for the "gnoma," or "dance-drama," in my honor, the musicians were already onstage preparing their flutes, drums and xylophones. The latter had large white keys, and three musicians sat on each side of them to beat out the *lutambas*.

Joseph had me stand up so the audience could see me, and then told them at length that I was going to be baptized the following March, at which there was stormy applause. The thunderous applauses reverberated, and echoed loudly. Some shouted "Bravo!" and stamped their feet.

Then Joseph said, "Miss Philippa, oh Miss Philippa, is it not wonderful now you can hear our own ancient Buganda instrument? Oh do you know that Buganda has existed since A.D. 1000? Why we can trace back our kings to the fifteenth century, we can! Now I will tell you about *Ennanga*, the Bow-Harp which is like the ancient Egyptian harp, and is played in five transpositions and also about *Endongo*, the eight-stringed bowl-lyre, and the one-stringed *Endigidi* fiddle. It a pity that you cannot hear the one stringed *Sekirulege*, but that can only be played outdoors. With these stringed instruments, we will play and sing in your honor, just for you, 'Nkwagala Kuyinga,' which means, 'We love you exceedingly much.'"

The audience and musicians now turned to me and sang, in exquisite hauntingly lovely, touching voices, full of sweet emotion:

Gwemperekera, muganzi wange, Omwana w'embuga,
Kulika kwogera, mukwano. Gwenziringana, mutayi, wange.

Then came "Akaliga," or "The Lamb Who Smoked a Pipe." Joseph now introduced five Ganda flutes: *Ensasi, Endesi, Entabitati, Ekiwuwa,* and *Enjogolo,* ranging from soprano to deep bass, and on them was played "Ensejjere Kawomera," or "Eating Delicious White Ant," while the singers sang, with quaint, capricious wit, to Joseph's direction:

Ensejjere kawomera gye palinnanga, Muganda wange.
O libera w'ani?

Now musicians and the audience sang, "Extraordinary Boats—Ohwato Nakawolele." The drummers demonstrated rhythmic, cylindrical and counting drums, and a couple came to the front of the stage—the man in a black Western suit with a leopard skin tied around his waist and posterior, and the woman in a long crimson and scarlet Baganda costume with a black sweater encircling her middle. They began to dance hotly, furiously, frenzied pelvises switching torridly, behinds quivering frighteningly, muscles twitching with orgiastic violence, as the drums beat pounded and boomed with malevolent joy.

The musicians sang repeatedly, "Dance joyfully, elders, dance!"

The insistent repetition had an erotic fury, heated, wild, savage, and exciting. Its throbbing seared into my brain and nerves, pushing them to violent reaction, as if some superficial veil of civilization had lifted, and I retreated to the primitive. Unaware of the blazing stares of those around me, I began to move and wiggle, until the music abruptly stopped. Now, a piece started about Kigula, the clown, who leads off a beautiful girl, singing and dancing to every herd of elephants he meets on the way.

Xylophones and drums began a short, staccato theme, and the man in the leopard skin leapt amazingly, lighting deftly on one foot in front of the *Embutu* drum. He beat it sharply, not losing a second, jumped again like a soring antelope, landed before the next drum, beat it, flew up like an eagle once more. The musicians sang the elephant chorus, "Wow! The Man He doesn't merely dance but sways!" Floating upwards with splendid virtuosity, the dancer leapt to the ceiling magnificently, like a winged deer, touched it partly with his stick, and landed just in time before the largest drum, hopping over it splendidly, with appalling dexterity. His convolutions and jumps grew higher, wilder, swooping with passionate fury.

Abruptly, the music stopped, with a sharp, piercing burst of pulsing, searing, fearsome sound. It was over.

The next morning, we all made the three-hour drive to Kampala.

When cars passed us on the road, clouds of swirling, gritty orange dust covered us. We drove past giant red ten-foot ant hills, flocks of tan and brown goats, miles of thick, brilliant foliage rich with yew-trees, boababs and cassias, and shoals of *tukals* like overgrown mushrooms.

We neared Kampala. Beer-parlors selling *pombe* (banana beer) and *waraga* (distilled spirits) thronged the roadside. Soon we were among the box-like, neat, unimaginative houses of Kampala.

At Makerere College, I practiced in the spacious auditorium. When I asked an African attendant to bring me a glass of water, he returned in minutes, grinning with elfin insinuation, and handed me a tall glass whose contents tasted thickly horrible as if they had come from a toilet. "Are you sure it's boiled?" I asked him. He giggled, "Of coorse he ees boiled, ha-ha!" and vanished. Soon the college dean came in, dressed in a white shirt and khaki shorts. I asked him if he thought it was really boiled. He said sharply, "Not possibly. You'd have to leave the school to get boiled water. Don't take things strange Africans give you."

Soon, I drove with Mr. and Mrs. Charles Leslie Holcum to their home high in the green hills. From their splendid garden, thick with flowers, frangipani, and purple bougainvillea, the view of Lake Victoria Nyanza, where the White Nile begins, was magnificent.

"How beautiful, how tranquil it is," I cried.

"Can't get too close to it," said Mr. Holcum. "Tsetse fly infected area."

"The fly isn't under control?"

"Not altogether. Lugard's Sudanese brought sleeping sickness with them here in 1891, killing a quarter of a million Baganda before the turn of the century. The danger is less now. Do you know one-seventh of Uganda's water, and Victoria is the world's second largest fresh-water lake?"

As he spoke, he took me into a quaint cottage, followed by a huge dark dog like the *Hound of the Baskervilles*.

The dog embraced me continually during the next twenty-four hours, opening door throughout the night, despite all barricades, and licking me with assiduous enthusiasm.

The Holcums and I had breakfast in the gorgeous garden next morning.

The dog stalked around me throughout, gazing with adoring eyes. "Yes he does seem to have taken a fancy to you," said Mr. Holcum.

"Does he love everyone so much?'"

"No! I'll say he doesn't. Doesn't like the Kabaka. The Kabaka used to come to see us often, but one day, as he appeared in the driveway, the dog knocked him down!"

The Kabaka of the Baganda, that is King Edward William Frederick David Walugembe Mutebi Luwangula II, was at my recital at Makerere College.

He had never attended a concert before.

When I arrived, five minutes late, he was already there, sitting on the front seat. The concert held up half an hour more while the crowd continued to pour in. Outside, a block-long queue of standees waited. All races, European, African, Asian, were there, the first time such an audience had ever come to a Makerene recital. Throughout my performance, they gave thunderous ovations.

Afterwards, Uganda's High Justice, Norman Wylie, said to me, "It was wonderful! Did you notice how the public wouldn't let the concert end after your last encore, and applauded for ten minutes until you came back and played again? That never happened here before. We never had such a crowd here before!"

Mr. Wylie, towering over me, looked quite handsome in his dinner jacket. About six foot six, he had a bluff, hearty, gay manner.

The Kabaka came to my dressing-room and invited me to visit him at Lubiri Palace next day.

King Mutesa II is a handsome young man, elegant in his well-tailored clothes. A Cambridge graduate, he speaks perfect, clipped, cultivated English, and put me tactfully at ease when I entered his sitting room at the white Lubiri Palace.

An Anglican, he is head of the Church of England in Uganda. He was exiled a few years ago by Sir Andréw Cohen, the former Governor of Uganda, but this caused such tension that he was allowed to return. The Baganda are devoted to him.

It was during Mutesa I's reign in 1862 that Speke discovered the Baganda, though Western Uganda's Mountains of the Moon had been known since Ptolemy. In 1875, Stanley visited Mutesa I, who was later succeeded by the unpleasant Mwanga, then Kiwewa, Kalema, and Mwanga and Kalema again. In 1890, the Anglo-German treaty assigned Uganda to Great Britain, and since 1852 the British flag has flown over Kampala.

Mutesa II seemed to me a modest, unassuming young man, without consciousness of the political intrigues that rage about him.

The other tribes fear that if Uganda gains independence, the Kabaka will assume rule over them all. The Kabaka was noncommittal on this subject, as was His Royal Highness, George Rukidi III, Omakama of the fiercely rival tribe of Toro, when I met him in New York, in November 1959.

The Kabaka was also noncommittal about the rumors of his heated romance with his wife's sister, forbidden by his position as head of Church of England, but he complimented me charmingly on my concert, and discussed abstract world affairs for awhile, showing intellectual perception and balanced judgment.

His Highness said, "I would like you to view our ancient drums. They contain our tribe's soul, and are named after our great heroes."

We went out to the bright sunlight, where the Kabaka graciously consented to pose for photographs with me.

The drums were in elaborate houses of intricate woven elephant grass and reeds—low, cool, and exquisite, they were artistic in style, original in outline.

The drums, of every conceivable size, of every type of animal hide, had bloody, exotic, fascinating tales connected with them. Some were three centuries old. Other reed-houses had flutes, trumpets, harps, and xylophones on the walls.

I was so enchanted, I hated to return to Masaka.

EARLY THE NEXT MORNING, Joseph, Mr. and Mrs. Basudde, a chauffeur, and I, set out in one of Mr. Basudde's cars for the Queen Elizabeth game park, 197 miles away. It took us six hours.

We were fried by the heat from the boiling sun that hung like an axe in the pitiless, glittering turquoise-blue sky. Dust swirled and sprayed over the narrow road, staining my new white dress a muddy orange. My hair got orange too.

We passed villages of round thatched mud tukals, and slow, tranquil herdsmen driving flocks of black and tan goats. We caught sight of the Great Valley.

Mostly we saw trees, magnificent, wild, tangled green masses of foliage. How wonderful to be where the earth was as God made it, where there were still more trees than houses, and more animals than people! Nature in her primeval glory! Without realizing it, we moved imperceptibly into the virgin bush of great animal preserve.

Suddenly, we glimpsed two olive-green Talapoins, staring at us with deep reddish-brown eyes from a tree-limb. We were intruders in their territory. Deer streaked in and out between the interlaced greenery of somber trees. Brown and white gazelles with black-tipped tails peered at us. Gnus with white beards, kudus, and elands flashed by.

Mr. Basudde began to take shots with the movie camera. As we passed aardwolves, cloven-footed okapi, and buffaloes, he suddenly told us to close the windows, stay still and say nothing. The reason was apparent when a lion walked into view. His golden mane was bedraggled, tangled, and dirty, but he had patriarchal dignity in his soft padded approach. He looked like an over grown kitten, tired yet arrogant. He neared the car and stared at us through the closed panes. His orange eyes looked amiable. We dared not move. In few moments he trotted away.

Mr. Basudde said, "Of course, they won't hurt you if the windows are shut. The gasoline odor obscures our smell then, and the animals think we and the car are just one large mammal, like a new species of hippo."

"Will we see any hippos here?" I asked him.

"At the river edge, we can see them from the water. They won't charge if we don't turn on the lights." We drove in the dusk to river bank. We watched them lumber gravely to the land. He went on, "It is a pity the hippopotamus is diminishing so fast. Do you know they once used to inhabit the Thames Valley in England? And now there are not so very many even in Africa. The whites destroyed hippo herds ruthlessly when they first came to Africa, killing them just for their hides. If you go to Liberia, you must try to see the species they have there—pygmy hippos that only weigh 400 pounds, and have greenish-black skin, and yellow-green stomachs."

We went to the Greek lodge for dinner. The dinner was good. The sanitary facilities were not. I chose a book from the library that I read until dawn by kerosene lamp-light.

Among the birds we saw next morning, were four-foot tall secretary-birds, with black and white bodies and big pink feet. They were strutting among the tukals of some Africans who lived in the park.

Mr. Basudde shot pictures of wild elephant herds, and said, "These are different from Indian elephants; in Africa both sexes have tusks, in India the female has small tusks, and you can sometimes see tuskless males. The Indian loves grass, the African prefers roots and thick branches. The African trumpets loudly when charging, not so the Indian. The African is largely undomesticable owing to the lack of a depression in the neck one could sit in.

To get some pictures in the sunlight, I left the car. There was a screaming trumpet-call from a nearby group of females and young bull-calves. One elephant charged. The others, like mammoth moving grey-black boulders followed, stampeding on the brownish-green sparse grass.

It was terrifying to see this violent example of mob in nature. Running faster than ever before, I made it to the car, the driver started it and we plunged through the thick bush. One wheel got stuck in some mud. At last we got free and journeyed on down the road. The elephants lost interest, and abandoned the chase.

Soon we met hippo standing at the edge. He had a portentous, well-fed expression, like a self-satisfied Dutch government official. We feared to move, as he might charge. For ten minutes we froze, immobile. Perhaps sensing our fear, he moved back, almost as though bowing to us. We rode on, and out of the richly-colored game park. Our car broke down fourteen times on the road back to Masaka. My hair and battered white dress were orange with dust when we arrived.

Before leaving for Entebbe the next morning, I met an African, who said, "I hate the Hindus! They bleed our country! They are worse than the Muslim

Indians, who keep the money they make from us in Uganda. The Hindus exploit us, and send the money back to India. Why should our wealth be poured into India? The Hindus despise us underneath. You never see a Hindu girl with an African, though many English girls have done so. This is a rich country, the greatest cotton-producer in the British Commonwealth. Why should they bleed us? When you return next year, things will be boiling!"

After I left Uganda, Joseph wrote my family saying, "Philipa coming here was a historic occasion!"

I was supposed to go to Madagascar before my return to Uganda in 1959, but conflicting schedules made it impossible for me to visit that land of my ancestors. But, in November 1959, I had the great honor of a two-hour interview with Philibert Tsiranana, President and Premiere of the Malagasy Republic, at his Waldorf-Astoria suite. He was handsome, a stylishly dressed man of forty-seven with a charming, hearty, and jovial personality rare in a chief of state. Once he had been a country shepherd, and he still reflected a jolly, warm pastoral innocence. He seemed to have a great benevolent love for poor people, and said, "The people of Madagascar have great love and sympathy for the colored people of America in their struggle for full equality. We hope they will soon receive their full liberties. All men are brothers in God's sight. Race intermixture and intermarriage are good, for they help break the barriers and bigotry in this world." He sent me his autographed photo, and wrote me after his return to Tananarive. I was officially invited to perform in Malagasy Republic in May 1960.

When I actually returned to Uganda, in 1959, hostility and fear hung heavily in the air. The innocence had been replaced by suspicion, the naiveté by torment, the affectionate simplicity by intrigue.

Uganda was really boiling.

No mixed audience attended my Kampala concert. Only English people, looking not hearty and enthusiastic, but nervous, secretive and scared.

Again, I visited King Mutesa, in response to the phone call he made to me at C. L. Holcum's villa, personally inviting me. He received me in a different room of the white Lubiri Palace, this time—one more luxurious and beautiful. He wore a well-cut black suit, and was as urbanely handsome as ever. He made no comment on the storm that was gathering among his people, on that approaching emotional hurricane. However, he invited me to visit him, as his guest, at his Summer Palace, out in the country of the rolling green savannahs, on my next voyage to East Africa. ⊞

CHAPTER 16

Royalty and Food Poisoning
Nigeria, Dahomey, French Togoland, Ghana, Ivory Coast, Liberia, Senegal, Morocco 1958

I N January 1958, I flew into Kano, capital of Northern Nigeria. Once it had been a great slave center that only fell to the British in 1902. Now it was dry and dusty, and looked much like the Northern Sudan.

At the airport, I met a young man named Muhammad Abdullah, who had come to meet someone coming in from Khartoum on my plane. This person had not arrived. Perhaps he had thought the plane would be even later than it was leaving Khartoum, and had missed it.

Muhammad Abdullah was pacing up and down, looking very nervous. He had the golden skin and blue eyes of many Semitic Fulani, and wore western clothes. He was about five feet nine.

We began to talk. I told him I had only a few hours there before going on to Lagos. He offered to take me into the city. I left my bags at the airport and got into his tiny, very beat-up looking, English car, and we rode into town. As in Khartoum, no women were visible. The city looked like a combination of Omdurman and Khartoum — only, if possible, dustier.

Muhammad was a Muslim. He had a clean-cut face that did not seem at all fierce.

There was not much to see in Kano. Ocher-colored houses, box-like government buildings, the murky waters of the Jakara stream, some fine Arab horses.

Muhammad began by promising to show me the "most beautiful mansions," ended by apologizing because he could not find any. As we bumped along the dusty brown streets, he told me a fascinating story about the giant, Daniel.

"He is eleven feet six inches tall! You cannot imagine how big he is. He was already eight feet five inches when he was seventeen! He eats enough for four. For breakfast he eats thirty slices of yam, and they say he eats lions for lunch! He drinks buckets of water every day, and he can break through a concrete wall! Daniel Onwubuta is a legend here—if you were staying longer, I would take you to meet him!"

Muhammad was eager and enthusiastic, and quite put out that I was leaving so soon for Lagos. "Oh, those Southern Nigerians! We had a civilization when they were eating each other. They are barbarians. The climate is horrible there. Once you get there, you'll wish you were back here!"

Indeed I did, for the ghastly humidity of Lagos was the most steaming torture that I had ever felt. When I stepped off the plane, an English lady was waiting for me.

"Mr. Shillingford sent me," she said. "I'm going to drive you out to the Ikoyi suburb to Chief Bologun's house, where you'll be staying. He's the Minister of Research and Information, and lives near some of the other Ministers. They have a beautiful new house. It's all modern. They just moved in. It's a pity—the house was designed to be air-conditioned, but the conditioners haven't arrived from America yet, so the house is blazing hot, because it doesn't have any of the porches or thick walls that make other houses a trifle cooler here."

We went out to her car. Just walking a few meters in the broiling heat seemed like a great athletic achievement. Yet, outside, were Nigerians cycling down the road wearing long, heavy, velvet robes and fur caps.

"You'll be giving two concerts at the college. The radio station sent their piano over. By the way, Minister Mbadiwe wants to see you, too. He says he remembers visiting your parents in the States so well," she went on.

"How do you stand the heat here? How do you keep up standards and everything?" I asked her.

"Standards? Ha-ha! Well, we spend one-third of the time in bed, one-third of the time losing our tempers at the servants, and one-third of the time counting the days to our next leave! Oh, it does get you down. Sometimes I feel like there's a little red devil on top of my head, just sitting there! I don't think the Africans are used to it. They suffer as much as we do. Those heavy costumes? Well, even if you have nothing on, you're not any cooler here."

In an hour, we had arrived at Chief Bologun's house. It was most impressive. Everything in it was brand new, and mostly from America. Chief Bologun came downstairs to greet me. He was pleasant looking, with charcoal black skin, humorous black eyes, beaming face, and a jovial personality which made it seem as though the cares of state did not get him down. He was the nicest-looking man I saw in Nigeria. He wore long white robes, and a high round white cap. Chieftainess Bologun appeared soon, wearing a white blouse, and a brown striped Nigerian skirt, with a brown and green turban on her head. She was coffee-colored, good-humored, and laughed a great deal.

I went upstairs to the luxurious modern suite they had assigned to me, and found beautiful flowers on my dressing table. They were from a lady connected with the MRA house there. I telephoned to thank her. She invited me to visit the MRA house that evening.

At dusk a car arrived to drive me there.

The Moral Re-Armament house was a beautiful mansion that had formerly belonged to Mrs. Gwyndolyn Wynter-Shackleford of Accra, an old friend. When we arrived, all the members of the house came downstairs to greet me. They included a Dutch couple, a British couple, and two African couples, who seemed all to be living in perfect harmony. Their children were playing together in the highest good spirits. A new baby had recently been born to one of the British couples. Evidently, it wanted to see me too, because it let out a lusty wail, as soon as I arrived. I went upstairs and held it a while, and then it went to sleep in perfect contentment.

When I returned downstairs, dinner was served. We had pleasant conversation, but I did not feel like eating much.

I was sizzling with the heat. I had worn no stockings, but all the other ladies had. They were the only women in Lagos who had the fortitude to bear nylon stockings.

They showed me a color film, "The Tide of History," that made me cry. It was beautiful and idealistic.

When I returned to Chief Bologun's my bedroom was so stifling that I could not sleep. Open windows and an electric fan made no dent in the humidity. It was as hot at midnight as it was at noon.

The next afternoon, the Bologuns took me to lunch with the Mbadiwes. Their six-year-old son came along with us, for he was betrothed to Minister Mbadiwe's daughter, age seven.

The Mbadiwe house was almost the same as the Bologun dwelling. Evidently, all the Ministers' houses had been designed and furnished to the same plan.

The engaged couple began to chase each other around the living room, playing leap-frog over chairs and couches, with gay and sprightly lack of ceremony. In fact, Miss Mbadiwe kicked and punched Master Bologun without the slightest reverence. They were quite accustomed to the fact that they would one day be married, and, indeed, Minister Bologun had already commenced to pay his son's dowry to Minister Mbadiwe.

The latter, clad in long yellow and brown striped robes of heavy linen, and with a jaunty leopard-skin fur cap on his head, led us in to the dining table. He presided with Falstaffian jollity over the long mahogany table laden with the highly-spiced dishes of a typical Nigerian meal. His wife, a small, attractive tea-leaf colored woman, wearing a white nylon American blouse with a green Nigerian skirt, sat at the table's other end.

The courses were fried curry-plastered bush-fowl, drowned in palm oil; palm oil chop with burning red peppers; curry-smeared rice, *fufu* in red pepper *pili-pi-li,* dried bananas and plantains swimming in spiced orange palm-oil. As I ate, I recalled the ant-stew I had consumed in East Africa, made from heaps of flying ants with their wings plucked off, stirred in a muddy paste and boiled with leaves, the mixture tasting horrible, like sand, fuel oil, rubbish and rancid cod liver oil.

On January 15, I played a children's concert; it was packed. After giving a Lagos recital for adults on January 16, I flew to cool, dry Jos, in the tin and columbite mining area. Much of its surrounding countryside is eroded, and one sees strange weird shapes of soil formation sticking up from the dusty ground like Neolithic idols.

My room at the Hill Station Hotel was beautiful, tranquil. It overlooked a private aviary that held a glorious troop of birds dark blue yellow-billed starlings, grey and white parrots, ground hornbills, yellow, orange, green and blue parakeets, tiny birds like thimbles! A very old turtle waddled beneath.

Jack Spicer, a British government official, asked me heartily, "Why did you come now? Our piano only works during the rainy season!" He drove me to see the piano, which he had been tuning — a true labor of Hercules. Jack had spent the last two days on it, assisted by the vicinity's sole musician, an ancient Englishman, who had not tuned a piano in forty-six years.

The piano, a haggard scarred Pleyel that had once been brilliant, needed a facelift. Flashlights had been kept in her during the rainy season, and water dishes during the dry one. That had not sufficed. The sounding-board had an immense crack which filled up during the rainy season, opened in the dry. Now it was gigantic. As he tuned, the ancient Englishman, bent and bowed from a half-century in Africa, told me hair raising tales of the huts whose courtyards were paved with human bones that he had seen when he first came to Africa, decades before.

My two concerts that day drew crowded houses. After the last, five Chiefs ascended the stage to present me with two magnificent ebony book-ends carved with these words, "To the Most Gracious Philippa Schuyler, Remembrance from the African Chiefs of Jos."

Then there was a party in my honor at the home of mining inspector Peter Gaskill. The British resident, Mr. Weatherhead, was present.

A wonderful salad sat on the table.

A brown object lay amidst the tomatoes.

It moved.

"Ha-ha!" I said to Mr. Gaskill, "That looks just like a cockroach!" Grimly, he stayed silent. Then I realized that it was, indeed, a roach!

When I flew back to steaming Lagos, I was entertained by Ben Enwonwu, the sculptor. On my last day, a strange voice phoned me, saying, "He-he! This is Adah. Remember? I met you in New York a few years ago!"

I searched my mind. She had not given much to remember. Yet, I said, with enthusiasm, "Of course, I remember you!"

She asked, "Can you come to see me tonight? I can send a car for you at 7:00 p.m." Still trying to figure out who she might be, I agreed.

The car came. I went, not bothering to dress up, for I had an increasing feeling this might be the Adah Obi I had met in New York. The niece of Dr. Nwafor Orizu, she had come to America wrapped like a cocoon in her Nigerian robes, and violently defended African women's position to me, declaring indignantly, "I shall never straighten my hair! I will not be like American girl. I am Nigerian!"

As I reflected, the car stopped at a small stucco villa. I heard the loud sexy beat of a rock-'n-roll record. The banging, jumpy beat got louder, and happier, as I walked in.

There, in the middle of the tile floor, was an apparition. Luscious black skin slightly covered by a skin-tight white and gold sheath dress, her waist was no more than eighteen inches, and her bosom outdid Sophia Loren. She wore the sheerest nylons and high spike heels on her shapely legs. Her neckline was low, her skirt rose high above her knees, she wore large gold pendants. And her hair was straightened.

It was Adah!

She was dancing, strutting up and down the black and white floor, swaying like a breeze, jiving like mad. The recording machine blared,

Rock-a-baby! Rock-a-baby! Rock-a-baby! Roll!
Hey! Rock-a-baby, Rock-a-baby, Rock, Rock, Roll!

Adah had gone American. She had "un-purdahed" herself, fast. On January 22, Wednesday at nine in the morning, a black Renault car came to Chief Bologun's house. In it was a chauffeur and the secretary of Georges Apedo-Amah, the Finance Minister of French Togoland. They had driven in from Lome and had come to take me back with them.

I remembered Mr. Apedo-Amah well. For six years he had been a member of the French delegation at the U.N. sessions in New York. He was nutmeg-brown in color, of medium height, with precise elegant features and grey-white hair. The best-dressed African I had ever met, he was always dapper, well-groomed and stylish, whatever the occasion. He was also a highly educated man. Since the independence of Togoland, he no longer holds office there, which is a loss to the country. He now resides in Paris.

But in January 1958, he was still the Finance Minister, and lived over the Ministry offices in Lome.

His secretary, who was faultlessly dressed, took me to the car. We were en route to Cotonou and Lome. The three of us drove from Lagos to Iju, Otta, and Ado in the moist morning heat. Both secretary and chauffeur spoke exquisite French. This was a welcome contrast to British Africa, where many, especially servants, mumble in the most exasperating, unintelligible manner.

The countryside was beautiful, the dusty road lined with baobab, coconut and palm oil trees, or fields of guinea corn and sugar cane. Weary women were working the fields in the hot sun. In fact, whenever we passed a female, she was working hard, and if we neared a group of idlers, they were always men.

Whenever a car or truck passed in front of us, it sent choking clouds of orange gritty dust into the air, and onto us.

At the Dahomey border, we had to pass through customs. The officials were gallant, courteous, charming, and, though African, spoke splendid French. Even with a few words, they made me feel feminine, as though merely being a woman was something important, which I had not felt in Nigeria.

Porto-Novo looked surprisingly peaceful, considering its bloody history—some of the bloodiest cannibal rites imaginable were once performed there. Once it was said that the skulls of conquered kings were used as royal drinking-cups, and that the king floated his canoe in a tank of human blood. The Grand Customs were held on a king's death, and the Minor Customs twice a year. Both were ghastly orgies of slaughter. In 1791 nearly five hundred were put to death and eaten.

Accounts vary as to whether the army of Dahomey had two thousand women warriors or over eighteen thousand.

We passed a statue commemorating the 1890 treaty which gave France Porto-Novo and Cotonou. Suddenly, our tires sank deep in some rich red clayey soil, but we managed to move on through the undulating country.

I asked the secretary, "What tribes live in Porto-Novo?" He replied, "It is mostly the Nago tribe in Porto-Novo, but they have Yoruba admixture and speak the Yoruba dialect." Despite the heat, he looked as perfectly groomed as though he had just stepped from a Ministry in Paris. He wore a well-tailored suit, and a delightful tie, which set off his dark chiseled features just right, while I was wilted and steaming.

I asked him, "How many people are there in Dahomey?"

"One million seven hundred thousand, peut-être. One does not know for sure about any African country—we do not have the exact census as you do in America — one cannot count each person in the bush—and some tribes move location constantly."

I recalled to myself the story about the census takers who had gone to count a tribe in the French Sudan, and could not find it, for it had gone somewhere else.

Our car jumped like a grasshopper over stones, sand holes, mud and manure. Trying to avoid the cows and flocks of goats that stalked and gamboled across the road, we vaulted suddenly around bend.

A pink pig was in our path, and did not escape in time. The car wheel passed over its leg and broke it. The pig limped back miserably with an anguished squeal, which saddened me.

The car went on. We passed groves of lime and orange trees, and fields full of women working.

One difference I noted between British Nigeria around Lagos, and French Dahomey, was that in the latter, the women worked naked to the waist, in the former, perhaps due to British morality, they were covered up. The Dahomey women would have looked better covered, for a lifetime of field labor plus the strain of nursing each child two to three years, ruins any figure. Their bosoms were flabby, pendulous, no more interesting than the udders of so many cows.

"We're coming into Cotonou now," observed the secretary, "I hope we're not too late for the luncheon the Minister of Social Affairs is having for you—the mayor of Cotonou will be there too—it's a pity Sourous-Migan Apithy isn't here now, he's in Paris as our Deputy—he would have loved to meet you."

We were two hours late, but the Minister and the Mayor had waited, and greeted us at the latter's home with urbane and elegant charm. An exquisite luncheon had been prepared, and the chef, truly a great artist, had outdone himself for the occasion.

What a marvelous Olympian heaven for the stomach after the horrible British cooking of Nigeria! Shamelessly, I asked for more helpings. One course was a positively imperial fish, four feet long—I ate most of it—this fish was a poem, the chicken was an ecstasy, the salad was rapture.

We left Cotonou, regretfully, at tea time. The city looked wistful in the lengthening shadows, as if regretting the bloody past before the 1890 fire—but half-resigned to its neatly ordered present.

We crossed the border from Dahomey, named after the Belly of King Danh the Snake, to French Togoland, once under German suzerainty from 1884 to the end of World War I. This country benefited from Teutonic influence for the solid educational foundation given by the Germans caused the Togolanders, after Togo's separation into French and British Trust Territories, to be the cleverest, most intelligent in West Africa. When they emigrated to neighboring lands, they often incurred the jealousy of other Africans.

Marvelously well-dressed as usual, Georges Apedo-Amah was waiting for me at the Ministry in Lome. He took me upstairs to his flat above the Finance offices, saying, "I'm having a little party for you tonight out on the terrace—about two hundred people—I've been trying all day to tune those two uprights so you could choose between them—they're both terrible, but I don't think there's another in Lome."

He was right. They were horrible, once worthy, but now ravaged by the tropical humidity, with great vacant spaces of missing or tuneless keys.

George's flat was in taste. There were many books of poetry and philosophy, for he was a very cultivated man.

The party was an event.

The women all wore sumptuous Paris styles, and were better dressed than any I ever saw in France. Champagne was served.

The next morning, the President of the National Assembly took me sightseeing, and to his home for lunch. His house, tastefully furnished, was much cooler than the steaming streets. We listened to symphonic records, including Bizet's, "Les Pecheurs de Perles," which I had never heard before. Two hours passed swiftly.

When I returned to the Ministry, no one was there.

I tried to practice on the dreadful uprights, but I felt trembling weak, and dizzy. My hands shook, I felt cold despite the incredible heat. My head was whirling. Trying to exert self-control, I told myself, "You can't be sick. You can't! There's too much ahead."

A French lady entered she said, "You don't look well. You look terrible! I have a small room with an air-conditioner, if you'd.

"WHERE IS IT?" I cried, and when she pointed the way, I plunged in the room like a diver. What a heavenly, glorious coolness! Running to the machine, I embraced it. Never was anyone so glad to see anything.

That evening, in a large room decorated with African rugs, Georges showed me a mahogany table piled with bolts of cloth and ivory statues, and said, "Choose anything you like for a present, a little remembrance of Togo—nothing is too good for you!" Charmed with his generosity, I would have taken them all, they were so gorgeous, but I restrained myself.

We attended a gala party at the chief hotel, where everyone was chic, and well dressed. On our return, a messenger from Accra was awaiting me. His English was atrocious, but I finally made out that he had been sent to tell me, it was urgent that I come to Ghana at once.

Georges and I tried to telephone Accra long distance, but the connection was hopeless. We screamed, shouted, but music kept coming over the line, as though it were mixed up with a radio broadcast. We decided I must leave at dawn.

Mr. Apedo-Amah placed a car and chauffeur at my disposal, and I left Lome, with the messenger, at dawn. I was wearing a red silk dress with white polka-dots, and only found, after I got into the car, that a big hole had been bitten in the skirt by some insect the night before.

How monotonous, wearisome, and slow, the trip was!

To our left was the greyish-gold beach from which, years before, the shameful cargoes of bleeding black bodies had been shipped to the slave-hungry Americas. To our right stood coconut palms and dew-dripping travelers' palms. Now, the grimy red dust swirled in the steamy air as our black car passed bony cows, pigs, goats and swarms of sinister-looking tukals. Even my sunglasses clouded continually from the choking dust, but I hesitated to remove them, and expose my eyes to the sun that relentlessly hung in the lapis-lazuli heavens. I asked the messenger his name three times before I could understand his mumbled reply; it was "Shakespeare Ka Bagesui.'

"Are you a Fanti?" I inquired.

"No! I am Ashanti!" he muttered, with an affronted look. About five feet eight in height, he wore a pink shirt over gray-green pants, had a broad nose, panther-black skin, small eyes rather close together, and looked as though he would not tell the truth even if it were in his advantage to do so.

"Are you a Christian?" I asked, hesitantly, wiping off a thick acid rivulet of sweat that dripped down my cheek.

"I am animist! I am proud to have religion of my ancestors. For a while I go to mission school, but do not change what I believe. Our religion is intricate and most elaborately involved," he replied with insinuation.

"What is it?" I asked, as we passed some half-naked girls in a millet field. "Is it possible to say?" he asked, as though confiding a secret.

"Please tell me."

"Oh, can I, can I really?"

"Yes, you can," I said, starting to eat a mushy, blackened banana.

"Ah! Perhaps I will relate to you a tale, a little tale of our Ashanti people, that may give you more idea than you imagine, not less but rather more," he purred, with a sidelong glance.

"Okay," I said.

"We do not really mean, we do not really mean, that what we will say is true."

"Do all your stories begin that way?"

"Yes. This is about a mother with eleven children. When she cooked them food, they ate it all, leaving none for her. She told the silk-cotton tree, saying, 'I shall send my children here. Kill them with your branches.'"

"Rather bloodthirsty, wasn't she?" I interjected.

"Do not interrupt. When the children neared the tree, Number Eleven told his brothers, 'Mother must have sent us here so the tree could kill us. So cut sticks and throw them at the tree.' They did. The tree tried, but was unable to kill them. The children returned to their mother. Again she fixed them food, and they ate it all, leaving none for her."

"Greedy, weren't they?"

"Do not interrupt. The mother begged the sky god to kill her children. He put a leopard, a snake and broken bottles in a pit, and covered it over to seem like a path. But Number Eleven was clever. He had his brothers throw a club, and it fell through the path to the pit, so they knew to avoid the danger, and went safely on to see the sky god."

"Did he kill them?"

"Let me tell you. He had stools placed on a thin covering over a deep hole. But the children were clever, did not sit on the stools, and were not killed. Then the sky god commanded the children to go to Death and get her golden snuff-box, gold chewing-stick, gold whetstone, and gold fly switch. They went to Death's village. Death, who had ten children, gave each of the human children to one of hers, and kept Number Eleven for herself."

"Did she eat him?"

"Lighting her teeth red, she tried to devour him. But Crafty Number Eleven said, 'Death, I am not asleep. Bring me your golden pipe to smoke, and I may fall asleep.' She brought it, and he wheedled the gold chewing stick and gold whetstone from her in the same manner. Death sprang again, and he said, 'I'm not asleep. Take calabash, splash in it, cook me a meal, and I may fall asleep.' Death left, and Number Eleven ran to his brothers crying, 'Flee!'"

"Did they escape in time?"

"After they fled, Number Eleven cut plantain stems, put them where his brothers had laid, and covered them, so when Death came to eat Number Eleven's brothers, she made a mistake and ate all her own children instead! Then Number Eleven stole all the rest of Death's gold things and ran away, crying, 'Ha-ha! I made you eat all your own children!' Death chased Number Eleven, but he climbed a silk-cotton tree and urinated on her, while his brothers swam across a big flooding river."

"Did they leave Number Eleven behind?"

"Of course. He could not swim. He turned into a stone. Death picked up the stone to throw across the stream at the children, and the winds bore it aloft. Number Eleven turned into god, and Abosom, all the lesser gods of the world, were descended from him."

"Is that the end of the story?" I asked, amazed.

"This is my tale, which I have related, if it be not be sweet or if it not be sweet, take some elsewhere and let some come back to me."

He had finished. He fell silent, and, with a sly glance began to smoke a cigarette. Now we were nearing Accra. Little girls in red tutus scampered down the roadside. We passed mammy-wagons with big signs on them, like "Ghana Best in the World," "Jesus Saves Us," and "We Love Great Ghana." Shakespeare pointed to the fields we passed, and said, "Look! Look! These are *Ghana* fields! Those are Ghana cows!"

I replied, "They don't look any different from fields in French Togoland to me."

The road got better. Asphalted now, was less dusty. Entering Accra, we soon reached the Ambassador Hotel. Mrs. Shackleford, a prominent business woman, whose late husband had founded a great bakery system, met me in the lobby. We embraced and she took me to the second-floor suite we would share together. A sensitive, highly cultured woman, she was dark, with finely-drawn features.

George Padmore, the Prime Minister's chief advisor, visited me that evening. I had known him well in London. He told me, "The Portuguese were the first whites to make permanent settlement in West Africa. Reaching the mouth of the Senegal River, in 1444, they came to the Gold Coast in 1471, building Fort San Jorge in 1782. The Dutch captured it in 1637, and the Dutch West India Company built many more settlements. The Swedes built Christianborg Castle in 1661, before the Danes ejected them. The Danes sold their Gold Coast holdings to the British in 1850, and the Coast became a British Crown Colony in 1874. In 1901, Ashanti and the Northern Territories were made British Protectorates. Now our policy is one country, one people, one destiny, so, since our 1957 independence, we are becoming integrated into one common citizenship.

Mr. Padmore had dark-brown skin and refined features. He spoke in a cultivated, nasal, disciplined voice that showed his scholarly training.

The next morning, he took me to Christianborg Castle—that great, white, building that could tell eerie tales of its days as a slave depot and lunatic asylum, before settling into its present respectability.

George Padmore and I sat a while in a cool room overlooking the swirling white-green waters of the turbulent sea. Then we went to greet Prime Minister Kwame Nkrumah, whom I had not seen since he had left America, years before when I was a child. He seemed no older now. A tall, handsome man with a noble, spiritual glow, he was, one knew at once, a man of destiny. It was inspiring just to be in the same room with him.

Dressed in a well-cut white suit, he put me at ease immediately. I thought him one of the most charming men I had ever met.

We talked about world events. He seemed tremendously interested in hearing impressions of the socioeconomic situations of the countries I had visited. I found him keen and alert, eager to learn and absorb new ideas, realistic yet idealistic, with a humility tempered by realization of his mission as a leader.

An hour later, Mrs. Shackleford and I flew to Kumasi. I played there that evening. Afterwards I tried to re-wash the white dress I had worn to the Uganda game park. The orange dust had never completely come out, and my scrubbing made it worse for the soap was a peculiar yellow, which stained the dress even more.

The next morning, Mrs. Marcus Garvey, widow of the noted West Indian leader, escorted me to the Royal Residence, to meet Prempeh II, King of the Ashanti people, who had become Omanhene of Kumasi in 1931, and in 1935, the Asantehene. A wealthy trader before his accession to the throne, he is the nephew of the previous ruler, and comes from a dynasty three centuries old.

"Nana," or "grandfather," which the King likes to be called, was dressed in beautiful robes. They looked like the flowing toga of Roman days. With wise gracious manner, he spoke to us for a while on world affairs, then presented me with a wonderful bolt of hand woven royal kente cloth. Its magnificent intricate design was gold, yellow, red and green, and only three such bolts existed in the world: one was made for King Prempeh, one for his chief wife, the Queen, and one was given to me.

I FLEW BACK TO ACCRA to play at Achimota College, which means "Speak No Name." Mr. Gbeho, an adorable jolly man, who had composed the National Anthem, presented me. Before I started, Prime Minister Nkrumah came backstage to wish me luck. And at intermission and the end, he returned to congratulate me. I was overwhelmed.

Finding I was in distress because there was no plane, train, or boat to take me to my Ivory Coast concert, he made the splendid gesture of giving me one of his cars at my disposal, with two chauffeurs, to make the twenty-four-hour trip. George Padmore saw me off when I left the next morning. But despite the luxurious comfort of the Prime Minister's car, the journey was wearisome for all the radiant, glorious, greenery. Wild rubber, mango, kola palm, orange, cocoa, and mahogany trees sped past us. Coconut palms, cotton trees, fields of yams, plantains, beans and peanuts, dotted the countryside. To answer the call of nature, we stopped at taverns and huts. The privies would have a square box of earth and shovel beside "the hole." One spaded the earth into "the hole" after using it. After one visit, I returned to the car to find it crawling with roaches.

We passed many stark naked little boys, tripping by the road. It grew dark. We stopped at a tavern to hear a rebroadcast of my radio concert, beamed throughout the country. We set out again. The millet and guinea corn fields were dim. Tall shea trees loomed like masked witch doctors above us. The gloomy blackness was terrifying.

When we reached the border it was closed. We spent a few hours in a weird rest house with no plumbing, no lights, and only a hard bench to lie on. It was crawling with bugs.

At dawn we set out again. Soon we were covered with orange dust, choking, suffocated. We lurched into Abidjan late that afternoon.

Now, we did not know where to go. Someone directed us to the Governor's mansion. It was not the right place. Someone directed us to another Governor's mansion on the opposite side of the gleaming city.

We went there, and I sent a note into the Governor, but he did not receive me. I was angry and embarrassed now, and roasted by the vicious heat.

We drove back to the city now, and searched for the American Consul, but could not find him, for the Consulate had just moved to a new building, and no one knew where it was. I stopped at a bar to get something to drink. They had no fruit juice, so I asked for milk.

They would not accept Ghana currency at the bar, and rejected my French francs as only being worth half of French West Africa money.

Finally someone told us where the Consulate was. I limped up the flights of steps to the office, but he was not there. I waited. Eventually, he arrived.

"Where have you been? Where? We've been so worried. You sent a telegram? What telegram? We'd better find Mr. Galliatzsky, so you can give him a program to print for tonight. You sent one? It never came," he said excitedly.

We ran downstairs, and he drove me to a wonderful white modern air-conditioned hotel. Carol Dunbar, the wife of the vice consul met us there. She took me to my room.

"How wonderfully cool this is! It's like an icebox," I exclaimed, as we entered.

"Yes, it's a help in this weather."

Carol Dunbar had beautiful red-orange hair that was well contrasted by her turquoise cotton dress. She wore no makeup. She was very interested in MRA.

"I played at Dr. Buchman's home in London, "I said, "It's a wonderful mansion that formerly belonged to Clive of India." I told her of my deep admiration for the spirit and message of MRA, how I admired its international humanity and its absolute standards and that this would certainly be a better world if its inspiration could reach more people.

Carol agreed that human nature could be changed.

She left. A splendid supper was sent up from the dining room. Now I had been thirty-two hours without sleep.

That night, the modern theatre impressed me.

The concert was taped for rebroadcast.

When the reception in my honor, ended, I returned to the hotel at 2:00 a.m. At dawn, the Dunbars drove me to the airport. I was sorry to leave bright modern Abidjan, with its clean white freshness, and French style. Monrovia would be a sharp contrast.

As the plane settled at last, on Roberts field, Liberia, I thought to myself, "How can I stand this? It's hell playing classic music in soggy, damp tropical heat. It's been too fast—Accra concerts on the 26th and 28th, Kumasi recital the 27th, that twenty-four hour trip to Abidjan on the 29th, the Abidjan concert on the 30th—and now concerts in Monrovia on the 31st, tonight, and Feb. 1st, in Dakar on the 4th and 5th, and Morocco on the 7th and 8th! It will kill me."

President King of the University of Monrovia, met me at the airport, and drove me over the long, uneven road to the city. We passed great tangled age-old forests. It was the most malevolently twisted, most barbarous jungle I had seen in Africa. The trees, like petrified giant's legs, stood with a sinister slyness, as though silently waiting for you to dare to enter, so they might strangle you.

The forest was supreme here, arrogant, monstrously proud of being stronger than man's puny civilization. The teeming leaves were like leering elfin faces.

We reached Monrovia, which sat like a cross old man at the edge of the woods, tenacious of what he has hewn out, but too feeble to do more. He is tired, and the poisonous enervating heat makes the finishing of any plan, the completion of any project inordinately difficult.

The sea rumbled like an angry serpent, hungry for human flesh.

At the hotel I was taken to the top floor, built in honor of the visit of Prince Bernhard of Holland. We walked up uneven, shallow grey stone steps, each step a harrowing distance from the next.

My concerts at the beautiful new modern university were packed with elegantly dressed people. I played on two ancient moldy uprights. Both were minus a few keys. President and Mrs. Tubman received me, most affably at their residence.

The other guests there were smartly dressed, in well-cut laces, silks, linens. The garden was hung with long, gay strings of colored lights. Rows of Cadillacs were parked outside.

During my stay, I was entertained splendidly.

Sometimes the houses had elegant, well-styled furniture from the u.s., but were themselves crazily uneven with irregular stair-wells, erratic walls and floors, and whimsical ceilings that often were capricious.

Yet, one thing to be said in Liberia's favor, is that, among the coastal Americo-Liberians, women have a dignity of position not often seen in Africa. Nowhere else on the Continent did I see a woman in a similarly responsible position to that of Angie Brooks, the Attorney General. An attractive woman, who does not allow her prominence in a male profession to detract from her femininity, she also showed her brilliant, astute side when she chatted with me in American Ambassador Richard Jones' garden.

There are other good sides to Liberia. The iron in the Bomi Hills mines, the best anywhere, is 68.8 percent pure. There is no Communist threat, no over-population. And Liberia's animal life is rich, colorful.

Robert Spelton, an American missionary living in Monrovia, told me he had often seen such creatures as, "fruit bats with gigantic heads, red-and-blue lizards, red bush pigs, greenish colobus monkeys, Diana monkeys with brilliant red-orange thighs, spotted hyenas, waxbills, six-inch long scorpions, hartebeest, and lemurs—not to mention porcupines, antelopes, chimpanzees, leopards, chevrotains, buffaloes, flamingos, vultures, duiker, dramatically colored weaver birds, and crocodiles."

We were sitting in the California-style patio of a Liberian friend's house. It was stifling humid. "Is the climate always atrocious?" I asked.

Mr. Spelton, who was about fifty, with a beaming, cherubic face, and who must have been suffering in his tight collar and white linen suit, said, "Oh no! You've just come in the wrong season, that's all!"

It was odd that no matter what time I came to any part of Africa, I was always told I had come at exactly the wrong time to catch the right weather, which was "really wonderful."

"What products do you have besides rubber trees?"

"There are kola, cotton, palm, fig and bread-fruit trees—and of course the gold, sapphire, garnet and diamond mines."

"Is it true that diamonds smuggled from South Africa and Sierra Leone used to be brought here to get false certificates that they were Liberian gems so they could be sold on the international' market to defy the Oppenheimer diamond syndicate—and not so long ago, at that?" I inquired, fanning myself desperately.

Mr. Spelton looked aghast, and changed the subject. "I'll show you photographs of some of the native tribes later, if you like. I have slides showing the Kru, Bassa, Grebo, Pudu, Tchien, Kra, Geh, Gio, Mano, Kpelle, Buzi, Gbunde, Gbande, Mende, Kisi and Vai peoples."

Later, I was told that the Vai, and a Moroccan Berber tribe, were the only African peoples to evolve an indigenous alphabet and written language before the coming of European influence—this classification excluding Arabic and Amharic, which are both Semitic tongues.

I saw some examples of the Vai seven-letter alphabet, which gave the impression of being quite clever pictographs.

These Liberian tribes are quite distinct, and do not necessarily practice the Golden Rule. My father once told me, "When I was on safari in Liberia, I had boys from half a dozen different tribes with me, but they would not eat with or speak to each other."

While Mr. Spelton was showing me his scrap-book, he said, "One of the most fascinating tribes is the Mano. Their religion is based on ancestor worship, contact with the ancestors being made by means of wooden masks—they think man has four souls, and that animals, trees and stones also have spirits."

They, the Mano, also have an intricate, involved medical system.

Abortifacients are in common use with them, and appear to be safe. One is the root of the cotton tree, another is the wana shrub, one leaf of which, they say, acts effectively in a day. They treat coughs with oranges mixed with salt, and burns with palm oil mixed with soot. Both male and female circumcision are practiced.

For treating impotence they eat the scraped bark of the black kola tree; or they tap the bark of a wild rubber tree, and drink half a cupful of the latex mixed with palm wine.

Recently, I told an English friend, Mr. Mclean, who had lived for fifteen years in the Congo about the latter remedy, and he said, "Why, I should think it would kill them—unless the palm wine acts in some inexplicable way to dissolve the rubber. Once on the Lever Brothers plantation I managed in the Congo, an African woman tapped one of the rubber trees and drank the latex. In a few minutes, it congealed and hardened within her, putting her in the most tormenting agony. A doctor came and opened the abdomen, but the rubber had already spread like octopus tentacles through the vital organs, strangling them, so that she died, writhing in the most ghastly pain."

Mr. Spelton told me, while showing me some photographs of the thick Liberian jungle, "—not until 1824 was the name Liberia created, though American-freed Negroes began coming to the coast here in 1821, and only in 1847 did the settlers declare the land an independent republic."

"Was cannibalism practiced here before they came?"

"Uh, yes. In the most grisly fashion. One quaint derivation of this took place after the circumcision ceremonies—what had been cut off from the boys was dried and made into soup for the girls to drink—and what had been cut off from the girls was dried, and made into soup for the boys to drink."

"Does this still go on?" I asked.

"It's not frequent. The Americo-Liberians have attempted to eliminate it. Of course, one doesn't know everything that happens in the depths of the bush."

The day before I left Monrovia, I stayed in a beautiful villa by the rolling sea some distance from the city. It was owned by a prominent businessman and his red-haired wife. It was exquisitely furnished and pleasantly cool. The bathroom was immense with gorgeous black tub and toilet and jade-green basins. The fact that no water ran in them was incidental beside their splendor. There was a lovely library, too.

Everyone talks about theft in Monrovia, but I did not have a thing stolen while I was there, although my suitcases were open since the keys had long since vanished. In fact, in all my travels, the only place where I've had anything of significant value stolen, was in the U.S. One describes Monrovia with apologies. Dakar with superlatives.

You would not think they were on the same continent.

Dakar is gorgeous. The Paris of Africa.

One third of a million inhabitants. One tenth are Europeans.

When I arrived at the Dakar-Yoff airport on February 3. André Liotard and Rolf Jacoby met me. Rolf Jacoby was U.S. Cultural Attache, André was Director of the Service d'Information de Presse et de Documentation du Gouvernment Generale.

"Have you been in Dakar long?" I asked Liotard as we entered the sleek black French Government limousine with its white-garbed chauffeur.

"I was born 272 kilometers from here, at St. Louis, in 1910 my father was a French Huguenot Missionary."

"You must know French Africa well, then!" I exclaimed, as we passed the gleaming eight-story Hotel Ngor, and drove towards the City. "I left when I was four, and didn't come back until 1955. I've held this post since November 1956," Liotard said.

"It must be exciting!"

"In a way. Sometimes I miss Antarctica, though—the peace, tranquility, the sense of being far from the jungle of mankind. I went there first with the British in 1946, and then I headed two French expeditions that went in 1948 and 1949. The last time, we stayed a year—myself and eleven other men."

I was thrilled to meet a polar explorer, one who fulfilled the Greek ideal of simultaneous intellectual and physical development. Liotard had a strong face, a face that might haunt one, a face not from Cezanne or Delacroix, but from Velazquez or Goya, it showed wisdom, sardonic irony, and compassionate tolerance of humanity's frailties.

"Was it cold there?" I asked, realizing that was not quite original.

"Naturally. But no one had a cold. During the entire year, no one had a cold. What did we eat? Penguin's eggs! And canned goods from France. What animals did we see? Seals, of course. No, no polar bears! You'll have to read my books, 'Terre Adelie,' and 'Man and the South Pole.' I'll give you copies. Do you see that three-story red brick building there in African Colonial style? With the ten steps leading up to it? That's where I work, 125 Rue Vincens. It used to belong to the Grand Conseil. Now, we use the whole building for the Cinema, Information, and Press Bureaux."

"Where are we going now?" We drove through spacious streets lined with solid white houses.

"To the Hotel des Gouverneurs, where the Governors of French West Africa stay when they visit Dakar. You will have the Ivory Coast governor's suite."

It was a sumptuous modern suite, worthy of a governor. The most expensive, stylish furniture, smart decor, chic lamps, exotic pillows, smoothly running bathroom equipment.

Monsieur Jobert, another French official gave a dinner party for me that evening. Guests were there, of every conceivable background, mingling with complete freedom. One French official said to me, "How is it you're still single after all your travels?"

"I don't want to marry unless I'm tremendously in love."

He gave an ironical smile, bitter, yet strangely gentle, "Is it not sufficient to love a little?" He seemed to gaze through me with a distant, cold, sensuous, yet tender look.

I moved away.

Another official said, "You must be happy to be away from Monrovia."

"The climate is so wonderful here. What a relief not to be broiled anymore! I love this cool dryness. What a nice place to live! But, then, Liberia never had the advantage of being a colony, so there was not the money and technical help from an outside nation to make their capital city impressive. How old is Dakar?"

"It was a simple fishing village in 1750, and only became a city a century ago. However, Goree Island, only three kilometers east of here, has a long history. Discovered by the Portuguese Dinis Dais, in 1444, it was taken by the Dutch in 1617, captured by the English in 1663, re-captured by the Dutch in 1664, taken by the French in 1677. In 1693, the English attacked, but were repulsed in July. The war with the English recommenced in 1755, the English won it in 1758, the French recaptured it in 1763. There were more struggles with the English in 1793 and 1797, but the English lost. Slavery was abolished in 1818, long before it was abolished in the United States. From 1857 on, Goree's history merges with Dakar's. Do you know Dakar's population has increased two hundred times in the past century?" he added.

"Why don't more people come here as tourists?" I asked him.

"Tourism is increasing. It's a wonderful drive down from Morocco. The road starts in Casablanca, and winds down through Mazagan, Safi, Mogador, Agadir, Tindouf, Fort Gouraud, Atar, Akjoujt, Nouakchott and St. Louis."

Many rounds of drinks were passed before the dinner, an elaborate French meal, was served. The next afternoon, Don Dumont, the American Consul, and his beautiful Morocco-born wife, gave a party in my honor. That evening, I gave a recital to a full house at the Theatre du Ville.

Afterwards, Mr. Senghor, manager of the theatre, and nephew of the great African poet, Leopold Senghor, gave a reception for me at his exotic modern flat. As everywhere in Dakar, people of all colors mixed without the faintest embarrassment, hostility, or awareness of difference. Two towering black Senegalese musicians in bright galabiehs stood in a corner playing colorful instruments of hides over wooden frames, with lute-like strings. There was a hypnotic sensual quality to it. They must have sung and strummed the same melody four hundred times.

Besides Leopold Senghor, and his nephew, Peter, Luz Iberia, the Spanish dancer, and Racine Kane, important official, were there. Racine, a tall handsome African, was an example of the best type of Muslim, educated, elegant, and evolved and modern in spirit. Born in Kayes, in the French Sudan, he was a Sorbonne graduate, and had lived in Europe for seventeen years.

"I loved your Beethoven Sonatas tonight," he told me. "My favorite composers are Bach and Beethoven. But you do Ravel beautifully, too. You have the French spirit."

"I adore French literature. Balzac, Zola. "My favorites are Lamartine and Sartre. I really admire Sartre's *Respectful Prostitute.*"

The next afternoon. I gave a private concert at the Residence of the French Haut-Commisaire, Mr. Gaston Cusin, before a select group of French and African elite, in a sumptuously furnished room. In the second row sat a large woman wrapped round with layers on layers of impressive veils, she looked like a monument. A wealthy Senegalese business-woman, she had singlehandedly made a fortune in the transportation business, though illiterate.

I had dinner at another official's home. The lobster was grey. They told me brightly that it had been left over from a party the previous week. Despite its strange taste, I took two servings.

At the Dakar-Yoff airport, that night, as I checked in for the Casablanca plane, a handsome blonde woman came up and embraced me.

"I am Marion Mill Preminger!" she exclaimed. "Wonderful to see you. You look like a movie star. I won't have to change anything. You are my daughter."

"Oh, yes! I read your book, 'All I Want Is Everything'."

When we boarded the plane at ten that evening, I tried to sleep. Impossible. I was repeatedly sick.

When I asked the steward for help, he handed me a small square that looked like granulated sugar. I asked, "Should I eat it?" He replied, "Yes." I had never eaten white sugar before, but I thought that perhaps in an emergency it was the thing to try. Sickness had obscured my sense of smell, never very keen, but in the middle, I realized it tasted strange. I sniffed it closely. It was not sugar, but camphor.

When I landed in Casablanca, Dr. Francis Hammond and his wife, both American friends, met me and drove to Rabat. The trip seemed endless. At the Rabat hotel, my nausea continued for twelve hours. Finally, in desperation I ate ten tablespoons full of charcoal, and the retching stopped, but it left me desolately weak.

The next night, I drove to Casablanca for a concert though my stomach felt aflame, and as if riddled by bullet holes. As weak as if all the blood had been drained from me, I summoned nervous energy and played for a crowded hall at the Automobile Club. The two-hour drive back to Rabat seemed to last ten years.

The next afternoon, I gave another recital, under the patronage of Ambassador Cavendish Cannon, and Her Royal Highness, Princess Lalla Aicha, Morocco's leading feminist, and eldest daughter of Sultan Mohammed V. Her younger sister, Princess Lalla Nezha, a beautiful girl dressed in smart Western clothes, attended the performance, and was photographed with me afterwards.

Then, there was a long reception. I slept four hours. At five in the morning, I was en route for Tangier.

Spanish officials were still at the border, though international rule of Tangier had supposedly ended in October 1956.

This was a historic day. The "retreat of the peseta" was occurring with all possible accompanying hysteria and skulduggery. Once in Tangier, I was not allowed to leave. No one would be let out for ten days. The border was closed to keep people from escaping with smuggled pesetas. Through influence, I got a secret written pass to leave, but, on recrossing the border, I was searched relentlessly throughout my anatomy.

The drive back to Rabat was torment.

It seemed twice as long as the drive north, my stomach tortured me, the road was bumpy, we were held up by flocks of goats, or strolling men in djellabahs.

A reception was given in my honor in Rabat that evening. I left the following dawn.

Driving towards Casablanca in the early morning light, I wondered what the future would hold for the women of Morocco, those strange secretive women, in their long grey shapeless robes like nun's costumes.

Lalla Aicha had set the example, but few had the courage to follow her.

The country, despite the chiseled modernity of Tangier, Rabat and Casablanca, looked back to ancient days of cruelty, to the arrogant seven-century rule over Spain, to the proud brutal epochs when Europe's ships had trembled before the Moroccan pirates, paying exorbitant tribute to these bloody buccaneers.

Yet, I felt dissatisfied on leaving Morocco.

I flew to Paris, drizzly, dull, dark and gloomy.

I already burned with longing to return to Africa, to its blazing sunshine! Europe seemed decadent, dead, Africa the hopeful one, so old yet so new! ⊞

CHAPTER 17

The Ants of Usumbura, Birthday in the Congo
Ruanda, Urundi, Belgian Congo 1959

CENTRAL AFRICA TEEMS WITH an astounding fecundity of insect life. Fighting furiously, with primeval ruthlessness, for breathing-space in this still near-savage area, are red ants, termites, scorpions, tsetse flies, beetles, spiders, mosquitoes—sinister, endless, poisonous, boundless.

Only a few decades have passed since huge armies of a million driver ants would regularly march across the terrain, devouring entire villages as they passed. Usumbura, the administrative capital of Ruanda-Urundi, still has ants. My hotel room was full of thousands of big black ones. Beat from two nights without sleep, I had flung myself across the bed when I entered, and dropped into unconsciousness. An hour later, when I woke up, I was covered with ants from head to foot. So were the walls. What I had thought was checked wallpaper was an army of ants. I fled to a table, jumped and trembled with fear when the slithering insects raced on relentlessly after me, like diabolic visitation.

Kicking and stamping, brushing them from my clothes, pulling them by handfuls from my hair, I was disgusted and scared stiff. Then, noticed an ant nest hanging upside down on the ceiling over my bed. The ants had been using the bed as a stepping stone on their journey home. I moved the heavy bed to the other side of the room, and put a table under the nest.

They continued to crawl in from outside—but from then on they did not disturb me. They kept to their side of the room, and I kept to mine.

I was pretty glad to leave Usumbura two days later.

I was tired of all that "togetherness."

The food in the hotel dining-room was good, but expensive. The morning after arrival, towards the end of January 1959, I walked outside the hotel looking for a store where I could buy less expensive food. I found one, but it was rather drab—with no attempt at decoration, just rows and rows of canned goods piled on top of each other. The place was Greek-owned, and the dark-haired, olive-skinned, sharp-featured young man who waited on me, plied me with questions about the whole world, especially the Near East, when I told him that I was on a world tour.

"My name is Demetrius Omorlogolou," he said. "I was born in Rhodes, but I lived for years in Cyprus before I came here. Have you been to Nisosia? No? You've been to Istanbul? Did you know any Greeks there? I had some friends who had their businesses wiped out in the anti-Greek riots there. Do you think things will get worse in Lebanon? How do the people seem to feel about King Hussein in Jordan? Do you think he'll be assassinated? I know a lot of Greek merchants in Khartoum. Did any of them come to your concert?"

His questions, and my replies, went on for an hour. Only one or two customers came in during that time. He offered to show me around, then, and leaving the store in charge of an assistant, took me in his land-rover through the dusty streets.

We ended up in a bar, where he ordered beer, and I ordered fruit juice. "I should think you'd take wine in a French-speaking country," I said. "No. People don't drink much wine here. Throughout the Congo, as well as Ruanda-Urundi, beer is the favorite drink."

"What do the Africans like to eat here?"

"Manioc is one of the staples. The Watusi eat peas and lots of milk. In the Congo, in provinces like Kasai, they like wheat, corn and manioc mixed together, served with such meats as zebra, elephant and hippopotamus."

"Do you go to the Congo often?"

"Fairly often. Sometimes I drive to the Albert National Park, in the depths of the Central Graben Rift. It's a hard journey, but the animal life is wonderful," he said. "Oh, you can really drive on the roads here? I've been on some horrible roads in Uganda," I said.

"This is quite a crossroads. Roads to Kitega, the native capital of Urundi, Kigali, the native capital of Ruanda, Costermans-ville, Shangugu, Uvira, Astrida, Rumonge, and lots of other places branch out from here."

"Do you like it here?"

"One gets bored," he replied slowly. "And now, one gets nervous. One doesn't really know what will happen, since the Leo riots. What will the Africans do? What will the Belgians do? Of course, this is a United Nations Trust Territory, taken from Germany, and handed to the Belgians to direct in 1919, so the situation is not the same as the Congo, but we're still nervous. None of these people are ready for self-government, that's evident. The Belgians should fight to keep the Congo—they should have brought more Belgians here in the first place—King Baudouin should never have made that announcement promising independence to the Congo—it's premature. It will touch off a hornet's nest of troubles. I'm afraid the Belgians have a defeatist attitude now. Why shouldn't they fight for the Congo? It will just be a mess if they leave, with tribe fighting tribe, and the common person worse off than before."

"And what about the Greek, Syrian and Armenian merchants? A lot of us will be scared to stay if the Congo becomes independent. Of course there is no sense of unity whatsoever between the Congo tribes. One can almost tell by looking at a Congolese what tribe he comes from—inbreeding has so stratified their physical characteristics."

"Do you know, I meet a lot of Americans who seem to think Africa is all one country? Eleven million square miles and all one country! It seems impossible to make them understand that Africa is hundreds of languages, and hundreds upon hundreds of tribes with totally different customs. Europe is tiny compared to Africa, like a kitten compared to a lion, but no one confuses the Scotch with the Sicilians, or the Welsh with the Albanians—yet they make far worse mistakes of ignorant generalizations and blanket thought about Africa. Every religion, every race, every custom is in Africa," I said.

Getting excited, he began to talk faster and faster, more volubly. He told me about the Watusi, or Watutsi, who are not Negroes, though dark in color—but are really Hamitic Nilotics who have lived in the Ruanda area for hundreds of years—those splendid, pastoral, cattle-raising people, the tallest in the world, the males often passing eight feet.

"You know, they have a strange caste system, with the Pygmies forming a hereditary serving-class," he said.

"Do they practice cannibalism?" I asked, softly.

"No. But there are occasional revivals of cannibalism among such tribes as the Bwaka, in the Congo—and one hears that even now, every month, among the Basala Mpasu in the Luiza territory in the Kasai province, at least one human being is killed for cannibalistic purposes, the victims being generally so well chosen that complaints were not filed about their disappearance," he replied, and ordered a third glass of beer.

It was raining now, the water seductively falling in a sparkling glass sheet. Then a bucketful of rain came down. The temperature was a little warmer than a typical September day in Belgium, yet one felt so different, one felt throbbing with a blood-rushing excitement, yet wary, watchful, dubious yet speculative, anxious, yet eager to descend into the unknown where one might lose, find, or destroy oneself.

The air seemed teeming with ghostly images. Like the pagan African, one could almost feel the spirits of the deceased and the unborn, watching, and one shivered despite the too-pleasant warmth.

"What was the reason for the cannibalism practiced before the Belgians took over the Congo government in 1908?" I asked.

"Partly for tribal rites to absorb the strength of the dead, but also because of the love of the taste of human flesh," he replied, taking out a pack of cigarettes and lighting one.

"Why should anyone like to eat human flesh?" I murmured.

"It has a sweet, soft tenderness compared to the stringy muscularity of the wild animal flesh which was their main source of protein, and irregular at that. Mostly, they had to depend on starches like manioc, which grows boring, I presume. One old man said to me, 'It was much more courteous for me to devour my friend, than to let the worms eat him,'" Demetrius Omorlogolou laughed.

"Have you seen any strange customs in the Congo?" I asked softly.

The red metal table, round, scratched, worn with the elbows of a thousand drinkers, seemed to whisper with us in an intoxicating, indistinct humming, as if the voices of spirits were hungrily listening to us.

"Now, the Baluba have a custom of artificially swelling the human female vaginal lips by pricking or injections, to give them a better hold on the male organ and thus increase passionate excitement — though it later causes difficult childbirth," he murmured, going on to tell me of the other queer and more shocking practices.

Suddenly, the rain began to fall in greater torrents. Two Belgians plunged through the watery flood and rushed into the bar. We changed the subject. They stared at me curiously. Demetrius asked me, "How do you have the courage to travel around the world alone? You're not afraid?"

"No. It is my destiny. One must go forth to meet one's fate. It is all written. Often, when I reach a place, I know that I have been there before, in some dream, or in some former life — I have the intense feeling that I am revisiting what I have long known. I have ten nationalities in my ancestry, and that may be what attracts me to all countries — I am trying to find myself."

When the rain lessened, Demetrius drove me back to the hotel, telling me strange stories of the Greek underground during the war, and of Cypriot terrorists, on the way.

It was almost lunch time. Against my better financial judgment, I entered the dining room. The frightening tales I had heard might have upset me too much had I been alone.

I saw a figure bent over one of the tables in front of me that looked oddly familiar. He was studying a menu. Then he began to gesticulate to the African garçon who hovered over him. He began to shout in Spanish. I looked at him. Our eyes met simultaneously.

"¡Madre de Dios! ¡Felipa! ¡Que maravilloso!" he shouted, and rushed over to embrace me, almost knocking down the flustered waiter as he passed. "What do you do here? God has brought you to save me from my suffering!"

"Antonio! What are you doing here? I thought you were in Paris?"

"Oh, in Paris they were cruel to me, cruel! And, in Germany, cruel! And cruel in Israel, and cruel in Egypt! And I am only sacrificing myself to save my pais—I serve, I only weesh to serve—I am not a playboy to waste my time on zee woomans, I give up all for my country—and they are against me everywhere. This is a terrible world. No one appreciates my idealismo!"

"But what were they cruel to you about, Antonio?"

"The guns for my revolution! ¡Mi revolucion! I must keel the traitors."

The others in the dining hall, all Belgians except the waiters, cocked their ears, listening sharply, with the alert look of hounds. "Antonio," I said harshly. "Callese la boca. Don't talk about that now, in a public place. Are you crazy?"

"Felipa! How you speaks like that to a Spanish gentleman? You rude and cruel wooman. You must treat me with respect." His handsome, sombre, sensual face now shifted capriciously to a new expression of dissatisfaction.

He complained about the food. It did not suit his ulcers. He had spent the morning dressing, and then came to breakfast at eleven o'clock. "The cruel waiter" had said that was too late for breakfast, and that he would have to order lunch. "The cruel waiter" spoke muddled French with an African accent, and did not understand Antonio's Spanish, English, or (equally incomprehensible) French with a Spanish accent. "¡Que lio! I am tortured. You must save me, Felipa!"

I ordered our lunch.

After eating, we left the hotel, and walked through the city. With the dramatic suddenness of the tropics, the rain had ceased as swiftly as it had begun.

We walked and walked, leaving behind the box-like European dwellings that looked just like those in Kampala, and reaching a native sector where the Africans watched us with a curious, speculativeness. And, indeed, we must have seemed an odd sight, weaving in and out among the drab, simple houses, I dressed in an orange Chinese cheongsam, and Antonio in his superbly-cut Parisian suit, and both of us talking in animated voices about Venezuelan revolution.

"You see, after we have conquered all Panama, and all Colombia, we will pass around the Goajira Peninsula, and enter the Gulf of Maracaibo, and capture Maracaibo itself—and all the people will rise up spontaneously to join us, and then we will march on to take San Cristóbal, Merida and Trujillo. Then we spread to San Felipe and Valencia, and strike forth to Caracas where we will be met by new forces that have sailed over from the Panama Canal! *¡Maravilloso!* Will be like French Revolution, *'Allons, enfants de la patrie, le jour de gloire est arrivee!'*" said Antonio, with spontaneous enthusiasm.

Wincing at his dreadful French pronunciation, I remarked, "But, Antonio, you'll need a big army to do all this—how many men have you got?"

"Twenty or twenty-five. There will be more. First I must get the guns. That is harder. I was rejected in France—*fue terrible*. I speak to them for four hours without stop, telling them how I must overthrow everything in my *patria*, and bathe Panama and Colombia in blood, and they were heartless, and refused me—my soul is scarred with that refusal. And in Germany I explained about my suffering people, and how I must capture the Panama Canal, and they would not even listen! And then go to Israel, and explain how I hate the yanqui influence and how it must be driven from South America, and they say cannot help me, and I get nowhere at all in Egypt—because they are angry that I have been in Israel. *¡Desastre!*"

As he spoke, an old man with a grizzly tufted beard, deep scars on his lynx-black face, and a long necklace around his wrinkled neck, of carved ivory ending in leopard's teeth, stared at us quizzically.

I guided Antonio in another direction, and said, "You can't tell people what you want the guns for. You're trying South Africa next? Well, for God's sake, don't tell them!"

"Not tell them? *¡Madre de Dios!* I must be honest! I am descended from Cortez! My great-grandfather fought with Bolívar. I cannot tell a lie!"

"But you won't attain your objective if you tell it to everyone!"

"Oh, you disgust me! You are Machiavellian. And I am pure, I am a *Santo*. I do this for San Antonio, my patron saint—and for my mother, how I love my mother—sometimes I think I love her too much! Too intensely! Too like a lover. It anguish me!"

Now we passed a whole group of Africans, some in white shirts and shorts, some in ill-fitting dark suits and tattered derby hats, some in Muslim galabiehs and little caps.

I suggested to Antonio, "We'd better return to the hotel."

"Yes. *¡Sí! ¡Sí!* Why you take me on this dreadful long walk, I don't know. I am tired. My shoes are all dirty. You have not the heart. Now I will have work up appetite—and I don't dare eat tonight, because of my ulcers. You are cruel. I don't speak to you."

He stayed sunk in sulky silence all the way back to the hotel. When we were seated on the veranda, he muttered, "You make me nervous. I am very nervous man. Why I come here?"

"Oh, I'm sorry, Antonio. You know I think you're wonderful. It's such a surprise to see you here."

"Yes, yes," he said vaguely, looking anxious and discontented, as though suffering twinges of pain. "You know, I go to Addis Ababa after I leave Cairo. I hate Ethiopia. Awful. No nightclubs. No chic. Food made me sick, all that red pepper. I sent my card to the Emperor, and asked what day I might call on him and his *esposa,* and he never even replied! *¡Insulto!* And I am descendant of Cortez. What he think I am—just a playboy? And then I go to Nairobi. Terrible. People wear guns everywhere. And then I visit Kampala. I could not stand Uganda. Woomans are too ugly. *¡Madre de Dios!* The most ugliest woomans I ever meet in my life. They frighten me. I run to airport, take first plane out to anywhere. It take me here. Now, I take first plane out to Johannesburg. Excuse me, I go change the shoes. These shoes are dirty. Your fault. Your *culpa.* Dreadful walk. I go. Don't go away. You be here when I come back, you rude and cruel woman!"

After I had waited for an hour, I went back into my room. After half an hour, there was a knock on my door. It was Antonio. I let him in.

"Is a very peculiar room you have here," he said, critically, as I showed him a seat on the side of the room away from the ants.

"We leave by next plane for South Africa," he announced.

"No. I do not like South Africa."

"Then we go to India, Japan, anywhere! Yes?"

"No. I have work to do. I have a tour ahead."

"We stop tour!" he said positively. "I buy you everything!"

"But I *like* to tour. It is my life. I like to perform."

He rose in angry disgust and paced the floor, "Three times I have ask and you rejects me!"

"Please come sit down *over here!*"

He exploded, "You cannot order me! I am Spanish gentleman! I walk where I wish!" Suddenly, he leaned down and started brushing furiously at his trousers. "Look at thees!"

"Oh, I'm sorry!" I cried. "I'll get them off!"

"But thees is awful! What you do me for? Witch girl! You puts ants on me? *¡Adiós! ¡Adiós!*" he strode out furiously.

It was raining torrents again. When it cleared up for a while, I passed through the lobby to the street, and saw him sitting in a corner morosely pouting. He expected me to apologize. I did not stop. Our worlds were too different.

The wet roofs and dripping trees gleamed like molten gold in the momentary brilliance of the sun.

A group of white sisters stopped to chat with me. I asked were there many Catholics in Ruanda-Arundi. They said that 40 percent of the people were Catholic. I told them I had read the *Nun's Story*. They smiled.

"We now have 158 students studying higher education in Europe," they said. I asked them about a giant black man, as thin as a rail, who was passing accompanied by two shorter men carrying an umbrella and packages for him.

"He is a Watusi lord," they said.

"People in the United States think the only lords in Africa are white."

They laughed. "We have a four-way caste system here," one said. "The Watusi are the overlords, masters of the land; the Belgians are the administrators; the Bahutu until the soil; lowest are the pygmies who only hunt."

Next morning a car drove me through more rain to the airport.

While waiting for the plane I fell into desultory conversation with an ugly, gaunt, man, whose eyes burned with a feverish brightness.

"What is your name?" I asked him.

"Paul Soigne. And yours?"

"Philippa Schuyler."

"Where are you from?"

"Guess."

"Indonesia?"

"What made you think that?"

"You have a Dutch name."

"I'm from New York."

"Are you going to the Congo?"

"Yes. To Elizabethville. To play at the new university."

Mr. Soigne said, "You should visit the Louvanium University just south of Leo, too. Of course those are not the only schools in the Congo. There are over twenty-five thousand primary and technical schools."

"What about those riots in Leopoldville? Will it be dangerous there?"

"Not now. That's over. For the present. I have something here. Look at some of these books, why don't you? There are some beautiful pictures of the Bashilele."

He reached into a package and handed me some lavishly printed brochures filled with stunning photographs.

"These are wonderful!" I exclaimed.

He gave me some more booklets which I scanned one after the other. One showed pictures of the side blown antelope horn wind instruments, lyres, lutes, zithers, curved harps and drums in use in the Congo, and said that the Konda tribe, around Lake Leopold II, had developed polyphony in vocal music. Another described the Albert, Kagera, Garamba and Upemba National Parks, with their rich collections of animals such as dwarf elephants, aardvarks, red buffaloes, black antelopes, dwarf chimpanzees, white and black rhinoceri, bustards and metallic blackbirds. Laden with books, handbags, camera, sacks, music, cans of vitamins, coats and shoes, I staggered across the airfield and into the plane, feeling like a dromedary, and wondering what adventure would meet me in the great primitive yet modern Congo that would be such a surprise to Stanley, if he could see it now.

The rich Katanga province lies in the eastern Belgian Congo, very near the Rhodesian border. It is seventeen times the size of Belgium. Elizabethville is the capital.

When I arrived at the airport, I was surprised to find that the cable I had sent four days before from Khartoum had not, apparently arrived. No one was there to meet me.

I waited. I talked for a while to an air pilot, a Belgian named Jacques Fuligineux. He was tall, with dark brown hair and clear-cut features that were only marred by a look of aggressive smugness.

"Do you live here?" I asked him.

"No. I'll be going on to Leo soon."

"What's that?"

"Leopoldville. We always call it Leo for short—like we call Elizabethville, E'ville. E'ville is sometimes called 'the copper capital,' while Leo is the capital for the entire country. There's quite a rivalry between the two cities. Of course, the climate's much cooler here—Leo's terribly humid."

"Is E'ville a very big city?"

"There are 170,000 Congolese, and 14,000 Europeans—of course, most of the Congolese live in the native section, except for a few servants."

"Is it true that the servants are only paid fifty francs a month?"

"Oh, I think it's more than that, now."

"Is there very much polygamy among the Congolese in E'ville?"

"Why, in all the cities in the Congo, there are more male Africans than female. The males come to the urban regions to work, leaving a surplus of females behind in the countryside. Sometimes they leave one wife there, and have another one in the city."

"I'm going to play at the new university here. Is it true that it's interracial?"

"Yes, but it has a small student body, and a limited curriculum. It has cost an enormous amount of money, so it's been the subject of heated debates in the Belgian Parliament. You'll like some of the buildings. The theatre is the best in East Africa, or any part of Africa, for that matter. The Haile Selassie II Theatre in Addis Ababa is much bigger, but this one has more tasteful styling."

Then another Belgian passed by us, looking as though he had lost something and was looking for it.

He said to me excitedly, "Are you the pianist? You are? Where have you been? We've been looking for you for two days? You've been in Usumbura? What were you there for? You sent me a cable four days ago? But I just got it ten minutes ago. Your concert's tomorrow, January 29. We thought you weren't coming!"

He was a tall, well-built man in a grey tropical suit. He had the same satisfied look the pilot had, mixed with an agreeable urbanity.

The pilot and he bowed unenthusiastically to each other, and this man, who was a government official, led me out to his car. He drove me in various directions, explaining, "You'll be staying with your old friend Gustave Rougon."

Gustave Rougon? Then I vaguely remembered he had assisted Paul Fabo in presenting my Brussels debut in 1953. After the concert he had asked me to translate one of his books, on African art, into English, and serialize it in my father's newspaper. As I had not done so, I had been punished by not hearing from him for five years.

The government official left me and my bags at a one-story yellow house and drove off. A servant let me in.

Gustave Rougon appeared. He burst in, like a leopard, in a gust of tremendous enthusiasm. "It is wonderful to see you! How long can you stay? Only two days? But you cannot leave so soon! You must stay two months, three months, four years! It is wonderful!"

He acted as though he had last seen me a week before, not five years before. He wore a white tropical suit, and had dark brown hair, sharp features, and black-rimmed glasses. He had a self-satisfied look, too, but mixed with energetic self-concentration. Gustave was constantly in motion. No grass would ever grow under his feet. With a tone of caustic irony, he said, "You look better now than you used to. I would never have been interested in you as you were."

I winced, wondering what had been so contemptible about me before.

I was wearing a red cotton cheongsam, from Hong Kong. It was tight-fitting, and slit high on both sides to reveal most of my legs. He said firmly, "I like that dress. It is a wonderful dress! You must never wear any other dress. You are mine! From now on, you are my little Chinese girl. If you ever look at another man, I kill you!"

Very soon, his servant brought in some dinner for us. We sat on either side of a modernistic table. Gustave exclaimed, "This is a celebration! Today is my birthday! You arrived as a special present for my birthday!"

"How old are you?" I asked.

"Too old!" he said, brightly.

"No, tell me how old are you."

'Too old," he said, less brightly.

"Forty?"

"No."

"Forty-two?"

"No."

"Forty-four?"

He did not say anything, but looked gloomy.

"Forty-seven?" I asked.

"NO!" he said furiously. "Eat your soup before it gets cold! What are you waiting so long for?"

His black and white cat, who sat on the table throughout each meal, drank some of his soup. "Is it a male or female?" I asked him.

"A hermaphrodite!"

"You mean, he's altered?"

"What does that mean? Ha-ha!"

"Well, what is his name, then?"

"Stanley! After my book on Stanley!"

"Which book?"

"You don't know? You don't have a copy? It came out in *The Ants of Usumbura* 1954, and it was sold everywhere. Of course it was sold in America. What do you mean you never heard of it! I'll give you a copy and you can make publicity for it!"

Shyly, I said, "I'm writing a book now, too."

"Wonderful! You will include a chapter about me. That will make it a best-seller! I shall write the preface. And you must dedicate it to me—'To my love, Gustave Rougon'—you must use my photograph on the frontispiece—I'll give you one, now."

He walked over to a shelf, and took down a large photograph, flourished it in the air, and said, "This was taken when I was more beautiful." He took out a pen, and signed the photo in red ink—"To Philippa, with deep affection, from Gustave." He said, "You will use this next to the preface."

We resumed eating dinner. Stanley alternately nibbled from his plate and from mine. Gustave asked, suddenly, "Would you like to marry a Belgian and have Belgian children?"

"Why not?"

"Fine. So that's settled. Now I'll tell you everything. I have two illegitimate children in Costa Rica."

"Costa Rica! Why there?"

"No, they're really in France. No, they're really in a convent in Belgium."

"How old are they?" I asked, puzzled.

"One is seven, and one is two."

"Who was their mother?"

"Oh, she died in Second World War!"

Gustave plunged into his rice with gusto. "I have illegitimate children in every country in the world!" he added, with enthusiasm.

"How nice," I said timidly.

"Would you like to have children by me?"

"Uh, why not?" I gulped. "But maybe you have enough already, you don't need any more."

"Children? I don't have any children. We've had enough to eat now. Come, let's sit down on the couch, and I'll make a sketch of you. You will use the sketch on the jacket of your book—by Gustave Rougon—I won't charge you for it!"

We went over to the couch. Stanley sat in my lap. Gustave adjusted me from one angle to the next, so that I would be right for the sketch. An hour passed. Gustave had now torn up five sketches and was started on the sixth. I asked him, "Do you still correspond with André?"

"André? André WHO?"

"André Gascht. You know, the poet. He's been so wonderful to me. You remember, you introduced me to him—he drives to all my concerts in Holland."

He interrupted angrily, "I haven't the SLIGHTEST recollection of having introduced you to him!" He glared at me. He tossed aside the sixth sketch, and said, "It's late now. Good night."

The next morning, Gustave had a party at his home for me. He insisted that I wear my red cheongsam. Quite a number of the Faculty members of the University were there. They all stared at the slits in my cheongsam.

Gustave introduced me to them as, "This is Philippa Schuyler. The great pianist. She is mine! My little Chinese girl! From now on, I am going to travel around the world with her, and turn the pages of her music! We will fly around like pigeons!" Then, he buzzed around among the guests, talking excitedly, in motion every minute.

Soon I had to leave for practice. Gustave drove me to the theatre in his red Jaguar. It was an ultra-modern structure, the last word in stylish originality. It was almost deserted, being the lunch hour.

I went through the aluminum doors. A piano, its lid raised, stood on the stage, waiting for me.

Pretty soon, I felt a pair of eyes boring into my back. I looked around. A Belgian in white shorts and open white shirt was staring at me from the front row of the modernistic seats. He had black hair, definite features, and a self-hypnotized look. I ignored him, and went on practicing. He moved closer, closer. He jumped onto the stage, and leapt at me, crying, "Just ten minutes!"

"Go away!" I screamed, and ran out of the theatre. Soon I had lost him. Now I did not know where to go. I walked through some mud and stones to the road. No one was in sight. I walked down the road a long, long way.

Then I saw a Vespa motor scooter approaching. A young African was operating it. He slowed down when he saw me. "Are you lost? Can I help you?" he asked.

"Yes. I want to go to the house of the Secretary of the University."

"Oh, you're quite a way from there. If you'd like to get on, I'll take you there."

"Why, yes, thank you!" I said. I got on the back of the motor-bike, he pressed the accelerator, and we sped off.

"I know some students at the University," he said. "You're going to play here tonight? Well, good luck. So you like the Congo. I'm glad someone does. There's no conception of the French idea here that all French Africans are Frenchmen and part of the French Community—we Congolese are not Belgian citizens—we're just here to be exploited by Belgium."

"But the country seems prosperous, well organized," I said, while trying to keep my cheongsam from blowing in the breeze.

"Umm. But how many Belgians have sincere personal feelings toward the Congolese? You can count them on your fingers. Most all of them have an attitude of arrogance toward the blacks—even those who are liberal in Belgium change when they get here. The Socialists have been responsible for almost all things in favor of the blacks here, and they've been constantly opposed by the Catholics, especially the Flemish Catholics. Why, the Protestants here are kinder and more liberal to the African than the Catholics."

We sped on. He let me off a few streets from Gustave's house, and drove away. I watched until his black figure disappeared.

Gustave was very excited when I arrived. "Where have you been? Where?" I told him what had happened at the theatre.

He said, "Ha-ha! Well, I'm not jealous, you know, I'm never jealous! Now, sit down and read the Tarot cards for me, I want to know my future. I'm disillusioned. I only came here out of idealism, you know. I gave up a very important offer to come here."

"What offer? Where?" I asked, sitting on the edge of the cream-colored couch, and shuffling the seventy-eight Tarot cards.

"In Ethiopia!"

"Ethiopia?" I asked, incredulously. "What would you do *there?*"

"Be a minister. Cabinet Minister."

I asked him to cut the cards.

He cut the deck at the Devil reversed and the Ace of Swords reversed.

"That's terrible," I said. "You're about to have a catastrophe."

He laid out fifteen cards. "Oh," I said, "that's very bad. You have Judgment reversed and the Traitor next to the Moon and the Eight of Swords. It's awful."

"Oh, that's just superstition. Let's have some dinner."

"I can't. I have to dress for the concert."

"What concert?"

"My concert."

"Oh yes, I think I'll come."

"How nice."

In half an hour we were en route to a party he wanted to go to first. As he parked the red Jaguar in front of a modernistic white villa, he asked me, "How much money will your book make? About two million francs? You must give it all to me, and I will buy a house with it for us to live in forever!"

We arrived at the concert just in time.

A small group of well-dressed Belgians filled the best seats in the striking circular hall. The concert went well. Afterwards, there was a reception in the Artist's room. Gustave buzzed around, talking energetically to everyone. On the drive back to his house, Gustave looked sad and disconsolate. He said repeatedly, "I am your father. Silly girl! Too old! Too old! You are my daughter. You are like eighteen. You are stupid, stupid, stupid!"

The next morning he looked even sadder. "You go away. What for you go away? Cancel everything. Don't go away."

We went to the airport at noon. The plane arrived on time.

Gustave came out on the field with me, right up to the runway that led to the plane. He embraced me dramatically, there, in full view of everyone. "My little Chinese girl! Goodbye!"

I ascended the steps into the plane. The door closed behind me. We soared into the air.

IT WAS HOT IN THE PLANE, and grew hotter as we neared Leo. The Belgian who occupied the seat next to mine, a short, thin nervous man, said, "I heard your concert last night. What a pity more people didn't come! Since the riots this month in Leo, people are afraid to spend their money very freely." He added that he was surprised as many people had come as had.

Yet in Leo, when I played at the Salle Albert there was a full house and no one mentioned the riots. They acted as if everything was wonderful.

Leo was damp, steamingly hot, but I saw no insects. One day, when I was driving with Mr. G. Dumont, the Procureur Général, through the clean well-laid-out European city, I commented on the white fog filling the air, "Why, this is like London! So much fog." He replied, "Not fog, insecticide. A helicopter sprays the streets and the air with it, each afternoon."

"A good idea. This should be done in Abidjan, Lagos and Paramaribo."

Leo, a splendid city, modern and gleaming, has broad boulevards, tall white buildings. The climate is a stark contrast to the relative coolness of Usumbura, which is 2,624 feet above sea level.

How I wished I had remained longer in Ruanda-Urundi to visit the Ruwenzori mountain-range, which rises at Mount Stanley to 16,800 feet, and was produced by an ancient upheaval of part of the continent's Archean floor.

In Leo's streets one saw many merchants in Muslim galabiehs, selling exquisite ivory, mahogany and ebony carvings. One Day, Henry Goldstein, a photographer, posed me by some of them, then he said, "You know, all the Africans for two blocks around were staring at your legs. Nothing is more sexually exciting to Africans than legs. Bosoms aren't considered interesting, for they are only for the suckling of babies."

"How many Congolese are there in Leo?" I asked him, as we drove out to a fine park, overlooking the Congo River, with Brazzaville on the opposite side.

"About 375,000. There are 22,000 whites. We'll have to leave the car here and walk. I want to pose up under Stanley's statue."

We left the luxurious bright red car, and went towards an enormous statue of Stanley, born John Rowlands in Wales, who had founded Leo on December 3, 1881, along with Captain Braconnier, Lieutenant Valcke, Lieutenant Le Marinel and Lieutenant Liebrecht. The statue dominated the terrain like a mighty elephant. Hovering nearby were three nine-foot tall black statues by Ianchelevici of Congo hunters and fishermen.

Then, Mr. Goldstein shot me cross-legged on a rail-fence overlooking the Congo, and drove me back to the Hotel Memling, to pose under a diabolic totem-statue in the lobby.

The Belgians of Leo feted me. One day I spoke with a Congolese of the Bakongo tribe, he had an open alert face, and large black eyes.

"Do you think Belgians look down on the Congolese as mental inferiors?" I asked.

"Some do. Some don't. The age of paternalism has passed. It's the Belgians who are stupidest themselves who look down on the Africans. But many of the Belgians who came here were nothing at home, and, suddenly being elevated to a prominence they had never before experienced, it went to their heads."

"Do you know any students at the Louvanium University?"

"Yes. It is only eight miles south of Leo. It was opened in January 1954, as the first university here."

"Is it true that it is integrated?"

"Not altogether. The students attend class together. Afterwards they go in different directions. White and black don't socialize."

"Have you heard of any dating between black and white students?"

"One case. A black boy dated a white girl, despite the prevalent disapproval. They fell in love. Pressure on the girl's parents was so intense she was forced to drop him. He fell ill as a result of this blow. To my knowledge, white and black students have only danced together once," he said.

"Is there really an integrated residential district around the college?"

"It's small and for show. Before the riots here in Leo last month, there were some whites who lived in the black city, but most had their homes destroyed by the rioting."

"Do you know of any interracial marriages in the Congo?" I asked.

"A few cases where a black man married a Belgian woman, but they had a difficult life on the fringe of the two communities. I know two cases where a white man married a Congolese woman. One marriage was not a success. The other was, because the husband was a businessman who lived in the native quarter and took on native ways."

"Can you go into the big shops in the European city and be waited on?"

"More often than formerly. Discrimination is greater in E'ville than in Leo."

"Have you ever thought of going to live in the Congo Republic across the river?" I asked him. "No. There's too much unemployment there. Too risky. I couldn't make nearly as much money as I do here."

Back at my hotel, I conversed with a Belgian businessman.

"Is it true the Belgians killed thirty-two million people during the Congo Free State era?" I asked.

"No. There were no census figures at all before 1910, so how can anyone know what the original population was, or how many people died before the Belgian Government took the Congo over in 1908?"

"How many people are there in the whole Leopoldville province?"

"There is 3,189,000 Congolese, and 33,500 whites," he said.

"Is the province really twelve times the size of Belgium?"

"Yes. Boma, the Congo's capital until 1926, is also in this province, not far from here."

Later, I visited the Dumont's splendid mansion. Mrs. Dumont was a real music lover who had once been a pianist. She was elegant and attractive, her beautiful white hair forming an artistic contrast to her serene youthful face and classic features. They had a wonderful collection of original Congolese paintings, which fascinated me with their marvelous colors and stunning ferocity.

One evening, the Dumonts took me to the home of the American Consul for a party. A Belgian there asked me, "What is your real impression of the Congo?"

"The Africans certainly look healthy. There is such an enormous difference in appearance between the robust sturdy Congolese, and the generally miserable-looking fella in Egypt."

I reflected on this on my way back to the hotel, afterwards, and mused.

Certainly, the Belgians have brought first-class technical and organizational methods to the Congo which have made it a rich, smoothly-functioning state that offers a higher standard of living than any of the free African nations. A physical miracle has been wrought upon the Congo. And it seems to have the lowest illiteracy rate in Africa. Leo is certainly an amazing city to find in the heart of Equatorial Africa. It would be a shame for this efficiency and prosperity to be destroyed by upheaval and violence. I don't think the Congo is quite ready for independence. What seems necessary in the Congo now is a spiritual miracle — for the Belgian minority to think and act in terms of human affection and equality of spiritual dignity towards the African majority, rather than merely with efficiency and organization.

February 3, the day I left, was hectic. I felt, gloomily, that almost insurmountable problems lay in my future.

Mr. Goldstein took more photographs of me, in shops, in front of modern office buildings. Then Mr. Dumont's secretary drove me to the wharf.

I walked down the wooden ramp to the ferry boat crowded with smiling, colorfully dressed Africans. As the ferry was about to pull out, I saw a man rush to the edge of the wharf. Mr. Goldstein. Dressed in khaki shirt and trousers, and holding an enormous package. He waved and tossed the package at me.

As we drew away from the shore, I opened it. It held seventy photographs of my Congo trip.

Despite my delight, I was still apprehensive.

I felt something strange awaited me in French Africa. ⊞

CHAPTER 18

Dr. Schweitzer and the Lepers Cannibal Country, The King's Necklace

Congo Republic, Gabonaise Republic, French Cameroons
British Cameroons, Nigeria, Ghana, Ivory Coast, Senegal 1959

I T TOOK HALF AN HOUR TO CROSS the Congo River, the great Hydra headed serpentine waterway that twists and turns its swirling brown waters through Equatorial Africa like a huge snake. Only the Nile, Mississippi-Missouri, Amazon and Yangtze Rivers are longer. It curves, sweeps, curls and arches for an estimated 2,718 miles, until, wearily, it flushes into the Atlantic Ocean. Brazzaville and Leopoldville lie, teeming, on opposite sides of the vast stream.

It seemed hotter, somehow, in Brazzaville.

I had a room at the Hotel de Relais. The woven straw chairs had oyster-shell shapes, the narrow bed had a blue bedspread, there was a small bathroom encased in metal walls, and there was an enclosed balcony, with more oyster-shells, outside the bedroom.

My room was in an annex, separate from the main body of the Hotel. I met a French official, in the restaurant, who told me the Cosmic Legend of the creation, as evolved by the Fan tribe. It seems, strangely, that the Fan tribe believed in the Trinity, in the concept of three Gods in one.

And this belief is ancient with them.

"Once," as Monsieur Paurelieu told me, "in the beginning, before anything existed, before earth, sky, plant, animal or man, there was God, and his name was Nzame. Nzame was three in one and one in three. His three selves we call Nzame, Mbere, and Nkwa. Nzame made the heavens, which he kept for himself, and the earth. He breathed upon the earth, and from his breath came forth the land and the water. Nzame made sun, moon, stars many beasts and plants. Then God made man out of clay. First he shaped the clay into a lizard. After seven days the lizard had evolved into Fan, a man. The three Gods in one gave him strength, power and beauty. They made him master of all the beasts. He surpassed the monkey, tiger and elephant. Man became vain and despised God and His authority, God destroyed the paradise He had created for him."

"God then made a new man, the father of us all, and made him make a wife from a tree. He gave them bodies and souls. The souls live forever. The man and wife were created to know suffering and death. They had three sons, one who was very bad, one who was very good, and one who thought of nothing. But Fan, who had been created first, can never die. He had defied God and still defies God. He is wicked, and tempts and taunts man. He is the source of wickedness and all evil and evil thoughts. Once Nzame came to earth and caused a maiden to have a child. He grew up. Once he almost died, but he came to life again, and gave laws to all mankind."

The French Middle-Congo had recently become the Congo Republic. Mr. Paurelieu told me that Mr. Christian Jayle, the new President of the National Assembly, would visit me that afternoon.

Mr. Jayle came at about three in the afternoon. We sat for a while in the oyster-shells in my room and talked. He told me something of the history of Brazzaville that had been founded in 1882, by Count Pierre Paul Francois Savorgnan De Brazza.

Mr. Jayle was a very nice-looking man, with white hair and strong black brows. Despite the heat, he wore an impeccable white suit that looked as though it had just been bought in Paris. He had intelligence and charm.

He took me sight-seeing. I especially liked the modern Catholic church St. Anne du Congo. It was the first modernistic church I had ever liked. He showed me the National Assembly. He showed me his own collection of paintings.

He introduced me to Jacques Quoirez. Jacques is the brother of the French novelist, Françoise Sagan. Jacques had a black beard, wore a white suit, and drove a red Jaguar. He was driving through Africa to amuse himself. Jacques entertained me elaborately during the remainder of my visit.

I gave a concert on an Érard as old as Methuselah. These were the highlights of my stay in the Congo.

My last memory of February 3, in Brazzaville, was of dancing the cha-cha-cha at the Hi-Fi Club with Jacques Quoirez. The Club was elaborately modern, with expensive abstract odd-shaped furniture, dark wine walls, and a luxurious bar.

The guests were smartly dressed, sophisticated and Parisian. Men of all colors were there, all equally urbane, charming and French in spirit, if not in origin. The girls were mostly French, and wore stylish daring gowns, and hairdos a la Brigitte Bardot, or Pascale Petit.

Jacques taught me the cha-cha, which I had never danced before. It was very late when I tore myself away.

GABON IS NEARLY HALF the size of France. But it has only 383,000 people.

On February 4, I rose at five in the morning after two hours of sleep, and packed to go to the airport. Jacques Quoirez saw me off. The trip to Lambarene was hell, pure, unadulterated steaming hell.

The Air France cargo plane was perhaps the worst in the world.

No food, no reclining seats, nothing to read, no air-conditioning. It was hot. Torturingly hot. It seemed like we stopped at every bush to take bananas off, and put more cargo on. Four Methodist bishops were on the plane, too. We got to Lambarene. The hell was not over yet.

We stood for an hour on the tiny runway, waiting for the rest of the bananas to be taken off, and our suitcases to be rescued from the darkness of the plane. Then a jeep took us to the river's edge where a pirogue, manned by six lepers, sent from Dr. Schweitzer's hospital, awaited us.

The pirogue took one and a half hours to row, on the River Ogowe, the few miles separating Lambarene from Adominanongo, the site of Dr. Schweitzer's hospital. The lepers offered us bananas to eat for lunch, but I squeamishly declined. I was starving, half-broiled from the ghastly sun when we arrived.

Dr. Schweitzer, with Olga Deterling and Emma Haussnecht, were waiting on the muddy bank when we landed. Greeting us cordially, he told me he would have someone "fix" the piano, so I could play for him after lunch.

My first glimpse of him was unforgettable. He wore white tropical sun-helmet, white trousers, white shirt open at the neck. His face had the kindly, benign look of a practical saint.

Marion Mill Preminger, founder of the Dr. Schweitzer foundation in America, came to greet me. The tall, blonde ex-wife of Hollywood movie director Otto Preminger, was born in Hungary, and lived a gay life as an international socialite, before devoting herself to Dr. Schweitzer for the past eight years. Author of *All I Want Is Everything,* she spends part of each year at the hospital, and part in America, lecturing to gain money for its work. She is the godmother of all the children in Dr. Schweitzer's leper village, and brings them presents when she comes each year. She has a brilliant, expansive and generous personality.

I was taken to my room, a small wooden cubicle with screening front and back. I was given a pitcher of water to wash with, and a kerosene lantern. I was told to hold it down by my feet so I would not trip on a snake when it grew dark.

Soon the gong was struck for lunch. We went to the dining hall. I sat next to Marian, across from Dr. Schweitzer. It was a great inspiration to be so close to him. His face had strong lines of character, and beamed with integrity and goodness. The food was mostly grown at the hospital, bananas, plantains, sweet potatoes, salad, fish, and macaroni soup.

After lunch, Dr. Schweitzer asked a young European to start fixing the piano. A brand-new English spinet that someone had sent there as a present. It had never been used, because Dr. Schweitzer preferred to play on the black upright that stood against the left-hand wall.

The fixing was to remedy a number of the keys in the spinet that had become swollen and stuck owing to the excessive humidity. It took the young man two hours. While he labored, I spoke to a young German who had come to the hospital to help, but had fallen sick from an ear infection. His cheery, good-looking face, with its brown-beard was wrapped round with bandages. He said that the night before, greenish pus had started to ooze from one ear, and that Dr. Schweitzer had gotten up in the middle of the night to give him an injection.

He had just come from eighteen months of hospital work in the Sudan. I asked him about female circumcision there, and he said he had seen the operation performed, that it involved the cutting of the clitoris, the labia majora, and the labia minora. He said that among some tribes the wound was sutured by thorns held in place by threads wound round their projecting ends—sometimes a reed was inserted so that a little hole might remain, and then the girl's legs were strapped together for six weeks for the wound to heal.

I asked him if this custom took place in Gabon, and he said, yes, among certain tribes. He remarked that sometimes the operation was performed at the hospital because, though they disapprove of it, they felt it better for them to do it with sterile equipment where there would be no risk of infection, than for it to be left to some inept and careless midwife.

The piano was almost ready, now. Soon, Dr. Schweitzer came in with Marion, and asked me to play. The bench that went with the yellow spinet was too low, so I put about ten hymn books from the shelf beside the piano under me, and began to play.

Had I not been half-dead from fatigue, heat and lack of sleep, I would have been terrified at the prospect of performing before one of the world's greatest musicians. I played "Field Nocturne," Schubert's "Impromptu" and the Chopin "Scherzo in B Flat Minor."

After that, someone called him to supervise some building. I felt thrilled, overwhelmed and appalled that I had the courage to play for him.

That evening, after dinner, Dr. Schweitzer played Protestant hymns for all of us to sing in German.

He played on the spinet I had used that afternoon. They told me afterwards that he had never wanted to use it before, and so he always played on the black upright, which by now was rather battered.

After he had heard me play on the yellow spinet, he had decided he liked it, and he played on it from then on, and did not return to the upright. Then he asked me to play again.

Two lanterns were placed on the top of the spinet so I could see. They attracted swarms of insects, which fluttered around, and bit me while I played, but otherwise I would not have had sufficient light.

I played my composition "Manhattan Nocturne," "Jeux d'Eau" by Ravel, and the "Pictures at an Exhibition" by Moussorgsky. I forgot the sweat that was streaming down from me until my dress was a soppy rag, my mosquito bites and weariness, in the excitement of the great chords of the Promenade, Gnomus, Bydlo, Baba Yaga and the Great Gate of Kiev. And I forgot I was in this humid tropical room, playing before a living saint and his devoted, selfless attendants. I was lost in the vastness of Old Russia.

Dr. Schweitzer made some compliments to me on my playing that I shall always treasure enormously.

We all left the dining hall, and picked up our kerosene lamps that we had left in the vestibule outside. I returned to my room, washed and saw that one of my lamps had gone dark, and that the other was weakening. Never having lit a lamp before, I was sure I knew how.

I lighted some matches, and then threw them inside. No light.

Finally I fixed it just right. I left one light in the room and, merrily swinging the other, went out to the outhouse, about thirty meters away. When I returned, my room was full of soot. All of my clothes, books and music were blackened with soot.

How one little lamp could have created such a mess I cannot imagine. The reveille bell was sounded at six-thirty in the morning, but I was too sleepy to get up.

Later, Marion took me to see the hospital and the leper village. She had recently sprained her ankle, and wanted me to put on sensible shoes so I would not rip on a root, a branch, a snake, or some such obstacle.

I didn't. I put on some rubbers over my high heels, took umbrella, camera and sun helmet, and we set forth. Marion said I did not need the umbrella, and not to bring it. It would not rain. I brought it. It did rain.

We walked through a beautiful grove of fruit trees that Dr. Schweitzer had planted with his own hands forty-six years before. Our feet sank deep in the mud of the treacherous path. We passed a wooden bench on which was carved an enormous heart. Within it was written, "Marion Preminger—1952." There were other smaller hearts, for each year since then. Panting, we sat down to rest for a few minutes. The climb had been hard. "And imagine!" said Marion, with her delightful Hungarian accent, "you and I are tired after going half way—and Dr. Schweitzer makes this trip sometimes five times a day. He walks so fast one can't keep up with him. He has more energy than someone twenty years old. He is magnificent. I worship him. It makes me cry just to look at his face. After his dog, I am his most humble follower."

We went on.

The leper village consisted of many small houses spaced at regular intervals. The adult lepers were clothed partly in tribal costume, partly in Western clothes brought by Marion.

Many little children were running about. Marion picked up several and embraced them. She had not the slightest fear of contagion, but thought only of expressing her affection. They all called her "ma mere Marion," and seemed delighted to see her.

We went to a mud wall that was called *la place de la mere Marion*. It had a big heart carved on it. The dot over the "i" was written as a heart also. Marion always dots her "i" as hearts.

Marion picked up one of the lepers in her arms, and she and I posed for a photograph. She looked very pretty with her blonde hair framed by the white sun helmet, her aristocratic features etched against the dark brown of the mud wall.

Then we posed for a few more shots. It started to rain, a vast torrential downpour, the heavens drenching us in a sluicing spouting squalling deluge.

We raced back through the jungle.

We arrived at the main shed of the hospital and took shelter.

Marion showed me the pharmacy, where many brown bottles of drugs and chemicals lined the walls. Then we glanced into the operating room. A male patient lay on the operating table, being operated on for, I believe, hernia.

The rains abruptly ceased, like someone suddenly had stopped crying.

Marion showed me the wards now, where some patients lay in bunks. Outside, members of their families were cooking food for them over low fires on the ground. Some children were sitting in wooden boxes.

Dr. Schweitzer adores animals. He believes that living his religion includes not only kindness to people but to all living things. This is one of the most wonderful things about him. Marion took me to see some of his pets, a wild pig, a quaint-looking bird that seemed somewhat like a duck-billed platypus, and an antelope. She told me that once Dr. Schweitzer had been awarded a honorary Doctorate from a European University, and he had left the certificate on a table in his room, when he left for the day's work. When he came back he couldn't find it anywhere. His antelope greeted him with an elaborate expression of innocence. She had eaten the Doctorate!

Next, I saw the building for housing European patients, the building for the mentally ill and the food supply building.

The bell rang, and we went to lunch. Like the previous day, I sat next to Marion, right across from Dr. Schweitzer. I was overwhelmed when, as he had the previous day, he pushed towards me the special dish that had been prepared just for him, and said he wanted me to have it. Most of the food consumed at the hospital is grown here. Certain special delicacies, grown just in Dr. Schweitzer's garden, are reserved only for him. At each meal he gave them to me. Cucumbers, tomatoes, radishes, and certain fruits. I was touched by his kindness.

After lunch, he gave me five presents, a photograph of himself, signed, "To Philippa Schuyler, in remembrance of her passage through Lambarene. With all my admiration, Albert Schweitzer." There were three other signed photographs and a ring cut from a virgin tree, with his name etched into it.

I was simply speechless with gratitude. To even be in the same room with one of the greatest living Christians made me feel small and humble.

After dinner, that night, I played again.

It was a long concert. It lasted over an hour and a half. I played the Chopin "Fantasie," and two long Scherzi. I did the Griffes "Roman Sketches," the "Alborada del Gracioso" and other works by Ravel.

Then, I asked him whether he would like to hear a Beethoven Sonata, or something by Gershwin. It terrified me even to have the effrontery to suggest Gershwin to this noble and august thinker.

He said, "I would like to hear Gershwin." Almost trembling at my daring, I suggested the "Rhapsody in Blue." He said, "Yes, I would like to hear that, for I have never heard it before. I like to keep up with what is going on in the world."

I went to the yellow spinet and began to play. The heat was so intense, that even in the red cheongsam I had on for comfort, I was dripping with sweat. The keys, expanded by the humidity, were difficult to press down, and the ten hymn books underneath me were not too comfortable. The insects whirled around me and the four kerosene lamps, but I did not mind. The privilege of playing before one of the greatest men humanity has ever evolved wiped all that from my consciousness. He liked "Rhapsody in Blue."

Then I played the "Appassionata Sonata" by Beethoven.

There was quite a bit of applause afterwards, and Dr. Schweitzer honored me by making some compliments on my playing that quite overwhelmed me.

Then he went out to see an African chief who had come from many miles away to see him. He had waited an hour and a half, until I finished playing.

The next morning I rose at dawn, and had breakfast with the others. Dr. Schweitzer did me the rare honor of posing for some photographs with me.

Then he left. Several hours later, he returned with a motor launch. He had made a special trip to the Catholic mission to get their launch to take us back into Lambarene so we would travel more comfortably.

I packed and repaired one of my suitcases that had almost fallen to pieces after travel in eighteen countries.

When I was about to leave, he told me that he was going to write to the dowager queen, Her Majesty Queen Elisabeth of Belgium, and suggest that she hear me play when I got to Europe.

He kissed me goodbye on each cheek, and said to me in French, "You should not wear lipstick." He came down to the river bank to see me off.

I felt broken-hearted at leaving the presence of this magnificent Christian whose lofty devoted heart transcends sectarianism, whose noble example of generosity, heroic stoicism, and chivalrous self-sacrifice, will lend inspiration to humanity for all time.

One also regretted leaving the corps of benevolent spiritual self-denying nurses and doctors that assist him in his labors of love and devotion to mankind, and the firm, solid image of the substantial buildings he had erected with his own loving hands.

The motor-launch was well built, covered from the blistering sun, and made the journey to Lambarene in far less time than a pirogue.

We arrived at the river bank nearest the airfield. The four Methodist Bishops had come along too, though their plane, going in a different direction from mine, would not leave for several hours.

It took some time to transport us and all our luggage by jeep to the airstrip.

When we arrived, my plane had come. As we waited for its bananas to be unloaded, one Bishop asked Marion why Dr. Schweitzer had given up his brilliant career in philosophy, theology and music, to devote himself to the poverty-stricken natives.

Marion said sharply, "Because he believes in living his religion, not just preaching it!"

The Bishop fell silent. He and the three other Bishops had come to Lambarene to ask Dr. Schweitzer his opinions on the future life.

The sun blazed down, like a bright instrument of torture, on all of us.

Marion kissed me goodbye, sweetly, and said, "Well, I'll see you next in New York! Good luck. Success in your concerts."

I boarded the plane.

After infinite snorting and grumbling, it took off, like a sick, dwarf bird.

The plane, miserably uncomfortable, flew into the heavens, descending at Port Gentil, and at Libreville, which the French had founded as a haven for freed slaves, like the English founded Freetown, Sierra Leone.

The next stops were Mitzic, Bitam, and Yaounde.

Now we were in the French Cameroons.

Nearly four-fifths the size of France, with a population of 3,200,000, including two hundred African tribes, and 13,000 Europeans, there is something forbidding about the French Cameroons. On the map, it has a sprawling shape, like a gigantic powerful sculpture by the Nigerian genius, Ben Enwouwu. Yaounde, and the coastal city, Duala, are tiny spots of civilization in this vast, primitive space, like the two eyes of a giant.

Our plane landed at Duala. It was like an electric shock when I found no plane to take me to Kano.

Back in New York, I had been sold a ticket for a February 6 flight to Kano, where I could change planes for Jos, where I had a concert on the 10th, as well as one at a school near Jos on the 8th, and two in Ibadan on the 12th and 13th.

Now, in Duala, they said there was no such flight on Fridays, and no other plane would go there until the following Thursday. There was no way out.

I would have to miss all my Nigerian concerts.

No plane. No train. Impossible to go by car through the thick jungle and swamp land to the British Cameroons.

I drove to the city to see if the British Consul could help me. Unsympathetic, he indicated no interest in or possibility of doing so. I returned to the airport, where a young Frenchman came to my assistance. After much searching, he found a man who was flying to Fernando Po the next morning in his private plane, and who agreed to drop me on the border of the Southern British Cameroons. Not being an international airport, it was illegal for any but British planes to land there, without a permit which it would take a week to get from the British Governor in Lagos. Nevertheless, gallant as Frenchmen usually are, he agreed to take the risk for me.

The young man, who looked like a hero in a novel by Pierre Loti, spoke to me a long time after that, mainly about social questions and politics.

"You ask me my opinion about America. Well, I am prejudiced, not against any particular country, but against hypocrisy in general. Americans have a confused view of international relations. Why do they smear Europeans in Africa with the unqualified blame of being wicked imperialist aggressors, because the waters of the Mediterranean Sea lie between Europe and Africa?"

"The Americans, who were immigrants, or descendants thereof, from Europe, expanded across a continent, seizing the land from, and exterminating hordes of, the original inhabitants, and they blandly accept the fruits of that plunder without any consciousness of wrongdoing."

"And, speaking of that catchword, "independence," it was not the original inhabitants who revolted and expelled the European governments in the New World. In every case, it was the immigrants from Europe to the New World, who then cut their ties with the Old World, and ruled the New World themselves while still sitting on the backs of the New World's original inhabitants."

"In Spanish America, it was Spaniards and part-Spaniards who cut ties with Spain, and then still ruled over the Indians. In Haiti, an exception, the original inhabitants had long since been exterminated, and both Negroes and whites had been non-indigenous."

I said, "Tell me something about the Cameroons."

"The French Cameroons are under United Nations Trustship now, administered by the French. But don't think we exploit the country. Many a colonial or quasi-colonial territory is being vastly helped by the mother country. In some areas that are poor in developed resources, money has come from the pockets of taxpayers in France or England to support hospitals, schools, social welfare projects, airports, and other modern developments. France has poured millions into the Cameroons recently. Though France agreed to full internal autonomy last August, we still, in effect, administer the land."

As he spoke, he escorted me to a taxi, and said *au revoir,* his handsome profile etched against the blackness of the night.

Now I was driven to the modern, amazingly first-class hotel, better than many expensive luxury hotels I have seen in the Caribbean. My air-conditioned room had chic furniture, brown paneled walls. The bathroom held a small square tub, and, naturally, the ubiquitous bidet. The cheerful yellow dining room had exquisite cuisine, its waiters were polished, flawless.

I shared the table of a middle-aged Frenchman with a sardonic, weary face. Never had I seen anyone look so disillusioned. We talked about my stay in Lambarene. He seemed angry at Dr. Schweitzer.

"Why should he get so much credit and applause? Only the Americans think him a saint. I've known hundreds of Catholic nuns and priests who devote their lives to the Africans, as much or more than he has, yet who receive no praise or publicity for their actions, and seek none, who serve with complete negation of self, and only for the love of God!" he cried.

"Dr. Schweitzer does not seek the publicity the world lavishes upon him. Indeed, his great reputation as musician, philosopher, insures that the world's eyes will never leave him, despite his genuine humility. He, and all of us, appreciate the wonderful work the Catholic clergy do in Africa. Do you know many Catholic missionaries are here?" I said heatedly.

"Yes. They are self-sacrificing and brave. The risks they run in some of these lonely jungle missions are unbelievable. Living in the midst of primitive savages, among whom there are still occasional hushed outbreaks of cannibalism."

I thought back in horror to his words when I read, months later, of the attacking and burning of a French Cameroon's jungle mission, with the slain priests' heads carried away as trophies.

I had terrible dreams that night, but awoke at dawn the next morning with a strange sense of peace. Before going to bed, Charles Dickens' line, "Something may come of this. I hope it mayn't be human gore," had flashed through my mind, and my nightmares had been accordingly full of horrors. But the purity of the clear morning light made me think of Shakespeare, "I have almost forgot the taste of fears. I have supped full with horrors; direness, familiar to my slaughterous thoughts, cannot once start me."

With a feeling of rejuvenated happiness, I went to the airport. All problems were solved. I was wrong. They had doubled. It took a long time to find the French pilot. When I did, his plane was the smallest I had ever seen.

As he seemed kind and considerate, I got in, soon, we rose in the cloudless blue sky, passing over miles of diabolic jungle and swamps. Then we landed at Tiko. He hurriedly threw my baggage from the plane onto the tiny airstrip, and zoomed up into the air and away, like a comet.

The authorities rushed out. I had violated a regulation! I had to face them alone. I told my story over and over—how I had been at Dr. Schweitzer's for two days, where there was no telephone, how I had been sold a ticket in New York for a non-existent flight, and how I had four concerts in Nigeria, and did not want to disappoint the Nigerian people. The English official muttered, grunted and was unsympathetic—the Cameroon officials were delighted.

Mr. Eyo Oku, a smart-looking young African, took much trouble to look up air schedules for me, but there was no plane that could get me to Jos that day or the next. He phoned a private air transport company that owned the only charterable plane in the Cameroons, but the plane had left that morning, earlier, for somewhere in Nigeria, to have its yearly checkup. Its pilot had broken his leg, which was in a cast. And, had there been a plane, it would have cost me 600 pounds to charter it.

That afternoon, I flew from Tiko to Port Harcourt, which lies some miles from the Gulf of Guinea, on the Bonny River, in Eastern Nigeria.

It was hot, brown, and devilishly dusty. But at least I was in Nigeria.

It should be a simple matter to get up to Jos. It was not.

No planes were available for charter. No one knew anything specific about whether there was a railway or not. One man said he thought one could go by train past the Enugu coal-fields to the Benue River, where there was a railway bridge that might or might not be in order, and if one got over it, one could go on to Kaduna, and then take another train to Zaria, and another train to Jos. Another man said, no, that was wrong, one should take the train up to Kano, and fly two days later from Kano to Jos. Another man said, no, one should change at Kaffanchan to get a train to Jos, if there was one.

No trains would leave for some days. I decided to drive.

I asked various people how far it was by road to Jos.

One Ebibio tribesman looked at me craftily, and said, "Far." This was succinct, but did not help me much. I asked Kwa attendant. He grinned, giggled, and murmured, "900 miles," as though something about me were terribly funny. An Ekoi passerby stared at me blankly, and muttered, "700 miles." An Ogoni servant, who was at least six inches shorter than I, and who had a big head with the diabolical look of a circumcision mask, chuckled vaguely, and said: "He-he-he. Not so far!"

An Efik loiterer grew more garrulous, "It could be, could it not? Perhaps, 300 miles. Is it so? It could be so. Could it not be? And not more, but maybe less. Oh, maybe less. Could it, could it be, could it not?" He went on and on muttering to himself in a sing-song voice, as though he were on track and could never, ever get off.

A light-skinned Muslim Fulani from the North said, in such a soft voice that I could hardly hear him, "Five hundred." An Ijaw murmured, "Three hundred and fifty or sixty. Though by one road might be three hundred and forty. And by another might be three hundred and seventy, although by some calculations it could be three hundred and ninety."

I was exhausted, weak, hungry, dusty, dripping with sweat, and angry. I tried to find a taxi driver who would take me. At last, I found strange man, with eyes like bright beads, who accepted with alacrity, and said he would only charge me 20 pounds.

He said it was not far at all, and he could easily get me there in ten hours, if we start at sundown, drive all night, we could arrive at dawn.

I got in the shabby car. He drove through a twisted, weaving maze of grotesque side streets, and, at length, stopped before a decrepit house with a tiny eye-like door. The unsavory look of it made me nervous. He went inside, and brought out another man, saying, "Is my brother. Comes to show me the way."

I felt my first twinge of doubt. I forced myself to suppress it as they sat down, and the car started. The driver drove fast, as though he wanted to get out of town as speedily as possible. *Tukals,* lean-tos made of cartons and tin boxes, sped past us. Soon, there were less houses and more trees. Then it became almost all trees. The road was muddy and filled with stones and branches now. I began to think of all the trips I had taken by car in Africa the previous year, and, suddenly, remembered that before each journey the driver had always stocked the car with big drums of oil and water, and food and bottled juices to drink. This time, the driver had gotten no oil, no water, and no food. Seemed queer. Of course there would be no gas station for hundreds of miles. Every so often, the driver and the other man would turn their heads around, stare at me fixedly, and silently turn back again. I saw a small sign on the road. It did not say anything about Jos, or anything about Enugu, either, which was on the road to Jos.

I got nervous. I asked them to stop. They did not. I asked several times. They drove faster. Finally, I said in a loud voice, "You must turn back—I've forgotten something—I left my passport and all my money at the Cedar Palace Hotel."

After I repeated this several times, they slowed down. Eventually, asking me many curious questions, they drove me, reluctantly, back to the city, and stopped in front of the hotel, while I went inside. I had never seen the hotel before, but had heard of it.

I found some Lebanese standing in the bar, inside. I said that I was en route to Jos. One of them said, with a start, "What? To JOS? That's impossible!" He led me out, and took me to the office. He seemed amazed. I pointed to the men in the car outside. He shouted, "Why, you can't go! You can't do that. The next time we'd see you would be a picture of you found dead, on the front page of the newspaper. How could you put yourself in the hands of those villainous men?"

"I had to get to my concert in Jos," I said, telling him the whole long story.

He was shocked. He insisted that I cancel the trip. I was hesitant. He pressured me. I went and told the men I had decided not to go, and gave them two pounds. They took my bags out of the back of the car, gave them to me, and drove off.

My head ached. I felt futile, nervous, anxious, embarrassed.

The Lebanese said to me harshly, "Never do that again. Never. Never."

"But I had to get to my concert in Jos," I repeated.

"Concert! Don't be crazy. You can play another concert any time, you can't get another body."

"You mean it's that much of a risk?"

"YES. My God, you'd never have gotten there—the roads range from bad to terrible to non-existent."

"How far is it?"

"Over six hundred miles. Arrive in ten hours? Impossible. More probably four days. The last time I went, I took three men with me in a car stocked with provisions, machetes, gas, oil and water. Guns, too. At some places, torrential rains had washed the bridges away, so we had to stop, fell trees, make bridges over the streams so we could pass.

"I guess I should not have even thought of riding in such a dangerous area."

"You wouldn't have had to fell trees. They would have dumped you out of the car long before that. It is a dangerous area—the country of the leopard-men where hundreds of people have disappeared and never been seen again. No, it's not all in the past. Those secret ghoul societies still flourish, with unspeakable customs. They need fresh human bodies to increase their magic powers, even their borofima fetishes are anointed with human fat," he said brutally, going on and on.

He had me trembling inside with nervous terror when I finally ascended the flights of wooden steps in the courtyard which led to my top-floor room.

After a wretched night of solitary reflection, I went to the Port Harcourt jail the next morning, to distract myself by looking for Prince Nwafor Orizu.

Orizu, my first suitor, and the author of the brilliant book, *Without Bitterness,* had hypnotized the New York intellectuals in the 1940s with his superlative gifts, before distinguishing himself by embezzling thousands of pounds, being caught, and ignominiously incarcerated in Port Harcourt's jail.

Yet, once as an "African Messiah," he had inspired hundreds of his countrymen to go to schools in America so that they might learn the vital spirit of classless democracy—an innovation, since the Nigerian students had always previously studied in England. Though, even then, he had often taken liberties with the truth, confusing actuality with wishful dreams, he had exceptional talents.

Somehow, I felt the hunger to seek him out, to discover from this quixotic and inspired character some hint to the torments and solutions of modern philosophy. Perhaps, as he had sinned and reflected, he had found some new truth, or re-evaluated the past in some new, illuminated light, from the profundities and agonies of his soul. Perhaps Orizu was one of Koestler's "Crusaders without a Cross," who had strayed into evil in the attempt to discover that which was beyond good and evil, the meaning of the meaningless, and the futility of man's unevolved being, groping for unknown, unimagined truths.

If Orizu could bring me the answer to my own doubts, self-tortures, and inner questing confusions, I might gain an unexpected spiritual serenity, and learn truth and idealism from one who had sinned and repented.

I did not know that my visit would be foredoomed to failure, that destiny in its own unpredictable manner, would bring us together with him, later, in a way we had never expected. A new Orizu had been born from his trial and redemption, his crime and punishment, an Orizu whose book, "Before I Die," would reveal his new, chastened philosophy, an Orizu who was devoting himself to the teaching of young people at a High School in Nnewi State. Not knowing this, I sent my mind back to that day to the way he had been when I first knew him, years before.

He had certainly been colorful. Six feet tall, he would wear splendid robes, and was always exactly 100 minutes late. He proposed to me 267 times and would phone me five times a day to ask, "Would you like to be a Queen?" Every time I left the house, he would be waiting outside in a luxurious car to try to capture me, and, whenever our doorbell rang, it would be him. New York had lost its exotic flavor when he left.

He was not at the jail when I arrived. He had been released, after a seven-year prison term.

When I returned to have lunch at the hotel, in the large, hot, bare dining room. A young man of Greek appearance sat down at my table.

He was Neophytus Sophronious, born in Nicosia, Cyprus.

He worked for the Pearl & Dean Advertising Agency in Accra, and was on a tour through West Africa selling film advertising space in cinemas to small African businessmen.

He had a pleasant face, capable and dependable. His conversation was full of details about life in Cyprus. Later, he drove me in his station wagon through the dusty Port Harcourt streets to the European Club.

The hours sped swiftly until Monday, when I flew to Jos.

The air was cool, but chokingly dusty. Mrs. McDavitts, a Scotch official who had lived there for years, greeted me with, "Well, my lass, I knew you'd get here somehow—I told my husband last year, you're the most determined, resourceful girl I'd ever met—and I knew if it was humanly possible to be here, you'd arrive. True, it's a pity your Keffi concert was lost, but I wouldn't want to see you dead!"

Then Mrs. Heckman, an American Missionary, said, "His Highness Bwong Gwom, Great Chief of the Birom tribe, will attend your concert."

Chief Bwong Gwom did come, in white flowing robes and cap, having risen from a sick bed to do so.

He told me at the beginning of the concert that he would only be able to stay for one piece. He was still there at the end, "I liked it so much, I just couldn't leave!" he said. The Chief had a jovial, benevolent face, beaming and radiant.

On Wednesday, I flew to Ibadan, in the Yoruba area, the largest purely Negro city in Africa, and the capital of Western Nigeria. A colorful, expansive city, I liked it better than Lagos.

The new University was well built, in cheerful pastel shades. A teacher there told me, "—when this country becomes independent in 1960, it will far outdistance Ghana, for it has four times Ghana's area, and seven times the number of people."

Something told me to leave Ibadan a day early.

On February 13, I drove down to Lagos airport. The heat was overwhelming. I flew to Accra. The heat was overwhelming there, too.

The air was full of moisture. But none was in the water tanks.

There was a water shortage. A bad one.

Accra's reservoir facilities were only suitable for half the present population, and there had been almost no rain for months.

At Mrs. Shackleford's home, where I stayed, the water only ran out of the faucets at 3:00 a.m. She would rise then and catch as much as she could in tubs and basins; we all had to use the same water to wash in for the rest of the day. She would pour cologne in the toilet bowls after use.

The evening of my arrival, I was received by Prime Minister Nkrumah at Christianborg Castle. After I was introduced to his Egyptian wife, who was soon to bear his child, and her mother, we had a long conversation on world events.

When the Prime Minister's chauffeur drove me back to Mrs. Shackleford's house, it was late, and neither of us could remember the address.

We stopped at George Padmore's house.

It is easy to get lost in Africa. And telephones are rare. There are more telephones in Chicago than in the entire continent of Africa. Only 1,546,100 telephones to serve 220,000,000 people! Without George Padmore's help, we would never have reached our destination.

Kindly as ever, he was sweet enough not to mind being roused from his well-deserved sleep. He came downstairs in his pajamas and dressing-gown and showed us the way. He had always been wonderful to me. I did not realize that I would never see him again. George Padmore, the brilliant West Indian intellectual, who inspired a generation of fighters for Black Nationalism and Negro freedom, died seven months later, in September 1959, in London, of liver trouble and overwork. His ashes were brought back to Accra to be enshrined forever in Christiansborg Castle—a fitting resting-place for one who had contributed so deeply to the struggle that finally wrenched the Castle from white hands to black ones.

On February 15, I gave a radio concert over a nation-wide hook-up. A distinguished crowd was at the radio station, including many prominent government officials. Lord Listowel, the Governor General of Ghana, introduced my performance. The room in which I played was suffocatingly hot. In fact it was the hottest room I had ever been in my life. Apparently, it had no windows, and they had forgotten to turn on the air-conditioning before the audience arrived. So it was like being in a hermetically sealed attic, over a broiling furnace. It was completely without air. I arrived just before performance-time, and was told the air-conditioning could not be turned on now, because it would distract the radio public. Never before had I realized how dependent the brain is on oxygen. My brain was dead, a complete blank when I started to play. Not even the realization that several million people were listening could revive it from dull atrophy. My fingers seemed to move all by themselves. An agonizing concert.

It was wonderful to get up to Kumasi. I flew there the next morning. My first act was to take a bath. My second was to prepare for a concert at the Kumasi College of Technology, while the college officials placed luxurious arm-chairs in the front row of the auditorium for King Prempeh II, and his retinue, who would be coming that evening.

The hall was packed for my recital. His Highness was there, in Western clothes, and honored me by expressing enthusiasm over my performance. While we were being photographed together, he invited me to visit his Palace the next day at eleven in the morning.

When we drove there, we passed *tukals*, box-like English-built houses, beer-parlors, a cinema, flocks of goats, muddy roads, shops of canned goods and flowered cloth, naked boys, and little girls in red tutus.

The King wore a wondrous multicolored toga today, in contrast to his well-cut, black English suit of the previous night.

We drank fruit juice together, and "Nana," who is a genuinely sweet individual, besides being a Chief of awesome rank, talked at length in a charming, good-humored manner. He seemed like a very happy person, not worried about anything, genuinely young in spirit, spontaneous and gay. He said he hoped soon to take an air trip to England. For fear of accidents (an Asantehene cannot rule unless he is perfectly whole in body, uninjured, unblemished), his twenty-seven lesser chiefs had not wished him to fly before.

He gave me a stunning, large, heavy solid gold medal, with such intricate workmanship as the Gold Coast was famous for five centuries ago. A bright yellow-orange, it was the most brilliant gold I had ever seen.

Back in Accra, I was honored by a final audience with Prime Minister Nkrumah, who had made a special trip back from Takoradi in order to see me again before I left.

We drank tomato juice together in a room overlooking the turbulent, foaming sea. I recalled the discussions we had in New York the previous July, when I had dined alone with him in his Waldorf-Astoria suite.

He had asked, "Americans always ask me, 'Are you pro-America, pro-England, pro-Red China, pro-Russia, pro-this, pro-that?' What do you think I'm 'pro'?"

"I think you're pro-Ghana!" I had replied. And we then we talked about the wildly enthusiastic crowds at the Armory in New York that had mobbed him a few hours before.

Then a madman had tried to burst his way in, eagerly desirous of seeing the Prime Minister, but only able to be oddly incoherent when he arrived. He had to be kindly ejected. Then, we had finished the dinner of tomato juice, turtle soup, lobster, roast turkey, watercress salad and ice cream, while talking about his autobiography, his school days at Lincoln College, his early youth in a small village far from Accra, his philosophy, and his impressions of America. I wondered on this dark, mysterious evening, if he too, remembered that July encounter.

The Prime Minister, wearing a well-styled white nylon American sports shirt, and black trousers, was well-dressed in a casual, relaxed way. His deep, black eyes gazed into the distance in a visionary way, as though seeing Ghana's future. Though he seemed fatigued, his face still held that look of glowing radiance, of proud yet humble consciousness of mission, destiny, fatefulness.

As we spoke, the fierce waves beneath swirled and trembled in an ominous, voracious lurching, as though erupting from the depths of torment and antiquity. The Prime Minister seemed to watch them too, as though they held a secret message only time would unravel. Like the violent heaving of angry serpents they roared and slashed, as though ferociously longing to reach up to the exquisitely furnished room, and destroy it ruthlessly. The waves' thundering was like the drumbeats of the bloody, anguished past.

Between Ghana and Liberia lies the rich Ivory Coast.

Wealthy from exports of cocoa, bananas, timber and palm oil, it has only two and one-half million people in its vast 123,200 square miles.

Abidjan, the capital, is second only to Dakar in pulchritude.

Once it was a fishing-village. Only in 1938 did it begin to grow into a city. Now, its 120,000 people live in a gleaming, white modern city that outshines all the far-away Caribbean cities except Havana.

They had just had torrential thunderstorms when I arrived on February 18. So the flying ants had come out en masse. Myriads of them swarmed in the atmosphere—black, with thick bodies about three-quarters of an inch long, and long transparent wings. After flying a while, they may shed their wings, and crawl.

I stayed with Mr. and Mrs. Dunbar on this trip. They had an air-conditioned room for me. Carol Dunbar opened the window for two minutes to close the shutters outside when I arrived, and fifty flying ants hurtled into us.

We went to the splendid home of Economics Minister Jacob Williams, and his beautiful wife, for dinner. Mrs. Williams, who was fair, with classic features, had been born in Lambarene, at Dr. Schweitzer's hospital.

I asked Minister Williams if it would be possible for me to meet the Prime Minister Houphouet-Boigny. I was told he was not in Abidjan. But nine months later I had a long interview with Houphouet-Boigny at his Waldorf-Astoria Hotel suite in New York, and found him to be a formidably brilliant man, with an incisively intellectual yet practical and solid approach to internal and external affairs, and without the wild hot-headed chauvinism that characterizes some African leaders.

The Jacob Williams home had outstanding paintings by African artists on the richly-colored walls. One, in particular, haunted, magnetized me. A jungle scene, with brilliant flowers, serpents, and the vast intricate expanse of giant trees. The sunshine filtered in a weird, strange other-worldly way through the swelling leaves.

After dinner, we sat on the tile-flagged patio while insects lurched, zoomed and dive-bombed around us.

It was worse the next night, at my concert in Treichville. The hall was packed, and the fans had to be turned off onstage for their rumbling noise interfered with the audience's hearing. The lights were burningly bright. There was no breeze at all, and the stagnant air hung like a poisonous cloud. The new piano was extremely stiff, and one had to use force to get a ringing tone.

The ants came by dozens and dozens. Teeming myriads leaping, swarming in profusion.

At least three dozen were always creeping round the bottom of my flame evening gown, and two dozen more at my waist. They flew in my eyes. I was immersed in black clouds. If one hand was momentarily idle, I would pluck off handfuls of ants with it while playing with the other. More hordes always came. I finished the concert.

The next day, at a place where thousands of chickens were raised, I saw eggshells pierced by tiny beaks, then the bedraggled half-emergent figures, the adorable week-old ones, the less cute older ones—and then the charm vanishing imperceptibly until the chicks were squawking, strutting hens, pecking with vicious egotism.

Disillusioned, I fled to a woodcarving workshop, where the magnificent creations combined the best of Africa and France.

ROLF JACOBY WAS AT THE DAKAR-YOFF AIRPORT to meet me that evening.

"Where is everyone?" I asked. "Mr. Cusin?"

"Out of office."

"Mr. Liotard?"

"Out of office."

"Mr. Jobert?"

"The same."

"What happened to the French people I knew in 1958?"

"The DeGaulle regime brought a changeover. And Senegal's a Republic now—a semi-autonomous member of the French community."

"Have they obtained new jobs elsewhere?"

"Most have not. They are back in Paris, waiting."

Rolf Jacoby, the American Cultural Attaché, took me to the Ngor Hotel. We had dinner. He was a witty raconteur, with a droll, ironic humor, who held one spell-bound with sardonic tales.

The day of my concert, I practiced on a spinet at the home of Robert Coqueraux, who had lived for years in the jungle before coming to Dakar.

Outside it was dusty. A dust storm had descended on Dakar. It swept and swirled, strangling, choking one. It settled like a visitation on everything, spreading its grey cloak relentlessly throughout the city. If one put on sun-glasses, in a few minutes they were laden with dust.

When I went to the theatre, a lady with long ruby earrings, red-gold hair, and a shocking pink dress rushed up to embrace me. "Wonderful to see you! I am Luz Iberia, the Spanish dancer! Remember me?"

She showed me five scrap-books with pictures of herself dancing the Jota Aragonesa for soldiers in the French Sudan, fandangos for Volta natives, boleros for pagans in Niger, and sarabandes for Muslims in remote parts of Senegal. She had brought Spanish dancing to the strangest, most inaccessible spots of French Africa, to lonely officers and curious Africans throughout its vast desert and jungle-ridden areas of primeval land.

After my concert, which was full, Mrs. Dumont, wife of the American Consul, came backstage. "What has happened to you?" she exclaimed. "You're so different!"

She reflected and continued, "You play like a completely different person from last year. Everyone in the audience noticed! Your technique is the same, but now there is a spiritual glow—marvelous. What have you done?"

"In November I was baptized by Father Drew, in New York," I replied.

"That must be it. You can't imagine how changed you are."

Luz Iberia and two Frenchmen took me to Rolf Jacoby's flat—strikingly modern, with brightly-colored couches and pillows, oyster-shell chairs, anarchic lamps. Sartre and Joyce were in the solidly filled book-cases.

We drank fruit juice and argued heatedly about Dr. Schweitzer until 3:00 in the morning.

Rolf took me on a tour of the city, next morning. Many Muslim working-men were seated on the ground, eating rice and mutton with their fingers.

When I reached Luz Iberia's house, later, a sensuous, dazzling Seguidilla rhythm was resounding in the cool, dry air.

Luz let me in, saying, "Where were you? I was practicing while I waited for you. Is it not beautiful? I changed the record. Now comes Asturias." The voluptuous melody coiled sensually from the record-player, to enfold one in quivering incense of perfumed insinuation. One felt Spanish music was the most carnal, haunting, and perfidiously intense.

She began to dance the Flamenco, ardently, incomparably. Desire, seductiveness, tragic pleasure, were intermingled with burning languor, fiery lassitude, in a world of simple emotions, of red and black, that enraptured.

Then she showed me how to use the castanets, saying she sometimes practiced them four hours a day. It amazes one to see the control necessary to make the taps that seem so easy.

We returned to the Hotel Ngor.

En route to my second floor room, my heel caught on a stone step in a dark, unlighted entresol. I landed on my right fifth finger. Luz helped me pack, we drove to the airport. Rolf Jacoby was there, with a copy of *The Roots of Heaven* as a going-away gift for me. "Will you return to Africa?" He asked me.

"Yes. I am called by its deserts and forests, streams and sandstorms, as by a hypnotic drug, lured by its mystery, so new, yet so old...I will always want more." ⊞

CHAPTER 19

Hong Kong Days and Nights
The Palace in Kuala Lumpur
Alaska, Hawaii, Japan, Korea, Formosa, Hong Kong,
Singapore, Malaya: 1954, 1957, 1958, 1959

NCHORAGE, ALASKA, GRIMLY UNPREPOSSESSING, does not reflect the beauty of the marvelous skyline of the distant snow-covered mountains. And Anchorage's people come from everywhere, with no common unity of tradition or cultural heritage. But some are great characters, with the proven determination to conquer.

Such was Zula Swanson, a dark, walnut-skinned woman, who began as a maid, then ran lodging-houses for miners, gamblers, transients, during Alaska's wild days, and built a fortune.

Grace Bahovec was a formidable character, too, black as ebony with the strength of Hercules, the will to kill a bear single-handed, which she had done. She and her Slavic husband had settled on the savage wilderness of Baranof Island, made it and prosper.

She generously showered me for years with skins of otter, wolf, lynx, and wild mink—that she had trapped herself—and precious gems she and her husband had dug from the earth.

Once, they had a daughter exactly my age.

I admire both these strong, exceptional women enormously.

My 1954 and 1957 Anchorage recitals enabled me to see the sudden, star-tling growth of streets and houses, but it was still too brusque, chaotic, to inspire one with poetic ideas.

Hawaii, by contrast, was a glowing paradise.

Its cool lush perfection was a verdant haven.

In August 1958, when I flew to the island of Oahu, I was met by George Barati, the Honolulu Symphony's Hungarian-born conductor, Walter and Sabina Ehlers, of the Palama Settlement House, Jock Purinton, manager of the Waikiki Shell, and his beautiful, olive-skinned Chilean wife, Natalia.

They bedecked me with multi-colored lei.

Lisa Purinton, a tiny ivory-skinned girl in a blue mumu, embraced me.

"How beautiful she is," I said.

Beaming with maternal pride, Natalia said, "She's never worn shoes." A Mrs. Toppington, who wore red shorts, laughed, "Out here we think we're real dressed up if we put shoes on!"

The Ehlers, with Mrs. Toppington, drove me into the city. We passed very ordinary office buildings, restaurants. Mrs. Toppington asked me curiously, "What does Honolulu look like to you?"

"Like Los Angeles."

"What! How can you say such a thing? Imagine, coming to a city, and say-ing it looks like another city!" she snorted. We passed a particularly ugly set of grey buildings. On one was a sign saying, "Iwilei."

Delightedly, I murmured, "Is this the famous Iwilei district I read about in 'From Here to Eternity' and 'The Revolt of Mamie Stover'?"

Mrs. Toppington said dryly, "Well, it's closed now, thank the Lord."

"But what do six thousand men do?"

"Do? What do you mean, do?" she asked suspiciously.

"Oh, you know, do."

"Do?"

"Do."

"Why they go to symphony concerts, THAT'S what they DO!"

In silence, we passed trees, Americans in weird tomato-colored shirts, ugly buildings. I said. "Do you really think symphony concerts are enough, for all those men at Schofield Barracks?" She replied dryly, "OF COURSE. Men aren't animals."

"But, soldiers?"

"They don't need sex! The American soldier of today is a nice boy!"

"But surely, men must."

"No they must not. I don't know how much sex you've had."

"None at all, of course," I retorted.

"Then if you can do without it, MEN can."

Silence.

The next morning, I awoke early in my bedroom at the Ehlers' home, and went to the kitchen. Mrs. Toppington was there, looking vehement in a pair of revealing lilac shorts. I started to open a can of tuna fish. I pierced my finger and it bled. Mrs. Toppington said, angrily, "Well, why didn't you buy a can opener for your own use?"

That night, we drove to the Waikiki Shell to hear the Honolulu Symphony, with a Japanese pianist and a Norwegian singer as soloists. The Shell, dazzling blue, white and silver, shone brilliantly. The air was dry, brisk, and clear. The sparse public sat on chairs or on the ground, while romantic couples lay on the grass.

The orchestra, with its multi-national musicians, began, and soon played some dull Grieg Songs. I remarked, "The songs are awful. What a bore." Mrs. Toppington, who wore scarlet and a purple mumu splashed with pink trees, green flowers—with blue Japanese sandals and an orange ribbon for contrast on her yellow streaked hair said: "Well, if you put over your pieces next Friday with one-sixth the personality they do, perhaps you'll be moderately successful!"

The days passed. The Purintons took me to a park with strange trees and flowers, to a Buddhist temple with gold lotus-flowers on golden shrine, to a native-style restaurant where we overlooked a green pond, and the walls and ceilings were of dark branches intertwined with vines and blooms. And we saw a mountain-ledge like an eagle's nest where, whipped by the strong wind, one could gaze dizzily on the city below and a museum with faded relics of Queen Kamehameha.

As we drove, one day, I asked Mrs. Purinton, who was of Chilean ancestry, but looked exotically Eurasian, "Was the book *The Revolt of Mamie Stover* really true? Did she actually sleep with seventy-two men a day?"

"Oh yes, sometimes more, they say. She had the strength of ten horses!"

The moon glowed golden in the purple skies as I played to a packed house at the Waikiki Shell on August 29. The Gershwin Festival received tremendous applause, and the reviews next day were excellent.

On December 12, I returned again to Honolulu. This time Mr. and Mrs. John Kelly met me at the airport and drove me to their home behind the Palama Settlement House. As we all ate wheat germ, Mr. Kelly said, "I'm delighted you're playing my arrangements at the concert tomorrow."

"They're wonderful. I never thought Asian music could be so beautifully transcribed by a Westerner."

"You're too kind, but what you say is most encouraging. What am I working on now? A more elaborate arrangement of 'Arirang.' That song rises above nationality and sings to universal man, with both tenderness and strength. It evokes compassion for human suffering and courage—it has fortitude, determination to solve, surmount life's vicissitudes, to survive for a better future."

Walking to the spinet piano, he sat down to play it for me. He touched the keys and the noble melody soared upwards, full of soul-questioning, aspiration, hope midst degradation, soaring love for humanity, will to conquer, to leap blindly into destiny, to rise up to God. Though it rang first from the bloody, torn, war-swept heart of Korea two thousand years ago—it still sings triumphantly in our modern age of mechanical destruction, and cold science, to the lost human spirit, infusing it with new courage, new will midst despair! One legend says it originated when the crushed people rose in revolt against a despotic emperor. The rebellion failing, the people were slaughtered by the imperial soldiers, and thousands of patriots were led across the primeval Arirang mountain to be executed—this was the song that rose spontaneously from their hearts, to send their message, their feeling of unconquered love for humanity to the world for all time! I was silent when he finished, plunged into another world.

Quietly, he said, "I see that you feel it as I do."

"It speaks to the hearts of everyone, everywhere—it says that God's love can yet be for all—compassion can wipe out one's sins in tears and blood, that faith, sorrow, forgiveness can bring absolution—yes!" I replied, fervently.

"I'll give you a copy of it."

"Please, please do!"

He took down several pieces of neatly copied sheet-music from a wooden shelf, and wrote on the first, "A modest gift in tribute, to Philippa Schuyler—one who shares a deep respect for the people's music of the East—from John M. Kelly Jr."

The concert drew a large audience of Chinese, Hawaiian, Japanese and Americans. The lights were dim as I always like them, when I began to play.

The next morning, Mrs. Kelly, who was part-Tahitian, awoke me early. "Mr. Faricy just called. He wants you to visit him this afternoon. You must go. He's our most important music critic.

At noon, I was in Mr. Kelly's car, en route with him to the Faricy dwelling, my self-confidence sunk to its lowest ebb.

We parked and walked up to the Faricy residence.

Austin Faricy, in a white suit, stood on the stone doorstep.

He was white-haired, with a sensitive pale face.

"Come in, and play on my harpsichord!" he said gaily.

He led us into a large pastel-colored room that contained a clavichord and a harpsichord. The former was in a black case, with brown and black keys on the tiny keyboard. One wondered how Bach could ever have been satisfied with such an instrument, with a tone so small one could hardly hear it.

The harpsichord was wonderful. In a brown case, with two keyboards and seven pedals, its sharp sprightly tone made Scarlatti sonatas, Bach fugues come to life as they cannot on the too-rich piano. One grew convinced that early eighteen-century music should only be played on the harpsichord.

Then we bade Mr. Faricy goodbye warmly, went to visit Mr. Kelly's parents.

"Do you think I did anything wrong?" I asked Mr. Kelly, after we got to his car. "Maybe I didn't use the right pedals."

"Oh, I wouldn't worry. He won't be influenced by anything you did today. Anyhow, his comments were handed into the Star Bulletin last night—they'll appear Tuesday."

As we spoke, the car had ascended lush verdant hills, and risen, it seemed to the heavens. Now we looked down on thick, tangled, trees, a swarming mass of live greenery, galaxies of multicolored plants, flowers and branches, made joyous by flights of chirping birds. Bright vines wound around massive tree trunks. Soon we reached a steep incline and suddenly stopped before a house that rose like a yellow lily from the hill.

We entered, and were greeted by Mr. and Mrs. John Kelly Sr., his parents, an old couple perhaps in their seventies or eighties.

Though old, their faces were beautiful, rich and fine, with a spiritual serenity born of goodness, and shared love and devotion through the years.

They had bright humor, too, and made little graceful jests to one another, as though they had a droll secret they shared with each other, that no one else knew.

She wore a scarlet and gold mumu, and sat on the floor of their Tahitian-style sitting room, while he brought out his etchings and engravings of Asian and Polynesian types—soft gentle brown-skin girls with does' eyes—strong, muscular yet kind, unhurried fishermen—an old Buddha-like Chinese, seated in the lotus-pose.

Truly he was a great artist.

And not only in art but also in life. Fifty years they had been married, and one felt that no cloud had ever disturbed it. Fifty years he had been painting and sketching the flower-like island boys and girls.

And the two had gone hand in hand in perfect proportion. Art not interfering with life. Life not interfering with art. The two inseparable, and complementary, like two seasons at the equinox, like dark and light, like waves and tides. Mrs. Kelly served us green Chinese tea, and Mr. Kelly told us old stories of love and death and sailing and music and ancient rites and of courage and wisdom. The atmosphere was delicate and merry, waggish and refined, joyous and glowing.

Truly, I felt, this is the way life should be, the way marriage, the way old age, the way happiness should be.

Then the radiant old couple gave me a Christmas present, the nicest they could have thought of. One of Mr. Kelly's etchings of a Hawaiian fisherman, and a long distance phone call to my parents in New York.

They were five thousand miles away, yet in five minutes we had the connection, and the Kellys and I spoke what was in our hearts to my parents, who were so far away and distant.

I hope there will be no end to my Hawaii story, I hope I shall return many times to its sublime beauty and kind people. This episode did come to an end, but in the nicest way. Two weeks later, when I was in sparkling Hong Kong, with its emerald bay and sapphire sky, I received the reviews of my Honolulu recital. Mr. Faricy had written, "Magical musical phrasing, infused with ardor and creative searching."

And, in the *Advertiser*, Mr. Ed Knowlton said, "Stirring...prodigious...a performer with vitality, vigor, sincerity and power."

Indeed, I was delighted with Hawaii.

The flight was interminable from Honolulu to Wake Island to Tokyo. The great Tokyo airport was immense and as efficient as those in London or Paris. One felt a shock at the great change from happy, easy-going, relaxed Hawaii. Here there was no time for relaxation. Life was too stern, too bitter.

Two girls from the Sacred Heart University met me, drove me to the largest city in the world, and, at last, to the splendid, impressive University. Though new, it gave a feeling of tradition and serenity. Its students were neat, sober, polite, without the gaiety one sees in American college students, but rather with a look of weighty responsibility. There is a repressed look on the faces of Japanese women, even those of the more fortunate classes. Japan seems not a happy country—it is an admirable, efficient one, but lacks smiles of joy or the sense of space or relaxation. There is no space in Japan. It is an anguished nation—for too long, too many have crowded its small islands—repressing their personalities to fit neatly, each in his little niche. Here, human fortitude is stretched to its limit—then going beyond, beyond the limit, always beyond, without rest or respite!

> If you can make your heart and nerve and sinew,
> Serve their turn long after they are gone,

And so hold on until there is nothing in you,
Except the will that says to you, 'Hold on'!

—Joseph Rudyard Kipling

Courage, discipline, extracting the utmost from heart, body, soul, reach their peak in Japan. Yet they have deep feelings, though they are disciplined—the human heart does glow with inner fire, albeit subtly.

The sensitivity with which they can perform Western music brought new life, tender meaning to works I heard them perform. "Courage midst suffering" could be called the motto of the Japanese character. Poor limited diet, extremes of climate, austere philosophy, intensity of work, stoicism in pain—are the reality of their lives. You do not feel that "I" is important there—the ego has been submerged under the weight of colossal, nearly insoluble problems. Each human life holds a tragedy in Japan. Everything is crowded, swarming, teeming, and congested—small wood houses piled crazily next each other—narrow shops packed with profuse merchandise—tiny streets (when you visit friends they often give you a map they have drawn to help you find the way).

The Tokyo and Yokohama men I saw all wore Western suits, most of the women, Western dresses. The women do not feel kimonos—part of the long-gone more gracious era—belong in industrial age factories and offices. Westerners do not usually think Asians to be beautiful. I find them exquisite, with a touching, refined sadness lost to the more gross definiteness of the West.

I came to see why Asian philosophies are so hopeless, and depressing. The balance of man and nature has been out of focus too long there, too many human souls crowded too close together. Almost throughout the East a barren or childless wife is held in contempt, and it is not easy to alter tradition in ancient countries. Though legalized abortion has reduced the Japanese birth rate, the population still swells relentlessly.

I find Chinese art and philosophy far more sensuous than the Japanese, with their stylized, chaste purity.

My first impression of Tokyo was the substitution of bowing for the hand-shaking and kissing of the West. Every conversation subtlety, nuanced and perceptively graded according to the sex, is begun, punctuated, ended, by bows of manifold meaning and status and class of bower and bowee. Kissing has always been abhorred by the Japanese, though a few, radical members of the younger generation attempt it. I miss the elegant bows when I left Japan—for they seem more civilized than handshaking, which long arose as a device for ascertaining that there was no knife in the other person's hand.

My concert at Sacred Heart University on December 19 took place on a magnificent Steinway. Oddly, it was only in Formosa that I saw a Yamaha, a Japanese piano, which is better than many European or American models.

Among those attending the concert were Mother Britt, who had first heard me play years ago when I was a student at the Manhattanville Convent of the Sacred Heart; the Japanese wife of an old friend in New York; and Señor Prieto and Señor and Señora Perez, from the Embassy of the Dominican Republic.

Later, the Dominicans drove me through the glittering Ginza district, sprinkled with neon-lights and crammed with hurrying Japanese. Their sleek beautiful car piloted like a firefly in and out of the swarming, darting traffic. Eighty years ago, the Ginza was a small narrow thoroughfare that centuries had not altered. Now it is startling and impressive. The Mitsukoshi store is as large as Macy's in New York. The Kabuki Theatre and Embujo Playhouse are there, as are many bars, usually presided over by women.

Then we went to the Birobasha nightclub, where they had folklore show in honor of the Christmas season.

Looking at a pretty singer, I asked, "Why doesn't she have the Mongolian fold around her eyes?"

Señor Prieto replied, "Some entertainers here have it cut off by a surgeon. If they are low in funds, they may have one cut, then save for months until they can afford to have the other one done."

One day I saw the Zojo-zi Temple in Shiba Park. On another, Japanese schoolteacher, Teresa Tsutsumi took me to her home, where her mother had prepared tempura, kabayaki, dried seaweed and fresh persimmons for us.

The low lacquered table was set in a deep heated indentation in the floor which kept one's legs comfortably warm. After dinner, Teresa changed to a gorgeous traditional Furisode. It was an artistic undertaking to tie and arrange the under-robes, cords, and obi.

One day, I had the great honor of being presented to Michiko Shoda, now the wife of Crown Prince Akihito. The prettiest girl I had seen anywhere in Tokyo, she looked innocent, gracious and poetic, far more beautiful in person than in photographs. I was extraordinarily impressed by her sweet, elegant manner. She was so charming to me, I felt overwhelmed. She had noble cultivation, refined intelligence, and graceful humility. She was well-groomed in a simple, stylish white dress. Her mother, to whom I was also presented, wore a dark kimono. One felt that Michiko Shoda would fill her coming role with sincerity, dignity and simple greatness.

Japan is a religious country. There are 106,634 Buddhist temples, 100,000 Shinto shrines, and several thousand Christian churches.

A serious country, it is growing surprisingly modern.

One night I received a phone call from the American soldier whose Japanese wife had come to my concert. I told him, "Your wife is stunning. Aren't you lucky to be married to an Asian girl who treats you like a god! Who is humble and meek!"

Laughing heartily, in his rich warm baritone voice, he replied, "Meek? Not her! That's a thing of the past. She's a modern Japanese woman. Rules our roost. Rules me with an iron hand!"

Tokyo is bustling, vast, metropolitan. Seoul is grim, and desolate.

The Koreans look much more individualistic than the Japanese. The spiritual hostility between the two lands is still intense. A Korean intellectual once acidly remarked, "Chinese, Mongol, Japanese, Russian, Communist and American armies have brought only chaos and destruction to Korea to add to the destruction and chaos the Koreans are quite capable of creating for themselves."

Cynical words that match Korea's bitter history.

Sometimes called "The Land of the Morning Calm," a less calm nation would be difficult to find. Their past has been a gloomy record of bloody invasions, the present is dispiriting. Twenty two millions are crammed into South Korea's 38,452 square miles, making the population density over five hundred per square mile, one of the world's highest. Only one fourth of the land is arable, and the economy is dependent on U.S. aid.

One of Seoul's bright spots is the EWHA Women's University, whose solid stone buildings are a beacon of hope amidst the glum surroundings.

I stayed on the campus with some Methodist missionaries. On December 23, the morning of my concert, the water supply was cut off, electricity failed, and I injured a tooth.

The auditorium was too bitterly cold for practice, so I went to a mildly heated room behind the office which had a piano. A girl who came to help me raise the piano lid, dropped it on my left hand second finger, a disastrous accident which crushed its tip. An hour before the concert, the finger was still too painful to touch, and the lights had failed again. I prayed to Saint Jude. Just before the performance, the lights burst on again, shining brightly, and all pain, all sensation, left my finger until the following morning.

The audience loved "Arirang," and rose with enthusiasm when I played this glorious song that so nobly expresses their traditional courage. I received an ovation, and Miss Helen Kim, President of the University, embraced me afterwards, with warmest congratulations, and gave me a magnificent red and silver vase.

Taipei, Taiwan, was my next stop. There the more sensuous beauty of Chinese culture was apparent. The Grand Hotel was exotic. Gorgeous, sexy Chinese girls, like golden passion-flowers were everywhere. Their seductive cheongsams were slit high to reveal sinuous, exciting brown legs that could have inflamed an iceberg, or roused hedonistic ardor in the heart of the most confirmed misogynist, or decrepit nonagenarian country. Their faces were like exquisite, like dazzling yet subtle jewels that peered above their high collars. They convinced me that the Chinese, when well-fed, are the world's most beautiful people.

After lecturing before a thousand cheering students at the University, and being mobbed by them, I gave a concert at the Town Hall before two thousand people. The next day, I played for boy and girl students at the Military Music Academy.

One evening, I gave a private concert for Archbishop Riberi, the Papal Nuncio, and Señor Jose Villanueva, the Dominican Republic's Ambassador to Taiwan, in the Archbishop's house. A kindly cultivated music lover, Archbishop Riberi had hundreds of records and tapes of classic music. He was a wonderful and inspiring person.

Señor Villanueva, also a great music fan, loved to make tapes of classic music, and he recorded my playing of the "Pictures at an Exhibition," and later broadcasted it to the Chinese mainland.

Taipei was one of the gayest cities I have ever seen. Never have I attended so many parties in such a short time. I was entertained by Señor and Señora Larracoechea, of the Spanish Embassy, by Dr. Kiang, an importer, and his wife, by Mr. Jamal Bafi, the Turkish Ambassador (his wife and daughter both looked stunning in cheongsams), and many others.

I spent New Year's Eve at the Grand Hotel nightclub, with the Bafis, the Villanuevas, the Larracoecheas, the Venezuelan Consul, the Brazilian Charge d'Affaires, and others.

As I entered the ballroom where the brown-skin Filipino girl singer and band were gaily performing, I reflected on the interview I had just had with Premier Cheng Chen, Taiwan's second most powerful official, at his beautiful home, filled with exquisite Chinese paintings. I had enjoyed sipping shark-fin soup and Chinese green tea with the Premier and his wife.

The party was gay, uninhibited. Some of the diplomats' wives removed their shoes to dance. One song was dedicated to the Turks:

No, Charlie! You can't have three!
You can't have three and still have me!
No, Charlie! You can't have five!
You can't have five and stay alive!
No, Charlie! You can't have seven!
You can't have seven and go to heaven!"

On New Years' Day 1959, I flew from Taipei to Hong Kong. No one was at the airport to meet me when I arrived. The cable that had been sent to warn, or rather notify Harry Odell of my arrival, had never come. After much telephoning and confusion, someone from the airport drove me to Mr. Odell's home.

We went in a taxi to Victoria Bay, took a ferry across the river. He picked up his car where he had left it on the other side, and we climbed up and down hills until we came to rest on a stone ledge, got out and walked gingerly down a flight of narrow iron steps to the villa below.

Soon, Mr. Odell came. He was a wonderful figure of an impresario. He made me think of Mike Todd, Miles Ingalls — a Broadway agent I know, and Mr. Pickwick rolled in one.

"Great! Great! Wonderful to see you! What wire? Didn't get a wire. Why didn't you come sooner? Should have started publicity days ago. Concert will be tremendous! Absolutely, terribly, completely tremendous. Of course no one will come. Nobody ever comes to concerts here. All business here. City of London transposed to China. But it will be tremendous. Got any clippings? Got to have lots of clippings. Recent ones. Recent. Get any reviews in Taipei? We'll use 'em. Fast. Fast. Got to start fast. You're staying with me. Couldn't let you stay anywhere else. Got to watch you. Watch you. Bought a new piano especially for you to practice on. You can go practice now. Believe in doing things right. Right. Knew you'd have to practice. So bought a piano just for you. Right!" He had white hair, a portly build, and a kindly, amiable face. He looked as though he had never cheated anybody in his life, an unusual way for an impresario to look.

When I met Mrs. Odell, she was amiable, too. They called each other darling all the time, and seemed a very happy couple.

On Sunday, I went to Loke Yew Hall to practice. It was cold, so I brought an electric stove with me. After I had worked a while, I looked up, and in the front row of the auditorium, a dark man was sitting there, his eyes riveted on me.

I started to play the C major scale slowly, over and over, usually an infallible way of getting people, whom I do not wish to listen to me, to leave. He did not leave, I tired of C major, tried A minor, and still he did not go, but just stared at me, then said, "Play some jazz."

"I don't want to."

"The hell you don't. I said, 'Play jazz.'"

"You know, I really don't like to be listened to while I practice."

"Crissake. Whyn't you shuddup, an' follow orders?"

"Please go. You're making me nervous."

"Nervous!"

"What are you doing here?"

"An' I couldda gotten drunk steada comin' here."

"Then go get drunk now, and leave me alone!" I shouted.

"I came down from Japan on a seven-day furlough, an' I read boutcha in the noos-papers, so I figgered I'd come down to the auditorium an' see if yuh hadda cute figure," he added insolently, snapping his fingers.

"Go away."

"I wanna hear some jazz."

"Go."

"Aw shit, can't no dame tell me what to do." He got up, jumped at the edge of the stage, fell, started to climb up again. I ran off the stage in the opposite direction, through the first door I saw, slamming it behind me.

I waited a while, tried to open it again. It was locked. To get back in, I had to walk all the way around and come back in the hall the front way. He was gone.

Dusk had fallen and night had made the air chill. When I had first come, an attendant had plugged the stove in an outlet too far away for warmth to radiate.

Looking for a nearer outlet, I found one, almost next to the piano, plugged the stove in, and all the lights blew out.

The audience, that night at the concert, though not overwhelming in size, was enthusiastic.

The next day, the *South China Evening Post* said, "A brilliant piano recital was given at Loke Yew Hall by the well-known German pianist Philippa Schuyler." The *South China Morning Post* wrote, "Those who attended the piano recital by Philippa Schuyler, dynamic twenty-six-year-old American (not German) pianist, came away with of a feeling of awe. She left the audience gasping.... Mephistophelian!" The *Hong Kong Tiger Standard* wrote, "Dynamic, dazzling, brilliant!"

After making a recorded radio broadcast of Beethoven, Chopin, Field and Asian music that same morning, I met an interviewer from the leading Hong Kong newspaper, at a Chinese restaurant, the Ching Kok.

We sat in a softly-lighted corner of the nearly-deserted place. His features had an exotic look. Maybe he was a Eurasian. He wore a superbly-cut suit that looked as though it had been poured over him. His wavy black hair was flawlessly arranged, his nose classically perfect, his expression kind, amiable, though blandly aware of how handsome he was.

"How I wish I could play the piano like you!" he mused." Won't you tell me how you arrive at your interpretations? What inspires you?"

"Well, in the first movement of the 'Appassionata' sonata, I think of the book, *Adolphe,* by Benjamin Constant—it's romantic, tragic, a thinly disguised account of his love affair with Madame de Stael."

"Have you known love?" he asked me, slowly.

"Oh, it depends on how you define love."

"I mean romantic love between men and women, of course."

"Have you been in love? Have you been ruled by your heart?"

"I've been experimenting with emotions, sensations, most of my life. Women, like people, are never what they seem. Often, only the facade has been interesting, without revealing anything else profound," he said, his handsome profile etched sharply against the orange, gold and red of the Chinese dragon on the black wall behind him.

"I am a sensualist, yet conservative," he continued, as we began our shark-fin soup. "I am not a prude. I can love a woman without getting married, well aware that there is a subtle difference between an act of sex and an act of love. Yet I am not emotionally at ease, for I am philogynous by nature."

Eating some of the roast duck-skin with garlic and spiced sauce, I asked, "What does philogynous mean?"

He replied, while sipping some rice-wine, "It comes from the word philogyny, which means fondness of women. I am romantic by nature, but not so romantic as not to realize that regardless of the little romances one has on the way, one is ever seeking the big romance."

"Do you believe in freedom of women? In their equality to men?"

"A woman must be feminine, and content with her role."

"What is her role?"

He took some of the birds-nest's soup, and went on, "Certainly, I don't approve of complete freedom for women. Also, I am firm that a woman who goes to bed with any man she wishes is not much of a woman."

"Then you think all men should have as much pleasure as they wish, and all women should be saints?" I asked, sampling the sweet almond soup.

"Have I made you angry?" he inquired softly.

"Well, Tolstoy, whom I love, says, 'The only sin is to use a woman without loving her.' I feel it is terrible to use a woman as though she were a martini or a breakfast."

He ate a spoonful of bean sprouts and some Chinese asparagus, and replied musingly, "A man can have an affair with a woman without loving her because he is sensual enough and she is the embodiment of a woman with whom he is anxious to sleep with. But no heart is involved. The nuances are just not there. The one who loves always suffers more, yes, but there is an ennobling feeling about it. Love is to sacrifice."

"I don't agree with that."

"Do you know, I sense under your outer coolness, a running streak of romanticism and ardor which I like. I think the man who makes love to you will be the recipient of such a showering of emotions that the romance will be an indelible memory," he replied, helping himself to some shrimps and prawns, with an air of nonchalance.

"Who says I'd let him make love to me?"

"It's a strange thing about emotions or people—one never knows how they will develop. Stendhal says love is like the fever that is born, and spends itself without the slightest intervention of will—resembles the Milky Way, a gleaming mass formed by thousands of little stars, any one of which may be a nebula," he said. He then tried the sliced chicken with mushrooms, while dipped into the plate of pigeons' eggs.

"How long have you been writer?" I asked.

"Oh, years. I wish there was time to tell you about everything. I feel you would understand. I feel irresistibly drawn to your mind. But we could correspond. I sense in you a desire to draw me out. Let us write. Writing can be very pleasurable, even if it is an evanescent thing. It is the interval between what's annoying, like morality. One must wait for an answer before writing again, or the sequence goes out of course. I cannot help wondering how we would behave were we alone. When you leave, will I nurse a yearning for you? Strangely, the idea of a reunion is often more enthralling, more pleasurable than the union itself. But Fate must have brought us together for a purpose. There is a Chinese saying, 'If there is divine affinity between people, they will meet though they be separated by ten thousand miles, but if there is not this affinity, they would never meet though they lived in the same street,'" concluded Victor Fung in a soft resonant voice.

He wrote me many letters after that day, letters in which philosophy and emotion were delicately intermingled.

Months later, he came to New York to collaborate with me on a series of sketches of the Orient, to be called, "Hong Kong Days And Nights."

While there he presented me with some poetry he had written in my honor.

After leaving Victor Fung that January afternoon, I went to a party at the home of a wealthy British family. Everyone was well-dressed, and looked prosperous, contented, as if they gave no thought to the appalling, misery in which the million refugees from Red China lived a few miles away.

The hostess' elder daughter was a sexy beauty, with red hair, and wearing a skin-tight olive-green sheath, slit up high to show a transparent red lace petticoat and shapely legs.

"How can everyone seem so gay here?" I asked a bearded Englishman with a dissolute look, who had led me to a closed-in terrace.

"They are gay."

"But, how? With Red China so close?"

"We don't think of Red China's taking over. We close our minds to the possibility. Even if it might some day happen, we're too busy making money now to worry about the future."

"But if Communist China can shell Quemoy and Matsu."

"Communist China finds economic advantage in Hong Kong's present status. The island imports lots of food from the mainland, and provides a nearby market in foreign exchange. Red China must have foreign exchange to pay for imports from the non-Communist world, and for the espionage and propaganda it incites in the free countries. Hong Kong is the legitimate medium through which goods from Red China come to the West, and the illegitimate medium for smuggling and transference of narcotics from the mainland to be poured out onto the West, particularly America. The dope that costs a few dollars here, can bring a small fortune in New York. And it is through Hong Kong that Chinese overseas send money to their relations on the mainland." He broke off to drink some gin.

"Tell me about the refugees," I said, shivering. It was so cold everywhere in Hong Kong.

"The Government try their best to solve the problem. But its magnitude swamps them. It is one of the most tragic dilemmas of this epoch. Tuberculosis is the leading cause of death here, the living conditions of most of the Chinese refugees are so horrible."

Six other Englishmen now crowded us, so he stopped talking, and drifted away to get some more liquor. A British government official, with a pallid, waxen face that looked as though it had wasted away, began a tête-à-tête with me.

He told me the word Hong Kong derives from "Heung Kong," meaning "port of fragrance," and he mentioned such sights as the Supreme Court, the Gloucester Hotel, and Repulse Bay Beach, and the sugar-refining and ship building industries. He spoke of Chinese art, and told me sculpture had never been as highly regarded as painting in China. He said the number of stories in a pagoda must always be uneven, for Buddhism set less value on even numbers than odd ones, and that he had once heard of a pagoda on the mainland that was 360 feet tall.

At the airport, next morning, officials told me I could not fly to Singapore as the plane would stop an hour in Rangoon en-route, and I did not have the cholera shot required in Singapore from all Burma travelers. In New York, I had been told this cholera shot would be absolutely unnecessary. We argued. Then the officials spent an hour typing huge sheets of paper for me to sign, relieving them of responsibility if I began a plague throughout Asia.

I got on the plane. It landed at Rangoon. I did not get off. Lots of officials tried to make me do so. I kept them involved in arguing until the hour passed, the passengers had returned to the plane, and it had to take off. At the Singapore airport, I was sequestered. An hour slipped by in strife as I protested, "I can't have cholera when I didn't even get off in Burma!"

Then a contemptuous voice asked me, "Are you here through anyone's invitation?"

"Yes! Sir Percy MacNiece's."

"What!" they said, in a canonic chorus of amazement.

"Sir Percy MacNiece," I said again.

The effect of the word "Sir" was magical, instantaneous. Their resistance melted, their tones grew honeyed, words soothing, apologies effusive. Now, they said it had simply been a mere formality that I would only have to visit the hospital the next day for "a minor check-up," and was now free to leave.

My hosts in Singapore were John and Alison Mackensie, a charming music-loving couple from New Zealand. They lived in a spacious villa on Chee Hoon Road.

The next morning, I went to the hospital, a great grey grim acing building with big colored posters about insect destruction outside. The doctor did not even look at me. Stamping a paper, he said, "Return in two days." When I did, he did not look at me then, either, but stamped another paper, and said I need not return.

My concert at the Victoria Theatre was a great success. I had been a little terrified by the swooping and lunging of black bats backstage while I practiced.

Everyone was elegantly dressed at the concert. As four-fifth's of the population of Singapore is Chinese, they were the majority in the audience, although Hindus, Pakistani, Malays and English were also present.

I was impressed by Singapore's Bank of China building, with the great stone lions outside. But what I most loved were the temples. A pretty Chinese schoolteacher, Ruth Ho, and her brother, Dr. Ho, a physician, took me sightseeing. How wonderful to see that juxtaposition of many faiths — Hindu and Buddhist temples, Muslim mosques, Christian churches, often on the same street! Spotlessly clean were the Muslim mosques as far as I could see from the outside, for, naturally, being a mere female, I could not enter. From a distance, I saw Muslim men washing themselves at the courtyard's open faucets.

Over the entrance to one Hindu temple, was a gigantic wooden mass of carved painted bas-relief statues of gods and goddesses, intricate and weirdly-detailed. We had to remove our shoes before entering, and the inside was so dirty, as though years of ingrained filth were present, that our feet were black when we had finished looking at the altar, and the statues of jeweled goddesses in the weedy garden. The Chinese Buddhist temples, much cleaner, had elaborate red and gold decoration outside — one had huge painted yellow wooden tigers, fangs open, as though leaping, ready to devour you. Another had a great fifty-foot painted wooden statue of Buddha, around whose base were depicted scenes from his life. At the back was a secret chamber, with a reclining Buddha inside. Totally airless, the room almost suffocated me. The Chinese lady who officiated wished to show me the sacred foot print of Buddha, but the stale heavy air overpowered me with its pungent aromatic scent.

It was January 11. We drove through the teeming churning streets of Singapore, with their ever-present cunning business activity, which handles most of Malaya's bulging trade. Singapore on an exotic, but dangerous spot. Across the narrow Straits of Malacca lied Sumatra to the west, Borneo hovers languorously to the southeast, Malaya rose like a burning torch to the north. At noon, I flew to Malaya.

The memory of Singapore remained with me, though the winter and summer and fall which followed, through illness and joy, unhappiness and exultations, and delight and mourning over the death of friends.

I received many letters from John Mackensie, who was a poet at heart, despite his position as a leading official with Raumunia Bauxite Ltd., whose broad luxurious offices stretched, air-conditioned and serene, over nearly a floor of the great Bank of China building that watches cagily, great stone lions guarding its entrance, over the teeming multiracial streets of downtown Singapore, swarming with Hindus, Muslims Indians, British, Chinese and Malays. On February 5, 1960, I received this letter from him:

> It is now about a year since you left Singapore. I rejoice that you write so rapturously that the year has passed like a day.
>
> It is a delightful tropical morning and the harbor with its transient restful burden of ships of all nations looks pleasant from my office window.
>
> Singapore seems to be doing quite well under its new management—moderation triumphing, and an admirable restraint being exercised in forcing cultural unity on the complex racial elements. Life goes on much the same.
>
> Some superficial vice has been exorcised through licensing of massage parlors, reforming of hotel bars, cabarets, call-girls, and the closing of brothels, gambling dens, etc.—so aesthetically and culturally, the pruning knife of reform covers depravity's unlovely ulcers, even if it does not always reform the soul.

Write soon, Philippa. You are one of destiny's children, so always aim high, never settle for second best. May your art flourish and your heart have heavenly wings.

The Federation of Malaya, almost as large as England, lies on the southern part of South East Asia's Kra Peninsula. Four-fifths of Malaya is swamp, mountain, or primeval jungle area. There are limestone hills, high cliffs pierced with caves—some of which are used as Tamil temples.

One of these that I visited in January 1959, had 272 narrow stone steps leading to the enormous yawning cave mouth. The air inside was tranquil, heavy with reflection. In mossy recesses sat weird Hindu gods. Walking back over the green mossy earth with Chang, the Chinese boy who had brought me, we saw a clearing within the mountain. Ghostly, as the gateway to Hades, it had serenity, as if life had ceased.

Howling thunderstorms are frequent in Malaya. During my Kuala Lumpur public concert, the rains splashed wildly against the closed-in top of the stadium.

My piano, in the middle on a raised dais, was surrounded by tiers of benches holding four thousand people.

The heavy rain, as though resenting the refined ornamentation of the classic music I was playing, lashed with primeval rage against the roof. This buffeting fury was made weird by the flute-like trills of the birds who nested in the ceiling and were flying back and forth. The sodden air made the piano keys swell until they were stiff in the cruel heat. Acid sweat ran in rivulets down my steaming legs. My long red silk dress was a suffocating rug.

In one part of Malaya, 198 inches of rain fall each year.

It is crisscrossed with rivers, too, some of them strewn with tortuous rapids, precipitous gorges, where waters rush with satanic fury. Many islands lie off the east and west coasts. The Federation's eleven states are, Perak, population 1,220,633, Selangor, population 1,012,047, Negri Sembilan, population 365,045, and Pahang, Johore, Kedah, Perlis, Kelantan, Trengganu, Malacca, and Penang. Half of the total population is Malay, 37.5 percent is Chinese, and 11 percent Hindu.

Though Malays are almost all Muslims, the saying goes, "Scratch a Muslim and you find a Hindu, scratch a Hindu and you find a pagan." Their Islam is not fanatical, and beneath the facade of monotheistic purity, you can detect glimpses of murky magical beliefs from a more primitive age. I heard one tale about a Negri Sembilan woman whose husband left her for a young girl. A sorcerer advised her to steal her rival's used panties so he could cast a spell on them. He did. In two weeks, the husband left the girl, returned to his wife.

Kuala Lumpur is a fairy-tale city of exotic beauty. The government buildings are pastel yellow, pink, blue, looking like cake icing. The railroad station is an Arabian Nights dream, with fantastic turrets and arches.

In 1857, it was dense jungle, until Chinese miners traveled up the Klang River and found a tin mine there.

The settlement's first name, "Pengkalan Lumpur," or "muddy landing-place," was corrupted to "Kuala Lumpur." The British moved the capital from Klang to Kuala Lumpur in 1880, and it remained the capital when the Federation became independent in 1957.

My public concert was January 12. The next day, I gave a radio concert attended by two hundred school children in the afternoon, and a command performance for the King and Queen in the evening.

The room in which I played at the Istana Negara Palace was airy, and was reached by a staircase over which hung an immense black and silver cloth, a present from India. It was large and decorated in quasi-modern style. On various tables stood art objects, presents from various monarchs and heads of state.

It was an honor to play for His Majesty, Tuanku Abdul Rahman ibni Al-marhum Tuanku Muhammad, the Yang di-Pertuan Agong, Paramount Ruler of the Federation, and Yang di-Pertuan Besar of Negri Sembilan.

I felt relaxed, at ease, because the piano was excellent. I had already tested it two days ago, at which time I had also met His Majesty's beautiful black wolfhound. A select group of Their Majesties, the Royal Family, and some Cabinet Ministers, were present.

The Yang di-Pertuan Agong, born August 24, 1895, is eighth in line of descent from Raja Melewar, a Sumatran prince who founded Negri Sembilan's present dynasty in 1773. Negri Sembilan has retained the ancient Menangkabau matriarchal system under which the women own the land. In his youth, His Majesty studied law, was an Army officer, and served in many administrative posts.

That evening, he wore a satin brocade turban with a diamond crescent and star, a sword, and several medals over his satin brocade suit. His kindly face testified to a sterling character.

Her Majesty, the Queen, the Raja Permaisuri Agong, Tuanku Kurshiah binte Tunku Besar Burhanuddin, wore a long gold and black silk suit in Malayan style, with a form-fitting jacket and draped skirt, and Western shoes. Very attractive, she had black hair and brown eyes, and wore a diamond necklace.

After I played a long program of the classics, I gave, in response to a special request, the "Rhapsody in Blue" by Gershwin, which His Majesty seemed to enjoy particularly.

During the late supper, afterwards, I had the opportunity to converse with Their Majesties, and express my deep gratitude for their kindness.

Among the other guests were Mrs. Sardon, who had already entertained me in her home the first night of my stay in Malaya.

She, and her husband, Minister of Public Works Inche Sardon bin Haji Jubir, gave me a luncheon at their beautiful home next day.

Then the Minister, a fascinating personality and real self-made man, drove me around Kuala Lumpur, and through the lush greenery of the surrounding countryside.

Later, he showed me the vast public stadium, the most impressive I have ever seen, which he had designed and built, the Merkeda Stadium of Coronation Park.

Then, he took me to a Malayan movie, which made me laugh more than I had in months. The dialogue was in Malay, with no English subtitles, but the acting was so broad that I understood everything.

It was adorable. The hero was a little boy, beautiful as only an Asian child can be. His father, dying of tuberculosis, taught the boy to run after a handsome young man-about-town, call him "Papa" at all possible moments and attach himself to him. The young man tries to shed the little boy, but it is impossible. Then the boy plays cupid, bringing together the young man and the poor girl whom he loved but whom his proud parents had rejected. It was full of hilarious comic moments and heart-warming sentiment.

There was a great party on my final evening, and I longed to go.

Some American officials refused to take me because it would, in their opinion, "hurt their position." I was desolate. However, Minister Sardon was "delighted" to take me, and I swept in wearing my new red cheongsam.

All eyes were on me, the Ministers gathered around me, photographers rushed up. "How wonderful that you are wearing our Chinese dress!" they exclaimed. "You look just like one of us! Just like a Chinese Malayan girl!"

It was a marvelous party, with everyone treating me splendidly, with overwhelming warmth. The Americans glared feebly from a distance.

Also, I was entertained by Miss P. G. Lim, a Chinese attorney, and her English husband, who had an elaborate Chinese dinner in my honor.

I met many charming English people in Malaya, who, though reliable and honest, lacked the color of the Malays. Though one admires English sanity, efficiency, and ability to underplay, one grows annoyed at their skill in reducing the most passionate emotion to the level of a crumpet.

I met some Americans there, who seemed as out of place as ice cream cones in curry sauce. I met a delightful Australian, who insisted on obdurately saying,

"Good-O!" at every conceivable moment. I met some Frenchmen, who looked pale and ghostly under the brilliant sky, with the waxen dissipated look of fugitives from Sartre and Sagan. But the most conspicuous sight I met in Malaya, so rich from rubber and tin, was an unexpected one.

The hula-hoop.

Everywhere. Indulged in with gay abandon.

But, indeed, I had seen it everywhere, throughout the globe, in 1958 and 1959.

Around the world, across the globe, from the Congo to Formosa, from Senegal to England, from the Cameroons to Holland, Egypt to Argentina, from Surinam to Singapore.

The hula-hoop. It had swept everywhere. Everywhere—black children, yellow children, brown children, white children. All doing the same thing.

All doing the same thing.

All merry, and wiggling, jiving, shimmying, to the whirling of the hula-hoop. ⊞

CHAPTER 20

The Black and the White
Summing Up 1960

AFRICA IS THE MOST EXCITING continent in the world today.

Ten more African nations will become free in 1960—Togo, Malagasy Republic, Congo, Nigeria, Ghana, Somalia, Mali Federation, Ivory Coast, Dahomey, and Voltaic Republic.

On the walls, fences, sides of houses and theaters all over Madagascar in May, one saw a huge snarling wildcat, with PSD underneath it: this stands for PISOUDIA, the Parti Social Democratique of Malagasy Republic. The head of the party, and first president of Malagasy Republic, Philibert Tsiranana, had just won a sweeping victory.

I had the honor of accompanying President Tsiranana, his wife and staff, on their official independence tour of this ancient island, which for sixty years had been ruled by France.

We traveled by the president's private plane, railway car, and motorcade into the remotest villages. Malagasy Republic is a mountainous land the size of California with similar climate. Everywhere along the route there were festivals, balls, outdoor dancing and feasting. People waving flags lined the road, thousands packed the stadiums of the chief cities.

The Malagasy are small, graceful people like the Malayans. The eighteen tribes (which consists of five million people) speak Malagasy and French. The French had deposed the last queen, Ranavalona II, and abolished royalty, in

1896, and ruled since. There was no bitterness towards them now. In every speech, President Tsiranana stressed the need for Malagasy Republic to remain in the French Assembly of Nations.

"We must feel no prejudice towards anyone of any color, black, white or yellow," he often repeated. He spoke highly of the United States. The only thing he seemed to dislike about us was segregation. He said he thought the highest form of civilization resulted when many races mingled. He danced and talked tirelessly with his people and everyone loved him. He said that he never wished to forget that he was a peasant, and had been a sheepherder and cowboy in youth.

"Before the French ruled Malagasy Republic," he told me, "Madagascar had close trade relations with the United States. I hope they can be resumed."

I flew out of the island with the president as far as Nairobi. He flew on to Paris, and I to Uganda.

UGANDA HAD CHANGED FOR THE WORSE. The boycott of Hindu merchants by the Aga Khan's Ismaili Sect of Muslims had seriously injured the economy.

At a reception for Cardinal Laurean Rugambwa in Kampala, all the rival factions seemed to be present. His Eminence appeared serenely unaware of these hidden hostilities.

An African journalist whispered to me, "The Kabaka has lost five million pounds in revenue because of the boycott."

An English banker said, "The Hindus fleece the Africans and send their profits to India. World markets are down. There is too much emphasis here on cotton and coffee."

"It's all the Kabaka's fault!" an African woman said. "He married into the wrong clan, then wasn't satisfied and took his wife's sister. This shocked everyone because he is head of the Anglican church."

Among the guests was Joseph Kiwanuka, politician, boss of the National Congress Party, and director of the *Uganda Post* and *Express*. Two years ago, he had been arrested and jailed for plotting to kill the Kabaka. Kiwanuka was sharp, astute eyes behind gold-rimmed glasses. He dresses elegantly and makes an immediate impression. After a recent visit to Russia and Red China, he announced, "Now, I have money enough to kill hundreds of men! Interpret this as you will." To me he said, "Aren't you afraid to meet a notorious person like myself?"

His papers praise Russia and libel the West.

The Kabaka, King of Buganda, looked worried when I saw him. "Maybe I'd better take up piano playing and start traveling," he jested.

Soon after I left Buganda for another smaller kingdom, Toro.

Toro is a mysterious land in the Mountains of the Moon which have an eerie blue-fairy tale greenness. Water tumbles down the mountain sides like strings of crystals and mist hangs above the serpentine road. One would not be surprised to see elves and indeed pygmies hunt in this range. It was cold when we reached Fort Portales, Toro's capital.

The car unloaded at the Karuzika Palace gate. On the veranda as we passed in, I saw a throne chair covered with lion and leopard skins.

Inside, the four officials who had brought me crawled on all fours to the feet of the regal Omukama, or King, who rules Toro, George Rukidi.

The King whom I had met in America, welcomed me heartily, and invited me to sit beside him; after we had talked awhile, he told me I must call him "George." He is six-feet-three and I could not well refuse.

"How I love America!" he said warmly. "It is the greatest country in the world! How I love the industry of America! How I would like to return!"

Servants on all fours crawled in and out. One crawled up the stairs ahead of me to show me to my room. When the King was out of sight, he stood up and pointed out the Royal bathtub where I was to take a bath.

In a candlelit, brown-paneled dining room, I dined alone with King George and Prince Christopher, one of his six legitimate children.

"I have invited both the Catholics and Protestants to build more churches here," said the King. "We do not yet have any threat of Communism, but religion is the best protection against it."

The meal, completely British except for the fried bananas, was served by waiters who traveled on their knees with the help of one hand while the other bore aloft the dishes of food. The King regaled me with tales of his lion and leopard hunts for the rooms were full of his trophies.

Next day, I was driven in a Land Rover to a forest full of pygmies. On the third day, Prince Daniel, another son, in expensive Bond Street clothes, introduced me to some Toro noble women. They were tall and elegant with classic features and wore silk togas. They sang songs of their own composition using a seven-note scale which their ancestors had evolved without European influence. They did not seem happy in their polygamous households. The songs expressed infinite sadness.

The King walked with me through the courtyard to the Bayaisumba gate where a car waited to take me away. I hated to leave so gracious a monarch.

Next day I was in Usumbura again, to change planes for the Congo.

FOREIGN EXPERTS WERE ALL OVER THE CITY, for an U.N. mission had recently been there. Last year exports had been increased, and now there was a great fever of activity promoting irrigation and insecticide projects. Two new power plants had been built and research into methane gas reserves in Lake Kivu had been successfully carried out.

Whether all of this activity had wakened the Bahutu and caused them to issue their Manifesto of Freedom to the Watusi is not known, but a peasant army, I was told, had murdered some Watusi and burned their farms; and in retaliation the Watusi had formed the UNAR party and all of this had stirred up interest and action. A conference had been called for August in Belgium, and freedom from Trusteeship of these two areas might be expected in January 1961, after the General Assembly of the United Nations which decides such things had reviewed the situation. Disunion was predicted.

"We want no part of Ruanda-Arundi!" Congolese leaders told me when I reached Elizabethville. It was about the only point upon which they all agreed.

There is a great struggle for power going on in Katanga province, of which Elizabethville is the capital, between three political parties.

The Conokat, or conservative pro-Catholic party wants to have a federalized Congo so that the riches of their province, which is the base of Congo wealth and the site of the great Union Minière, which produces uranium, copper, cobalt etc., will not be drained off to support poorer provinces. In opposition to the Cartel party, composed of immigrant workers, the mines, leftist officials of the University of Elizabethville, and various anti-white and anti-Catholic groups. This so-called liberal party demands centralized state in which the riches of Katanga will be shared by all.

The third, or moderate party, the Congolese Union party could well be the saving of the Congo. Gabriel Kitenge, the newly elected representative of the Union party, told me:

> The Union party was founded equally to combat the conservatives of Conokat, and the leftists of Cartel. We do not believe in encouraging racism, black or white; or tribal division. We feel that civilization the result of the exchange of cultures. Thus, we have no hatred of strangers who, in good will, come here to work. We recognize the eminent services rendered by devout Catholic and Protestant missionaries, and we want them to continue. We believe in the spiritual conception of man, high moral standards, family unity and individual liberty, and the great Christian ideals that form the base of universal civilization. We want to keep the Congo united.

Mr. Kitenge thirty-six, tall, with a sincere face and agreeable personality. He was formerly surveyor and cartographer, had one wife and five children, and had never been involved in scandal.

The Union party is widespread, but lost membership recently when Moise Tshombe switched from the Conokat party. By walking out of the Elizabethville Parliamentary Assembly during vital session, the Cartel party had prevented the Conokat party from choosing a president for Katanga. It was rumored that this action would drive the southeast section of Katanga to secede and join Rhodesia.

In social structure, Elizabethville had changed for the better. The previous year, no Congolese had been in my audience at the university theatre, and none were seen in the best hotels. Now, the hotels were crowded with chiefs and half of my audience was Congolese.

"We are ashamed to be Belgians!" some colonials told me bitterly. "Freedom has come too quickly. There has not been enough preparation. It will mean civil war."

Other whites said, "King Baudouin was quite right to grant swift freedom to the Congo. The 120,000 whites here could never keep down 13,000,000 Africans once they decided to fight. Even if we had flown in 100,000 soldiers, it would have been a futile, bloody, long drawn-out struggle antagonizing all of Africa."

Some Africans said, "Belgium did not give up the Congo out of kindness. They saw the dismal fate of the French when they tried to hold onto some of their colonies by force. This year, the market for minerals is down, and the Congo has a deficit. It will not ruin them to give up our administration."

Some non-Belgian Europeans said, "Congo profits were never equally distributed in Belgium but remained in the hands of a few. These world financiers have reinvested their profits in Canada and elsewhere. It is us, non-Belgian whites, who have invested all of our money here and who are now left holding the bag. We'd like to sell out to American investors and leave."

A few Belgians said, "We'll stick it out, no matter what. It's our duty. The Congo needs us now more than ever."

In Luluaburg, capital of Kasai province, which provides 90 percent of the world's industrial diamonds, the struggle for tribal supremacy had become so violent that all public buildings were guarded by soldiers, there was a 7:00 p.m. curfew, and three-fourths of the whites had fled.

I gave a concert in Lusambo, another Kasai city, which was less tense.

Roger Nonkel, Assistant Commissioner of Lusambo, took me to visit the local jail which was so pleasant that Congolese frequently commit petty crimes just to get in it. For a poor Congolese peasant, jail can be a fine thing. It provides a clean bed, good meals, free medical care, protection from armies of ants and other insects, prowling animals, snakes and storms.

The prisoners who wish, work in the town, and return to the jail at night. There are shower rooms, an art shop where they make handsome ebony statues, and recreation time in the court yard with visitors. The prison band performed a concert there for me upon instruments they had made themselves, xylophones, drums, and horns. I met many embezzlers, several amiable murderers, and some unrepentant adulteresses.

I reached the Congo capital, Leopoldville, a week before independence. It was jam-packed with chiefs and their retinues, and foreign correspondents.

Many educated Congolese said to me, "Why does not America come to our aid at once? We need their help to establish canning industries, to show us how to breed better stock, and diversify our crops. Why don't they woo the hostile leaders like the Russians do? There is already a Congo trade mission visiting Red China. Why do Americans let the Russians take a lead?"

On June, 24 at six-thirty that evening after days of disputes, Joseph Kasavubu head of the Abako party was elected President of the Congo.

The beautiful, new Parliamentary building was packed with spectators who burst into wild applause when the tabulation for Kasavubu passed the 140 mark, thus assuring victory. Out of 213 votes, he received 159.

How will this cryptic, mystic, reticent, reputedly part-Chinese new president get along with Patrice Lumumba the Prime Minister, who is a born politician with a magnetic personality, and who is called a leftist? Without the votes that Lumumba threw at him, the election of a president would have ended in deadlock. Lumumba was once imprisoned for embezzlement, a favorite pastime here. Africans apparently do not look upon property quite the same way as we do.

King Baudouin arrived in the capital, Patrice Lumumba signed the Pact of Defense with the Belgium monarch, and tension eased.

On Independence evening, I performed American music before the new government, the president, prime minister and visiting notables.

Throughout that day and night, merry throngs paraded the streets, under the depressing, seven-starred dark-blue flags. In two days, riots started again. July 6, Congolese soldiers demanding pay raises, mutinied against their white officers, looting houses, raping white women, including nuns, in drunken fury. Frenzied sexual dancing and orgies in the native communes added to the savagery. In a panic, thousands of Europeans tried to cross the Congo into Brazzaville. In Luluaburg, whites were besieged until Belgian paratroopers arrived to rescue them; in Elizabethville, many whites were killed and Rhodesian troops massed at the border. The United States set up an airlift.

Forgotten were the great advantages the Belgians had brought the once-divided, disease-ravaged Congo, decimated by Arab slavers and tribal wars, giving it unity, and the highest health and literacy rates in Africa, hospitals, fine schools and clean, elegant cities, all turned back to them now. The average Congolese did not understand that continued prosperity depended on work, order and world markets. Kasavubu and Lumumba tried in vain to calm them.

I left for Ghana at the start of the terror, and found there a sedate and orderly celebration of Ghana's independence. I had been invited by President Nkrumah as one of the two guests artists of the festival; Paul Robeson, the other one, never showed up. Officials were embarrassed. I carried on my part, performing American music.

ARRIVING IN BRUSSELS, July 9, I found Belgians bitter about the Congo.

Italy stands out as the most enjoyable and artistic nation.

In March 1960, I played in fourteen cities there. People who had been strangers until my concert, embraced me and invited me to their homes. When I ventured on the street in Milan during Carnival, the young men cried out, "Oh che bella!" chased and serenaded me. In Messina, when I complained to the hotel manager that a young man had just tried to break down my door, he shrugged and smiled, "But that is il amore!" In Verona, I played in a thirteenth Century castle, complete with drawbridge; and I recalled Shelley's, "Old palaces and towers...all overgrown with azure moss and flowers."

If Frenchmen always make you conscious of being a woman, Italian men make you feel like a goddess. I think all artists must feel as Byron when he wrote, "O Rome...my country...City of the Soul."

One hears many opinions around the world on the stormy subject of what women should be and are doing to fit into twentieth-century society. A Japanese secretary told me, "Japanese women will not return to the slavery we used to endure. We still aren't free enough."

An Ethiopian matron said, "I'd never want to live in America — middle class women have to work too hard there. I have nine servants, and have never washed a dish or wiped a floor. The young American matron has to wear herself out. I can enjoy my children, spend my leisure entertaining for my husband."

A Norwegian business woman said, "There's no such thing as a girl over eighteen in Norway, who's a virgin. But I envy American women. The emphasis is on marriage in America. A Scandinavian man won't marry until he's settled."

A Ghana professional woman made this remark, "Polygamy serves a purpose for the ignorant, but lowers woman's dignity as a sex. I'd never let my husband take a second wife."

A Nigerian girl economics student commented, "Our society's fabric needs polygamy. What would surplus women do otherwise? Look at the mistresses' men in your Western world have—as they are not obligated to them, they can discard them at any time, and the women have no dignity of social position."

A Turkish diplomat's wife declared, "We Asian women have patience. Each man is really like a six-year-old boy. There is no exception. We are not anxious, impatient, or hurried. We let life take its course. We yield to a man, yet preserve our dignity. At forty, we are not worn and haggard like the American woman."

A French ambassador's wife said, "When I was at school in Paris, all the girls said they wanted an American husband, because they do all the housework. A Frenchman wouldn't wash a dish!"

A Dutch banker's wife told me, "The young Dutch people of today have good marriages. Neither tries to rule the other."

A Belgian official's wife said, "It's nonsense when Americans talk about 'the European woman' and how meek she is. That's unwarranted generalization. Every country in Europe is different, with different customs and traditions, and a different reaction to modern living. There is no 'typical European woman.' I've known some arrogant, domineering European women, and some who were meek. There is infinite variety of personality in Northern Europe."

A Swedish career girl declared, "Why shouldn't both husband and wife work and have a higher standard of living? The majority of women have always worked, since the beginning of time. The difference in the modern world is that women for the first time are allowed to enter a variety of professional and executive positions, in intellectual competition with men. But women have always worked."

An English member of MRA said, "The new world will be built by men and women working side by side, thinking not of competition, but cooperation, not of rivalry, but human tolerance, love and high standards of personal conduct."

I have found that foreigners throughout the world distrust the sincerity of the United States as a democratic power largely because of the racial situation in the South. We cannot uphold liberty and equality abroad, while permitting racial segregation and discrimination here. We cannot demand free elections elsewhere when those in the states where the Negro is most concentrated, are rigged in a one-party system. People abroad do not understand that we are a country of federated sovereign states but think of us as a centralized entity.

I feel a profound respect for all those Americans who have denounced this racial bigotry; especially for Dr. Frank Buchman who does something concrete about it in Moral Re-Armament.

America's material riches have blinded many of our young people to the realities of life as faced by most of the world. American youth seems too confident of security here, too unaware that all they are used to could be swept away overnight. We will not be able to maintain our leadership in the world without better education in the lower grades, as well as in college.

I am not sorry that I was a child prodigy. There is so much to learn, and so little time in which to learn it.

Childhood now is too often considered just the period for 'having fun.' That is why youth today seems to have lost respect for society. There is nothing to challenge the spirit when everything is made too easy. Youth is brave and wants to battle.

It is a shame to waste one's early years, for the memory then is most retentive. The works of music that I learned at twelve, are still firmly entrenched in my mind without practicing. Latin and French phrases, and Spanish conjugations that I learned at ten, can be summoned readily. German idioms that I memorized much later vanished when I did not use them.

I found the young people in Europe, Asia and Africa more serious and studious than here; and far more disciplined. I did not find that America was hated everywhere, as has been reported. In some places, they like us very much.

Despite the turmoil, threats, hazards, uncertainties, of this age, I love it, for I realize all human eras have been fraught with problems. I admire the people who are doing their best to shape the new world. I think there is great hope for the human race, and feel deep warmth of affection for all peoples, everywhere. ⊞

PHOTO: Fred Palumbo, World Telegram

ABOUT PHILIPPA DUKE SCHUYLER

PHILIPPA DUKE SCHUYLER, child prodigy, internationally renowned concert pianist, composer, author and journalist, was born in Harlem in 1931 (although there are documents noting her date of birth as 1932 and 1933). During the first fifteen years of her life Philippa won a broad array of awards, citations and honors.

For several years in succession she won honors in competitions sponsored by the New York Philharmonic Young People's Society, and on June 19, 1940 the New York World's Fair devoted a day to her where she performed her own compositions before an audience of 70,000. Philippa became the youngest member of the National Association of Conductors and Composers. During her lifetime she composed works for piano, orchestra and voice.

According to her parents, she began studying and composing for the piano at three. Josephine attributed much of her daughter's genius to this and a diet of raw foods. However, Philippa was raised around only adults who had an intense interest in scholarly matters and the arts; thus one could reason that her accomplishments can be attributed to constant intellectual stimulation and challenge. At the age of six Philippa made her first formal recital appearance, playing a repertoire that included her own compositions. Three years later, Philippa had nine of her sixty compositions published. She wrote and orchestrated a symphonic poem, "Manhattan Nocturne," which received first prize in a nationwide contest held by Wayne State University, in Detroit, Michigan. "Manhattan Nocturne" received its premiere performance by the Detroit Symphony Orchestra before an audience of 7,000 young people. The next season it was played by the New York Philharmonic Symphony Orchestra at Carnegie Hall for the final festival of the Young People's Concerts.

Also, among her accomplishments as a young composer were "Rumpelstiltskin," a symphonic scherzo, also prize-winning, which was premiered by Dean Dixon at Hunter College (CUNY) on his Youth Series. It was later performed by the New York Philharmonic at Carnegie Hall, and at Lewissohn Stadium, and was broadcasted to Europe by the U.S. State Department in 1946; and "Sleepy Hollow Sketches" for symphony orchestra, which was showcased by the New York Youth Orchestra. She also received an award from the United Nations Festival at Tarrytown, New York in 1950.

In 1965, Philippa composed what is considered to be her most ambitious work, the "Nile Fantasy" for piano and orchestra. It had its premiere in Cairo, Egypt on December 10, 1965 with Philippa as soloist accompanied by the Cairo Symphony Orchestra.

Unfortunately, the U.S., which had been intrigued with the child prodigy, turned its back on the young black woman as she entered adulthood. Philippa, like many other black artists before her, was forced to go overseas to seek a career and continued recognition. Thereafter she toured widely throughout the world as a concert pianist, giving solo recitals and appearing with the leading symphony orchestras of the world. Touring more than seventy countries, she gave command performances for Ghana's first president Kwame Nkrumah, the Queen Mother Elisabeth of the Belgians, was honored by the Haitian government in 1950, and by Emperor Haile Selassie of Ethiopia in 1955.

In addition to her fame as a piano virtuoso, Philippa used her travels as a musician to collect material to write five books and numerous articles. While performing in Haiti in 1950, she wrote a series of five articles about President Paul Magloire for the *Pittsburgh Courier*, thus launching her career as a journalist. Her musical tours often took her to countries around the world in the midst of political upheaval, and as a result, she began to write about them. She served as foreign correspondent in Africa for the *New York Daily Mirror* and the North American Newspaper Alliance.

Among her published books are *Adventures in Black and White* (1960), an autobiography, and *Who Killed the Congo* (1963), a controversial analysis of the Democratic Republic of the Congo's independence. A devout Catholic, she visited some 200 Christian missions in Africa and Asia and recounted her observations in her book *Jungle Saints* (1963). In collaboration with her mother, Josephine, she co-authored *Kingdom of Dreams* (1966), an analysis of the influence of dreams in human history and the connection between dreaming and symbolization, in general. There is speculation that her mother was solely responsible for writing the book, but having Philippa attached to the work helped it to get published. Her last book, published posthumously, *Good Men Die* (1969) was an account of the war in Vietnam.

Among her many accomplishments, Philippa frequently lectured. Fluent in French, Spanish, Portuguese and Italian, she lectured in the United States and abroad, specializing in the history of the missionary movement in Africa, as well as independence movements. Philippa believed she would not be seen as a respected speaker in the u.s. because she was African American, so she invented a pseudo-identity, Felipa Monterro. Being African American was a struggle for her, while abroad she let people believe that she was of Iberian ancestry and refused to identify as black in prominent American reference publications. In the early 1960s, under this assumed name, she traveled throughout the southwestern u.s. speaking on the threat of Communism.

In May 1967, while helping to evacuate a group of Vietnamese school children from Hue to Danang, Philippa Duke Schuyler was killed in a helicopter crash in South Vietnam. She was honored posthumously with a procession down Fifth Avenue to St. Patrick's Cathedral where she was eulogized by Cardinal Francis Spellman, Mayor John Lindsey and other notables. u.s. Congress members also paid her tribute in the Congressional Record. Throughout Philippa's life, her career and accomplishments were heavily documented by the press. *Time* and *Newsweek* chronicled her early life as a child prodigy. The Musical Courier, Musical America and the Music Journal ran articles concerning her career as a pianist and composer and the *Crisis, Sepia* and *Ebony* magazine wrote articles about her on several occasions. Her death was covered by *The New York Times* and other New York publications. ⊞

PHOTO: WNYC Archive Collections

ABOUT DEEMS TAYLOR

JOSEPH DEEMS TAYLOR (1885-1966), composer, critic, author, and radio personality, was one of the most influential figures in American culture from the 1920s through the 1940s. With his witty, clever, charming, and informative but unpatronizing manner, he almost single-handedly introduced classical music to millions of Americans across the nation. A self-taught composer, the New York City native wrote such pieces as the orchestral suite "Through the Looking Glass" and the acclaimed operas "The King's Henchman" and "Peter Ibbetson," the first commissions ever offered by the Metropolitan Opera. Taylor's operatic works were among the most popular and widely performed of his day, yet he achieved greatest fame and recognition as the golden-voiced intermission commentator for the New York Philharmonic radio broadcasts and as the on-screen host of Walt Disney's classic film, *Fantasia* (1940). ⊞

ABOUT TARA BETTS

TARA BETTS is an award-winning poet, author and scholar of African American and white French descent. She holds a Ph.D. in English from Binghamton University, and an MFA in creative writing from New England College. She has taught at Rutgers University, University of Illinois-Chicago, and the MFA program at Chicago State University.

She is also one of the co-editors of *The Beiging of America: Personal Narratives About Being Mixed Race in the 21st Century* (2017) and the Poetry Editor at *Another Chicago Magazine.* Her poetry has appeared in numerous journals and anthologies, she is the author of several poetry collections and chapbooks, including her latest book, *Break the Habit* (2016). A Cave Canem graduate, she held residencies from the Ragdale Foundation, Centrum and Caldera, and was awarded an Illinois Arts Council Artist fellowship. www.tarabetts.net. ⊞

OTHER BOOKS BY 2LEAF PRESS

2LEAF PRESS challenges the status quo by publishing alternative fiction, non-fiction, poetry and bilingual works by activists, academics, poets and authors dedicated to diversity and social justice with scholarship that is accessible to the general public. 2LEAF PRESS produces high quality and beautifully produced hardcover, paperback and ebook formats through our series: *2LP Explorations in Diversity, 2LP University Books, 2LP Classics, 2LP Translations, Nuyorican World Series,* and *2LP Current Affairs, Culture & Politics.* Below is a selection of 2LEAF PRESS' published titles.

2LP EXPLORATIONS IN DIVERSITY
Substance of Fire: Gender and Race in the College Classroom
by Claire Millikin
Foreword by R. Joseph Rodríguez, Afterword by Richard Delgado
Contributed material by Riley Blanks, Blake Calhoun and Rox Trujillo

Black Lives Have Always Mattered
A Collection of Essays, Poems, and Personal Narratives
Edited by Abiodun Oyewole

The Beiging of America:
Personal Narratives about Being Mixed Race in the 21st Century
Edited by Cathy J. Schlund-Vials, Sean Frederick Forbes and Tara Betts
with an Afterword by Heidi Durrow

What Does it Mean to be White in America?
Breaking the White Code of Silence, A Collection of Personal Narratives
Edited by Gabrielle David and Sean Frederick Forbes
Introduction by Debby Irving and Afterword by Tara Betts

2LP UNIVERSITY BOOKS
Designs of Blackness, Mappings in the Literature and
Culture of African Americans
A. Robert Lee
20TH ANNIVERSARY EXPANDED EDITION

2LP CLASSICS
Adventures in Black and White
Edited and with a critical introduction by Tara Betts
by Philippa Schuyler

Monsters: Mary Shelley's Frankenstein and Mathilda
by Mary Shelley, edited by Claire Millikin Raymond

2LP TRANSLATIONS
Birds on the Kiswar Tree
by Odi Gonzales, Translated by Lynn Levin
Bilingual: English/Spanish

Incessant Beauty, A Bilingual Anthology
by Ana Rossetti, Edited and Translated by Carmela Ferradáns
Bilingual: English/Spanish

NUYORICAN WORLD SERIES
Our Nuyorican Thing, The Birth of a Self-Made Identity
by Samuel Carrion Diaz, with an Introduction by Urayoán Noel
Bilingual: English/Spanish

Hey Yo! Yo Soy!, 40 Years of Nuyorican Street Poetry,
The Collected Works of Jesús Papoleto Meléndez
Bilingual: English/Spanish

LITERARY NONFICTION
No Vacancy; Homeless Women in Paradise
by Michael Reid

The Beauty of Being, A Collection of Fables, Short Stories & Essays
by Abiodun Oyewole

WHEREABOUTS: Stepping Out of Place,
An Outside in Literary & Travel Magazine Anthology
Edited by Brandi Dawn Henderson

PLAYS
Rivers of Women, The Play
by Shirley Bradley LeFlore, with photographs by Michael J. Bracey

AUTOBIOGRAPHIES/MEMOIRS/BIOGRAPHIES
Trailblazers, Black Women Who Helped Make America Great
American Firsts/American Icons
by Gabrielle David

Mother of Orphans
The True and Curious Story of Irish Alice, A Colored Man's Widow
by Dedria Humphries Barker

Strength of Soul
by Naomi Raquel Enright

Dream of the Water Children:
Memory and Mourning in the Black Pacific
by Fredrick D. Kakinami Cloyd
Foreword by Velina Hasu Houston, Introduction by Gerald Horne
Edited by Karen Chau

The Fourth Moment: Journeys from the Known to the Unknown, A Memoir
by Carole J. Garrison, Introduction by Sarah Willis

POETRY
PAPOLíTICO, Poems of a Political Persuasion
by Jesús Papoleto Meléndez
with an Introduction by Joel Kovel and DeeDee Halleck

Critics of Mystery Marvel, Collected Poems
by Youssef Alaoui, with an Introduction by Laila Halaby

shrimp
by jason vasser-elong, with an Introduction by Michael Castro

The Revlon Slough, New and Selected Poems
by Ray DiZazzo, with an Introduction by Claire Millikin

Written Eye: Visuals/Verse
by A. Robert Lee

A Country Without Borders: Poems and Stories of Kashmir
by Lalita Pandit Hogan, with an Introduction by Frederick Luis Aldama

Branches of the Tree of Life
The Collected Poems of Abiodun Oyewole 1969-2013
by Abiodun Oyewole, edited by Gabrielle David
with an Introduction by Betty J. Dopson

2Leaf Press is an imprint owned and operated by the Intercultural Alliance of Artists & Scholars, Inc. (IAAS), a NY-based nonprofit organization that publishes and promotes multicultural literature.

NEW YORK
www.2leafpress.org